HONEST TO
Goddess

Russia, Sophia and
the Celtic Soul

GERAINT AP IORWERTH

(crescent

First published in 1998 by Crescent

Crescent is an imprint of
Crescent Books Limited
36 Osborne Road, Warsash
Southampton, Hampshire SO31 9GG

ISBN 1 84086 001 4

A CIP catalogue record is available from the British Library.

Geraint ap Iorwerth has asserted his right to be identified as the author of this work.

Editor: Lesley Walmsley
Designer: Caroline Reeves
Illustrator: Richard Edwards
Colour reproduction and film output: Spectrum Colour

Printed and bound in Spain

Illustration on previous page:
Homo Sapiens as Microcosm, after Hildegard of Bingen.
(1998 is the 900th Anniversary of the birth of Hildegard of Bingen.
This German Abbess was developing her own Sophiology in the twelfth century.)

Contents

To Ann

Tra syllem, tydi a myfi, anwylyd,
ar yr heulwen yn ymgydio a'r feiston,
gwyddem fod yr haul a'r dwr
yn fyw...
Byw oeddynt.
Nid unwedd eu bywyd hwy
a'n bywyd ni,
ond byw oeddynt:
unben ac unbennes,
duw a duwies,
rhyw yang a yin mewn hwyl.
Ac eto nid oedd iddynt fywyd
ar wahan i'n cariad ni...
Ein bywyd ni a roddai fywyd
i'r ddeudduw direidus,
ein bywyd ni na allai fyth fod
heb gydiad haul a dwfr.

from the poem *Llanddwyn* by
Pennar Davies, Y Tlws yn y Lotws,
Llandybie 1971

An English translation by Geraint

As we gazed, you and I beloved,
at the sunshine coupling with the shallows,
we knew that the sun and water were alive...
They were alive
but with a life different to ours,
but still they were alive,
prince and princess,
god and goddess,
a yang and yin in joyful celebration...
Our life gave life,
our love gave life,
to these two playful deities,
and yet our life could never be
without the coming-together of sun and water.

Foreword

Honest to Goddess is a call to spiritual maturity. Its title may shock or dismay, but its purpose is to reintroduce us to the Wisdom or Sophia who is poured out upon all life by the Divine One.

Bringing Sophia back into our lives and worship brings a warmer colour to the sometimes pale cheek of Christian observance. This is not an unwanted intrusion, nor an orthodox one, for Sophia has been there as Lady Wisdom from the very beginning, labouring in the creation of life, and accompanying prophets of all ages. Her voice is clear in the sayings of jesus, especially where He, the great Sophianic reconciler, yearns over jerusalem, city of peace: 'You are the city that kills the prophets and stones those who are sent to you. How often I have wanted to gather your children as a hen gathers her chicks under her wings. But you have not let me.' And in our time too the shalom in our souls has been squeezed out by such killing indifference.

We have a Church and Christian history of our own making, and it is not always pleasant to look at. One cause is that by excluding Sophia we have sometimes neglected the spirit of Christ's commandments. Sophia, the Lady Wisdom, helps develop the potential which the Divine Spirit gives us so generously, and which we sometimes so grudgingly shrug off.

Sophia is sudden and surprizing. She comes in the moments of lightening-illuminated night, leading us through the spiritual deserts to the oases of refreshment. Many within the church have indeed lived her kind of passover existence all their spiritual lives, moving between a hasty bite and sup, never quite as comfortable or complacent as the settled souls, but willingly travelling on in the company of Sophia, hopeful of better times to come.

The prophetic words of Isaiah, 'My house will be a house of prayer for all peoples,' speak with the very accent of Sophia who will resolutely camp out in tents until these words become true. It is not comfortable, living with prophets, for inevitably thet are shunned by their neighbours as trouble-makers, perhaps because they are indeed inspired by 'the Spirit and the Bride?'

Sophia's message is to the street-wise as well as to the philosopher, to the nomad as well as to the cleric of any tradition. And let us not forget her most loved and yearned-after children — those trying to squeeze their souls into spaces where they will not fit, those who are betwixt and between, those on the boundaries, alienated ones who fall between the stools of heresy and orthodoxy, those who have opted out, the marginalized, the poor in spirit, and those scandalised by the lack of spiritual hospitality offered to them. This lack of hospitality has been the continual charge of the Divine against humankind: as the Son of Man had nowhere to lay his head, and the dove of reconciliation had nowhere to rest, so Sophia has also suffered exile and neglect.

Sophia's role of making sense of our personal spiritual pilgrimage through life is clear within these pages, as her call to maturity and growth are heard throughout the prophetic-books. She has laid her table since the beginning and calls the guests who are ready, to come and dine. The bread which she has kneaded and set aside, the matter from which all life springs, is now risen. It is good crusty bread, not the soft, processed stuff suitable only for infants. The discovery that gifted souls may indeed eat the spiritual food of their desire, that it was originally prepared for them by Sophia to encourage and support their life's pilgrimage, is a wonderful revelation indeed!

The call to renewal and maturity is being heeded throughout the Church today, drawing on a variety of sources, including the native British and Celtic traditions which were vessels of spirit long before the first apostles reached these shores. This inclusion, like the acknowledgements of Sophia herself, may cause some unease, but any renewal of spirit must always recognize the gifting qualities that spring from land, culture and background. We cannot grow without our essential selves. Whatever we cut out or exclude will never grow up with us, but will be forever childishly kicking and screaming in a back cupboard of the soul, distracting us from our spiritual pilgrimage. Finding a deeper hospitality of spirit is something we can learn from Sophia, if we adopt her nomadic method of living off the land, and gratefully acknowledge the welcome of the familiar and abiding co-ordinates of humility, gratitude and love.

In the pattern of Sergius Bulgakov and the many faithful followers of Sophia, the author's orthodoxy is strongly committed to the knightly championship of her. The Spirit and the Bride sing 'Come' and he has answered their invitation. The reconciliation of the Resurrection and its promise to all living things, not only to human believers, rings out with its Sophianic song of compassion within these pages — if we will only read, heed and understand.

Caitlin Matthews

Biographical note: Caitlin Matthews is the author of 30 books, including *Sophia, Goddess of Wisdom* and *The Celtic Devotional*. She teaches Celtic spiritual traditions worldwide.

Introduction

The Divine Feminine has come among us in a new way. We must attend to Her. We must listen to Her voice. Her message is of **Unity**, and **Reconciliation**.

Sophia is The Mother of a genuine *Oikumene* (Greek for 'the inhabited earth') and not of any one religion or spiritual path. She is the Mother of every one of us. Hers is the All-embracing way, promoting a global way of 'doing theology' that goes beyond the rigid dogmatism and petty sectarianism of patriarchal mentality, that so easily breeds intolerance and the injustices that issue from it.

Above all, Sophia is the Wisdom that calls us to work together for 'peace with justice', in so many parts of 'the inhabited earth'. I think especially of Jerusalem, the Spiritual Mother of so many of us.

Honest to Goddess is one written attempt at celebrating the return of the Divine Feminine to the heart of Western spirituality. Her message is of **Sovereignty** — her own and ours.

Writing as a Christian priest, rooted within my own ecclesiastical and native traditions, *Honest to Goddess's* message is nevertheless a universal one — a message that I hope will continue to help build bridges between all believers throughout the world.

Geraint ap Iorwerth.

Geraint ap Iorwerth
Pennal Rectory, 16 July 1997

The author cannot enter into personal correspondence.
Anyone wanting information about retreats, courses and pilgrimages should write,
with a stamped, addressed envelope, to:
Order of Sancta Sophia
Arduyn
Pennal
Near Machynlleth, Powys
Wales, SY20 9DH
United Kingdom

The Pennal Green Man

1. Sophia & the Green Man

An Invocation

In the Name of the Father, the Son and the Holy Spirit.

I call to Thee Divine Wisdom,

The Image of Divine Beauty and Power,

The Shining Body of Eternity.

This Soul of the worlds,

The Queen of Souls.

Descend to us in visible form.

Once again become incarnate in us and in all the world,

So that the Divine One may be all in all.   (after Vladimir Solovyev)

The future of living Christianity rests with the Sophianic interpretation of the world and its destiny.   (*The Wisdom of God*, S.Bulgakov, p. 39)

Tomb or Womb

The time of change is at hand. The Church as we know it is dying. The radical demands of the Gospel challenge us to acknowledge the death of Mother Church. This is not an easy task, and I have found it very traumatic for I love Her dearly. But She is old and tired. Generations have sucked Her dry, clinging immaturely to Her like leeches, unable to let go, refusing to grow up. She has been a wonderful mother to me, but, like all good mothers, She wants to see Her children stand on their own feet and become mature. We need not fear this image of the Church as an old woman or the toothless Old Hag, 'twittering away in the corner', as the current Archbishop of Canterbury once described her. She is the Wise One, and we need to listen to what She is saying. She knows that it is her time to die. She also knows that her dying is the celebration of things new born.

She is both tomb and womb.

The mystery that surrounds the passing of the old and the emergence of the new, has become an integral part of my spirituality. It is the mystery that has enabled me to face both ways at once — at least for the time being. In the words of The Preacher, commonly known as Ecclesiastes, there is a passage that declares

There is a time for everything

and a season for every activity under heaven:

a time to be born and a time to die,

a time to plant and a time to uproot,

a time to tear down and a time to build.   (3:1-3)

This has always been the Way of Wisdom, and honesty demands that we be true to it, for as the new millennium dawns this is not an either/or but, in true Celtic fashion, a both/and. In the Twilight between the ages we are called to celebrate birth in the dying, planting in the act of uprooting and building up in the act of tearing down. Over thirty years ago we were called by Bishop John Robinson to be *Honest to God*. As the second millennium comes to a close, we are being challenged to be *Honest to Goddess*.

Haunt of Eagles

I grew up in Northern Snowdonia, where my father was a parish priest in the University city of Bangor. Our home was about a mile or so from the Menai Straits, which divide the mainland from the ancient Druidic island of Mona or Anglesey. To the south we had an unobscured view of the twin peaks, Dafydd and Llewellyn, named after the thirteenth-century princely brothers of Gwynedd. On a clear day, the summit of Snowdon or "Eryri", as it is called in Welsh, is visible to the West. It means the Haunt of Eagles.

My mother came from a family of fishermen in Conwy, a picturesque walled town on the North Wales coast, famous for its castle. She loved the sea. My father's family were quarrymen, and his loyalty was to the mountains. Living in Bangor gave me the best of both worlds.

A regular childhood journey that made a lasting impression on me, was the six-mile trip to my paternal grandparents' home at Bethesda in the Ogwen Valley. A journey of stark contrasts, both sea and mountain greet you in that short distance. In less than half-an-hour, my sisters and I had exchanged our green playing fields for numerous grey hills of discarded slate. And yet 'the tips' were located within some of the most beautiful mountain scenery in Britain.

But it wasn't the breathtaking Ogwen landscape that captured my imagination during those early years, or the slate graveyards, where countless hours were spent at play. It was an ordinary, rather drab looking dwelling place, that we passed en route to Bethesda, called Halfway House.

I assumed that it was half-way between Bangor and Bethesda, but to this day I have not actually measured the distance between the two. What intrigued me was the fact that it was half-way to somewhere, a place in-between, neither one nor the other. Fascination with the in-between has remained with me to this day.

I was nurtured within two spiritual traditions. One was Christian and overtly religious, the public face of our family spirituality. The other was more private, spontaneous and un-labelled. The former was middle-of-the-road or 'Prayer Book' Anglicanism, as my parents called it. The latter was our love of the land and its history. I have since come to know and honour her as Sovereignty.

Anglicanism initiated me into the wonder and awe of worship: the fellowship of angels, saints and the whole of creation, in praise and thanksgiving to the Divine. It taught me the importance of spiritual discipline, the daily round of prayer and study, and a life tuned into the rhythm of many festivals and holy days. There was always something to celebrate. In addition to its sense of right worship and order, the Anglican Church appealed to me in two ways: one was the commitment of many of its leaders to the universal struggle for peace and justice; the other was its learning and scholarship. I hold my Anglican teachers in high regard as custodians of the Truth.

As I recall my formative years, I suppose I did think of the Church Community as more (though not exclusively) the domain of the Heavenly Father, while Mother Earth governed the outdoors, fully able to embrace everything in Her outstretched arms. And there was much to embrace.

It was (and still remains) a rich heritage, that gave me the feeling of being rooted to something solid and real. I was surrounded by so many 'llans' or sacred enclosures, that almost every step was a sacred act, every journey a pilgrimage of some sort. Within these sites were ancient churches, many of sixth-century foundation, dedicated to a host of Welsh holy men and women. Standing stones and cromlechs had incredible names, such as 'Barclodiad y Gawres' or The Giantess' Apron. My favourite lake was 'Ffynnon Lloer', which means Moon Well. We walked the ancient tracks, climbed the mountains and drove regularly through the narrow passes. The mountains and rivers were no less alive than the plant and wildlife that reigned in abundance.

Everything was alive. Even ruins were animated and had much to teach us — living stones. Everything had its own kind of empowerment — but it was a different kind of nurturing to that supplied by the Church. It was also a different kind of belonging.

Spaciousness

It was when I left home that the third strand of my spirituality began to unfold, though the seeds had been planted much earlier. This path took me beyond the tradition which I had been brought up in, although, paradoxically, clergymen were often involved, as well as a priest's wife — my own mother. I moved beyond the traditions of my birth and upbringing but not away from them. They became, in fact, a vehicle for a series of spiritual journeys and explorations. The paths I was to follow were not, in retrospect, separate and unconnected but led to one another in an ever-increasing spiral, a movement into greater and greater spaciousness.

The source of this movement was an ordinary, six-foot-square box room at The Vicarage, that my father used at least twice daily for private prayer, his secret communion with The Infinite. He shared the space with a vacuum cleaner and an ever-changing array of domestic items, from old picture frames to rolled up pieces of carpet of varying sizes. An old Victorian folding screen separated his kneeler and chair from the household odds and ends.

From my early teens I was aware of it as a place set apart, although there were no signs on the door demanding 'Silence' nor a religious drawing marking it out as sacred space. No matter what time of day or night I entered this small room, I immediately became aware of a reality so powerful that I could almost clothe myself in it. It was a Presence that went beyond anything that I could imagine, an intimacy that appeared to be at the heart of all things, a silence that somehow contained every sound in the universe.

I treasure the moments when I have not tried to label this reality. I never thought of it as being exclusively 'Christian', and knew that my father drew from a Source that was far greater than any religion could ever hope to contain. It belonged to no one and yet was available to all.

It was here that the various threads of my parents' spirituality came together. It was here that Wisdom began to weave together the different strands or colours of my soul.

Books have played an important part within this strand of my spiritual growth. They have been, and indeed still are, a valuable means of Grace. They offer a way of entering into a personal relationship not only with their authors, but also with the Spirit which animates their work. I still find it exciting to open a book and to feel each word and sentence pulsating with life, some actually dancing before my eyes. Reading is a total experience for me, an engagement with Truth that involves every part of my being. And this Truth is something alive and dynamic, not a reality that is static and frozen in time. It is the Spirit confronting and challenging us with the knowledge of ourselves within the divine scheme of things, a knowledge that is forever growing and developing as we progress and change in our thinking and powers of understanding.

The Grail Quest

My mother had always treasured a small book she had won in 1938 as a prize for doing well in an exam at her local Methodist Sunday School. It was written by a Welsh Methodist or Wesleyan minister, E. Tegla Davies, and entitled Y Greal Santaidd, which is Welsh for The Holy Grail. To this day I have no idea where my mother kept it. I never saw it lying around with other books. It's as though it appeared mysteriously from somewhere, for its stories to be read, and then, just as mysteriously, disappeared again. My mother promised the book to me, but when I left home to go to college, it was nowhere to be seen. I forgot about it for nearly twenty years, until my mother's premature death from cancer in 1989, at the age of sixty-three. Memories of The Holy Grail came flooding back to me in my grief, but my sisters failed to find it among my mother's belongings. My own search proved equally fruitless.

Three years were to pass by before I found my mother's Grail book. I claimed it as mine and brought it home.

Honest to God

My time at Theological College was a big disappointment — it was like living in a spiritual strait-jacket. I was asked to leave at the end of my first year, and I did. But it was not a complete waste of time. It was here that I had my first real taste of freedom, by coming to terms with an institution that had almost a pathological fear of it. Instead of providing the space where priests of the future could continue to grow up, it encouraged them to remain infants, little boys who were forever seeking a father's approval, be he earthly or heavenly.

Furthermore, I became dissatisfied with a theological tradition that was content to think of the Divine only in terms of a trinity of 'two males and an it'.

I discovered the rudiments of my own spiritual geography. I learnt about the scattering of boundaries. When to honour them and when to step beyond them.

I remained within the Anglican fold, however, or at least Anglicanism as I perceived it. Its richness and diversity has always amazed me. With such a broad spectrum of traditions, I felt sure that there was a place somewhere for my spirituality to unfold, and my Archbishop honoured that unfolding. With his support I completed my preliminary theological studies as a secular student.

At last I had room to breathe

Although I have remained on the edge of the Church as an institution ever since, I was ordained a priest in 1975 with Archbishop Gwilym's blessing. Anglicanism has since become a vessel — as good as any — for my continued journeying into the truth. Two churchmen, an Anglican bishop and a dean this time, were my intellectual guides when I found myself alienated from many of my contemporaries. Their scholarship helped deepen my understanding of Christianity, their witness helped me to grow in my faith.

I first came across Dean Inge, one-time Dean of St Paul's Cathedral, in my mid-teens, by courtesy of my father's library, in a biography by Adam Fox, called quite simply *Dean Inge* and published in 1960. After reading only a few extracts from his writings, I had been immediately fired by the spiritual reality, and indeed the adventure, that he spoke of. He wrote of a third element in Christianity besides the combative Catholic and Protestant elements, a spiritual religion that embodied the highest wisdom of the past, a tradition that was part of what he described as The Great Quest. It took me many years to find out more about this type of Christianity, but I knew that it was here that I belonged.

When Bishop Robinson hit the headlines in 1963, I was coming up to my thirteenth birthday. It was the year when I first met the Beatles, a few months before their TV debut on the BBC. I was to meet them again, four years later, when they attended an International Convention on Transcendental Meditation (TM) in my home town of Bangor, hosted by the Maharishi Mahesh Yogi. In 1963 I had no idea how famous the 'fab four' from Liverpool would become, neither was I aware of the impact that *Honest to God*, the title of the bishop's book, would have on believers and non-believers alike. Over a million copies of the book were eventually sold, and it was translated into German, French, Swedish, Dutch, Italian and Japanese.

It was during my first year in college, seven years later, that I found out why my father and his colleagues had referred to *Honest to God* as a bombshell. I found the bishop's book so challenging, that I started a library of what I called my 'honesty books'. Over the years they have become an important part of my continuing or Third Testament. If they are truly alive, then spiritual traditions are always growing and changing, and our Christian traditions are no exception. The Truth of the Gospel has to be regularly reinterpreted. As the twentieth century comes to a close, this task has become an increasingly urgent one. *Honest to God* came to epitomize this challenge for many of us.

Bishop Robinson's purpose was to launch a long-term initiative to look again at the basics of Christian spirituality and theology. His was a preliminary, exploratory start. He was going to 'map a new programme' (p. 133) for the Church. He called for a 'radical re-appraisal of the way that Christianity has been presented in the West, confident that the fundamentals would stay the same.' He wrote:

> We are still at the beginning of our task. But the beginning is to try and be honest — and to go
> on from there. (p. 141)

I believe that the key passage in the whole book appeared on page 124. This is what it says:

> What looks like being required of us, reluctant as we may be for the effort involved, is a radically
> new mould, a metamorphosis, of Christian belief and practice… It means that we have to be
> prepared for everything to go into the melting — even our most cherished religious categories
> and moral absolutes. And the first thing we must be ready to let go is our image of God himself.

Honest to God made an impression on people because of its openness and genuine concern for the truth. A bishop, in sharing his concern about the Church and its message, enabled both lay and clerical members to be more honest about themselves and their religious and spiritual beliefs. The debate may have been short-lived in ecclesiastical terms, but Robinson made it quite clear that his role was 'to get things going'. He certainly did that!

The *Honest to God* debate has continued over the years, both within and outside the Church, even if only among a minority. 'Honesty books', urging renewal in every aspect of the Church's life, continue to appear, but many in authority choose to ignore them — there are too many vested interests at stake, lip service alone has been paid to genuine renewal, the priority for the status quo is survival. Many within the Church refuse to face the truth that a religious establishment professing to renew itself while at the same time maintaining itself as an institution, is a contradiction. It means living a lie. Genuine renewal means the regular dismantling of religious structures — from within. There are signs that such a process is well under way. The current identity crisis within the Anglican Church, for example — especially in the light of the Church of England's decision in 1993 to ordain women as priests — shows that a major realignment is beginning to take place within British Christianity.

We are witnessing the birth of something different within the British soul. A new spirituality is emerging.

The Twilight Zone

For the last nineteen years I have lived in Southern Snowdonia. In 1978 my wife Ann, our sons Shem and David, and I, made our home in Pennal, a small Meirionethshire village, situated four miles from Machynlleth, where the last Welsh prince — Owain Glyndwr — was crowned at the beginning of the fifteenth century.

Although I was not immediately aware of it, the challenge of the in-between was soon to re-emerge in my life, this time with a greater intensity. It was a double homecoming: I was back in the town where I was born and I was back in my sacred space. This time, however, instead of Halfway House there was Halfway Valley! I had come back to live in the Dyfi Valley, the historic and geographical 'in-between' of Wales.

The River Dyfi is a special gateway to our national heritage as Welsh Celts. It was to this neutral strip of land that Welsh princes, the Pendragons, would summon the rival families of north and south, if they were to have any hope of forging them into a lasting unity. This has been the Dyfi's challenge down the centuries: the union of opposites.

But the Dyfi has come to symbolize another Gateway for me, allied this time to the uniquely Celtic way of perceiving the mysteries of life and death, of rebirth and renewal. It is the magical place where a bridge can appear to facilitate intercourse between the Otherworld and us. It represents a way of seeing and being that entails entering the Twilight Zone.

The bridge was to appear in the most unexpected of places.

St Peter ad Vincula

One of the most striking features of the parish church at Pennal is its' beautiful East Window, a gift of the

1873 restoration, depicting the Ascension of Christ, with Mary Magdala and the disciples looking on, crowned with words from the Fourth Gospel:

I ascend to my Father and your father, to my God and your God.   (John 20:17)

After a few years at Pennal, I became aware of a great imbalance in my life. The main focus of my daily devotion became the Ascension window. Apart from Christ's right foot, which points downwards, everything was too heavenward. Maybe it was the fact that the reredos obscured almost a third of the window, in places, and totally blocked out the bottom part? The reredos is a panel or section that you find in some churches immediately behind the altar. It can be made of any material, from ornate marble to a plain cloth, but ours was a fine piece of carved oak, fitted as recently as 1950. There was nothing wrong with it in itself. It was simply in the wrong place. It did not belong there. It spoilt the picture. Instead of drawing me closer to Christ, the window began to have the opposite effect. Christ was becoming more and more distant to me, or at least a particular image of Him no longer spoke to me. I became more and more disorientated. Some barriers in my life seemed insurmountable. But I would try to do something about one of them at least. The reredos would have to go.

During morning and evening prayers, I often thought up schemes for its removal. And then an ideal opportunity presented itself. The Parochial Church Council (PCC) decided to decorate the church, and in order to facilitate the work, the reredos would have to be temporarily removed. I was more than a willing volunteer for the task. I even dropped it on my left foot in the process, but the satisfaction of having finally removed this particular piece of furniture from my church, far outweighed the temporary discomfort I was experiencing.

The reredos was not put back. For the first time in over thirty years, the East Window was visible in its full glory. Nothing was hidden. It was to be many months until all was revealed.

The Ancient One

I cannot remember whether I was standing or kneeling before the altar at the time, but I was in the Sanctuary. There, in my church's holy of holies, was the Green Man. His eyes stared directly at me. I was face to face with the all-seeing and all-knowing one. He was clearly no afterthought on the artist's part, but earthed the Ascension. He too had an important part to play and brought a much needed sense of wholeness to the drama portrayed.

The window was complete after all. It spoke of a spaciousness that I never thought possible, least of all in a small Anglican church in the foothills of the Cadair Idris range. I should have known better.

The sanctuary became my bridge into the Twilight Zone, the Ancient One my personal guide.

Celtic Wisdom

In Teutonic mythology, the twilight stands for everything that is shadowy, obscure and dim. It is the place of partial illumination, a condition of imperfect knowledge. For Celts, however, the twilight zone is where wisdom is born. It is the entrance into Annwfn or Annwn, the Celtic Otherworld, the dimension where one acquires the ability of knowing the Truth in a special way, that sacred space where one begins to trust the 'in-between' that alone can illuminate and make sense of the opposites in life. It means learning to face both ways at once. Any religion that insists on a duality between light and darkness, body and soul, male and female, etc., has always been alien to the spiritual temperament of the Celtic people. In our world there is a natural rhythm that involves moving between the polar opposites, instead of pitting one against the other. Initiation into the Celtic mysteries means embracing the constant interplay of life and death, creation and destruction, order and chaos and even of heaven and hell.

Similarly, in cultures where the twilight is regarded as something negative and undesirable, the gods and goddesses have suffered the same fate. Banished to the netherworld, theirs has become a shadowy existence, beyond even the redemption that Christianity claims is available to all. They have been ridiculed in many cultures and ignored by others. In some cultures the immortals have even been declared mortal and killed off. I had not killed off or banished my deities although they lived in a part of my soul that was hitherto unrelated to my Christianity. There was room in church for my ancestors as well as for saints and angels. But the gods and goddesses were not welcome — until the Green Man appeared.

He heralded the coming of a new order and with it a new kind of sacred space. I did not have to keep 'the holy ones', as the Bible calls the gods and goddesses, in a separate compartment of my life any more, I could invite them into the sanctuary. They were, in fact, there already. It was not long before the Twilight began to work its magic. I was enabled to look at creation in a new way. I was more aware of its richness and wonder. The divide that was mirrored in my soul between heaven and earth disappeared. The depths became no less the domain of holiness than the height. I became a son of one world and celebrated the fact with the opening words of Cardinal Newman's hymn from the Dream of Gerontius:

> Praise to the holiest in the height
> And in the depth be praise.   (*Hymns Ancient & Modern*, Standard Edition, No. 172)

The challenge was to discover whether I could truly live these words or not.

The Green Man

The advent of the Ancient One brought with it many trials. It was a painful and traumatic time. We became engaged in a series of encounters that lasted, on and off, for a couple of years. There were some hard-fought contests between us. He may not always have been gentle with me, but he was always fair. His most challenging manifestation was as the Green Man. He became a trusted companion as I was led into the mysteries of the Otherworld.

I remember that there was a paradox when I first wrote down my description of him. The face of this Green Man consists of a leaf-mask but painted in gold and white! Gold represents nature transformed, in harmony with heaven. The combination of leaves (acanthus) and a human face celebrates the union of homo sapiens and the vegetable world. No matter how high we may ascend into heaven, the Green Man reminds us that neither we nor the animal kingdom could exist if the plant world had not remained at the vegetative stage. Every breath that we take is dependent on plants. Every mouthful of the wholesome food that they are, nourishes both body and soul. His is a benign and loving face, full of warmth and inspiration. He reflects a deep sense of confidence in our ability as humans to approach and use the cosmic intelligence which he possesses and imparts. But at times I also see a profound sadness in his eyes, as he stares, eternally, at the human abuse and rape of the elemental powers or deities (neutral in themselves) in his care. But in spite of this tragic sense of life, the Green Man continues to proclaim the words that enable the different aspects of Nature to be in harmony. These words are symbolized by the golden ribbon or meandering pattern that issues forth from his mouth. In this particular context he is the Teutonic god Odin or Wotan, creator of speech in all its manifestations, the outward flowing of creative breath.

Long before the advent of modern psychology, in ancient myths and ritual, the Green Man warns every generation that any attempts on our behalf to suppress or crush the powers of Nature will prove fatal to human well-being. These divinely created energies need to grow and flower. Ignore them and they will turn on us in a desperate attempt at self-recognition. They need to be approached with awe and humility, lovingly embraced and moulded into the creative work of art that we have the potential to be.

The Green Man transcends all cultures and ages. His is a truly universal role. This became apparent the more I researched into the symbolism of the Pennal figure. In addition to his affinity with the Teutonic deities, our Green Man is a link to ancient Greece and its mysteries. He is also Oceanus, the leaf-rayed, open-eyed deity of the Greeks, who imagined an immense river (self-contained and therefore with no source or outlet) which formed a watery canopy around the whole universe, the Supernatural River which embraces all seas within its waters. Represented in the window by a deep-blue river pattern, Oceanus is the eternal flowing movement of creation. He speaks of a harmonious and ordered world, one where every aspect of creation is in tune with each other. It is wonderful to realize that we belong to such a world of symmetry and beauty. But cosmos is always balanced by chaos. It was therefore no surprise, when I looked at the Green Man a few more times, to find that he had horns sticking out of the side of his head! In his primordial wholeness, the Ancient One is also Dionysius, the Horned God. He is the irrational power of life: spontaneity and wildness, ecstasy and intoxication. Dionysius, the god who wants us to feel everything to the core of our being, the fertility god who challenges us to journey to the centre of the earth in order to experience the creativity that lies at the heart of life.

Since the Green Man is the bridge between our native pagan and Christian past, it is fitting that in the guise of the Horned God he also points to Cernunnos, the Celtic Lord of the Wild Hunt. Half human and half animal, he reminds us of our links with the animal kingdom. With horns or antlers on his head, he is also the archetypal shaman, the wise-one-cum-healer, who travels between the different worlds honouring the unity and interrelatedness of all things. His experience teaches us that nothing exists in isolation from the Whole.

The faces with which my divine companion revealed himself to me were manifold, as were the blessings which came from our encounter.

A Native Christianity

During my Celtic initiation, unknown aspects of my personality emerged, each one seeking my attention and allegiance. But the Green Man had not come to draw attention to himself. His role was to prepare for the coming of the Lady Wisdom into the lives of many in our Valley, the return of the Goddess. It was through his mediation that I was empowered to explore Nature in all her beauty and wonder. His guidance enabled me to become more open to the Wisdom that lay behind all phenomena. By learning how to look 'both ways at once' I encountered true wholeness. I also caught a glimpse of that which partakes of divine and human reality, the Mystery that is Sophia. It was the Green Man who announced the dawn of her restoration. He was Her champion. No longer would She be out of reach for those who truly sought to embrace the reality which She embodies. 'By your desire the veils which hide me are withdrawn,' She said. She revealed herself to us in many and various ways. In addition to Her heralds in Nature, She spoke through the ancient words of Holy Scriptures, as well as addressing some in dreams and appearing to others in visions.

It was in honouring the land that we began to earth the Vision that Sophia had imparted to us. It was through the earth that She helped us to reclaim our ancestry.

We began to cultivate our gardens. At the Rectory we even hired an earth-mover in order to re-fashion the land. It was a time of great physical and theological activity.

We began putting things right.

The 'high places' were re-built. An altar was erected near two of my sacred trees. One, an Ash, like a living pole, has two arms forever outstretched towards the sky. The other, a Willow, overshadows one of many special places for worship and prayer. It is always a privilege to be near her and a delight to sit in her shade.

Although our garden runs parallel to a busy road, I'm always amazed at how peaceful it always is. It is like entering another world. Here, even the hard work of digging has ceased being a painful toil and has become a source of blessing, the sweat of my brow an anointing.

Overshadowing the whole site is *The Lady of the Mountain,* a solitary Beech that occupies the highest spot in the garden. She sees everything. Twin Oaks, nearby, provide a spacious canopy, a shelter from both sun and rain. At Pentecost 1993 I planted a small Tamarisk tree, a gift from a friend. To mark the Midsummer that followed, I planted a Rowan tree, one of two Celtic holy trees missing from our grounds. Trees played an important part in the spirituality of the ancient Celts. They still do for those in many countries who are endeavouring to follow the teaching of their native wisdom. Trees form a sacred calendar, where days and months are named after a whole range of trees that focus the energies and qualities of a particular time of year. For example, the evergreen Ivy occupies 30 September to 27 October and is symbolic of the tenacity of life. The Birch or *Shining One* (24 December to 20 January) is the cosmic pillar or ladder that links heaven to earth. My trees have become a very special source of knowledge and inspiration. I have learnt much by entering into personal relationship with them.

Of all my garden duties, caring for the trees is the sacred act *par excellence,* a special form of worship and devotion, moving prayer. As with the touch of fresh spring water from our well or the feel of rose petals, trees are also a tangible manifestation of the Divine. Living icons, intimate, sensual ways of relating to divinity.

The mystery of heaven is not divorced from the mystery of earth.

Sophia had come and 'tabernacled' among us, as the Bible describes it. She now laid the foundation and built Her temple. There are no barriers inside. All is sanctuary. All are welcome. We saw its many beautiful pillars and walked amongst them. We were especially drawn to two of them. One of them honoured our native spirituality. I shall never forget the excitement of discovering that we Celts had our *Old Testament,* our own ancient scriptures, written not only on paper but also in the very landscape itself. This pillar celebrates the wisdom of pagan, Druidic and Celtic lore. The Green Man adorned the temple with garlands, and gave me the courage to make a sanctuary of my high places

The Order of Sancta Sophia

In addition to honouring Sophia's tabernacling by entering into a new relationship with the earth, some of my parishioners joined me on Ascension Day 1987 in founding the Order of Sancta Sophia or Holy Wisdom. At first our aims were general in nature. We wanted to find out as much as we could about the Lady Wisdom, especially Her status in the Bible and church tradition. It became clear early on that her appearance was, in some way, related to the renewal and usefulness of the Church. With this went a new awareness of the meaning of prayer and spirituality. There emerged among some members a deep desire to develop our lives in a more contemplative manner. Not an easy vocation for busy Christians! But we took comfort from the fact that in Celtic and Orthodox traditions, no distinction is made between the spirituality of the lay person and those called to what the Roman Church describes as 'the religious life'. Through Christ the life of Grace is open to all.

As we gradually travelled into Sophia's universal nature, we found, paradoxically, a new sense of pride and empowerment in our own native identity and cultural roots. But the more we celebrated our own spiritual heritage, the more open we became to Sophia's presence in other religions and cultures. One tradition, in particular, resonated deep within me, and its history eventually came to embody the various stages of my early encounter with the Lady Wisdom. I refer to the Sophianic or Wisdom movement that emerged in Russia during the last quarter of the nineteenth century, and lasted until the 1930s. This is the second pillar of great power and beauty that supports Sophia's temple in our Valley. The reredos removed from Pennal Church has since become symbolic of many barriers encountered during my spiritual journey. None more so than my efforts to find out more about the Russian Sophianists, in view of the fact that I have no knowledge of the Russian language! My search for 'the Russians' became synonymous with my quest to discover more about Sophia.

A celebratory spirit pervades all our activities. Even the painful and sad occasions seem to be rooted in a deep sense of joy. No event was 'ordinary' any more. Sophianic reality is profoundly incarnational. The so-called insignificant things in life do really matter and speak volumes about one's spirituality. A simple poem becomes a mystic love-song. A familiar journey suddenly takes on the spirit of a Grail adventure. A plain-looking building becomes Camelot.

In groups of different sizes, and sometimes individually, we visited and thus honoured, sites and buildings important in our native heritage and in sophianic lore. Many of these visits coincided with major seasonal and/or ecclesiastical festivals. Samhain (the Celtic New Year) 1992 was a pilgrimage to Anglesey, the Druidic Isle, nicknamed *The Mother of Wales*, to visit prehistoric sites. The high point of the day was being huddled together deep inside an ancient burial mound at Bryn Celli Ddu. In 1994 we made a pilgrimage to Whitby, to mark the 1330th anniversary of the famous Synod held there. It was the occasion when Christians who followed the Celtic Tradition had to break with their customs in order to follow the way of the Latin or Roman Church. We returned to 'Whitby AD 664', not to commemorate the defeat of the Celtic Way but in order to honour the memory and courage of St Aidan and his companions who could not abide by the decision of the Synod and chose, instead, to return to Lindisfarne, Iona and the West Coast of Ireland, still free to honour their distinctive spirituality.

Sergius Bulgakov

In 1992 I visited two buildings contrasting both in history and size, one explicitly Sophianic in character, the other with a more veiled association with the Sophianic movement. On 16 May at about twelve noon I stood in Sancta Sophia, Constantinople, or Istanbul as it is known today. I too fell under 'the spell of that which it reveals, an all-embracing unity, harmony itself.' So wrote Sergius Bulgakov, one of the leading Russian Sophianists, after his visit to the domed church, built by Justinian in the sixth century, and dedicated to the Divine Wisdom. In this temple of temples (now, alas a museum), I knew that Fr Bulgakov and his companions had not turned to Sophia because there was something lacking or missing in their Christianity, but because they had discovered the Source of that which is Wholeness itself.

In June I visited St Basil's House in London. It was, at the time, the headquarters of the Fellowship of St Alban and St Sergius, an ecumenical Anglican-Orthodox society which Bulgakov.co-founded in 1928. In the chapel I saw the iconostasis (the screen that separates the main body of the church from the sanctuary) designed by Sister Johanna Reitlinger. Sister Johanna painted both icons on it and dedicated them to the memory of Sergius Bulgakov, her spiritual father... 'Our ever-remembered teacher and guide, in fulfilment of his prayers for the Russian Church' and 'in fulfilment of his prayers for the union of all Christians'.

Fr Bulgakov's Orthodox supporters hailed him as a great Christian sage and teacher, one of the most outstanding Russian Church leaders of his, or any, generation. Even his detractors could not but acknowledge him as a great scholar, a wise pastor and a devoted priest. And yet it transpired, after some preliminary research, that during his lifetime Fr Bulgakov was attacked by members of his own Church, and denounced as a modernist, a gnostic, a propounder of an alien doctrine and a heretic. All this came about because of the teaching he developed concerning Sophia, the Divine Wisdom. She came to occupy the heart of his experience of the Divine and consequently the theology that grew from it. 'Sophiology', as it is known, was the fruit of his life's work and devotion. And yet I found it strange that no mention of Sophia appeared in Bulgakov's English-language obituary. Furthermore, it is only now, fifty years after his death, that Bulgakov's writings are beginning to appear in English.

'Be healthy, be whole, be holy'

Members of the Order who live locally meet every week, in each other's homes, for prayer and meditation, study and fellowship. Saints' days and other holy days are celebrated with the sharing of the Holy Eucharist. Occasional day and weekend retreats are welcome aids in the pursuit of sanctity. Birthdays and special anniversaries are also occasions for social gatherings and fellowship meals. Members who live at a distance from the *Mother House*, as some have come to regard Pennal Church, make every effort to join us for the major festivals. There is still no physical Round Table at Pennal (at least not yet!), but the strong feeling of solidarity that exists among followers of Sophia is a reality that now spreads to many parts of the world.

In 1989 *The Upper Room* above the Parsonage house garage was renovated and furnished for the use of the parish and the Order. Built in the 1780s, and entered by stone steps from the outside, the room has become the focal point for most of the Order's activities. So tangible is 'the Presence' in this room that the space and atmosphere within has become a living embodiment of the Order's motto, — 'Be healthy, be whole, be holy'. A few years ago a sculptor friend of the Order, David Iona, presented a highly original piece of sculpture as a gift to the Order. It is a cross that celebrates the union of our Celtic heritage and Sophia. It now hangs on the north wall of the Upper Room.

Sophianic Liturgy

Another fruit of Sophia's presence is the emergence of a Sophianic liturgy. Still in its rudimentary form, these acts of worship have grown out of our relationship with the Divine Feminine. It has become increasingly difficult to honour profound aspects of our spirituality in alien forms of expression imposed from without. It is in and through the heart that all our human faculties are drawn together. The outward expression of an intimate Divine-human encounter, authentic liturgy must therefore be rooted within the rhythmic beating of a passionate and loving heart. Members continue to produce their own prayers and hymns, in addition to discovering a wealth of material from other traditions that speak personally to them. One of my first discoveries was the following from the Jewish mystical tradition. It occupies an honoured place in our devotions, and I have put the words to a simple plainchant.

Sweet hymns and songs will I indite
To sing of Thee by day and night
Of thee who art my soul's delight.

How doth my soul within me yearn
Beneath Thy shadows to return
Thy secret mysteries to learn.
Thy Glory shall my discourse be,
In images I picture Thee,
Although myself I cannot see.

In mystic utterance alone.
By prophet and by seer made known
Hast Thou Thy radiant Glory shown.
My meditation day and night.
May it be pleasant in Thy sight
For Thou art all my soul's delight.   (Jewish Hymn of Glory)

The following is a prayer written by a member of the Order. It also highlights the theme of GLORY that appears to be synonymous with Sophia's presence, in this case as She emerges from the depth of the earth:

Awake my Queen
For you have dwelt too long
Within the dark recess
Of this hidden cave.
How my heart grieves to see you
Forgotten and neglected.
Come close, my love,
Remain within my arms
Until strength returns
And you can face the dawn.
These precious moments
Will all too quickly pass...
Soon I must wrap you warm
Within your royal cloak,
And place upon your head
Your pearl encrusted crown.
For we are caught
On the very axis of the Universe.
Drawn inexorably
From darkness into light...
Soon you will step forth
Into the hearts of your waiting people.
In their hearts you will find
Your kingdom and your power,
In their hearts you will witness
The celebration of your Glory.

(AMH)

The Universal Christ

My parents nurtured my sisters and me in a broad type of Christianity. We were taught about the Universal Christ who owes allegiance to no religious label, least of all Christian ones! I valued greatly belonging to an Order where its members had no desire to follow a narrow kind of Christianity, or any other religion, for that matter. The memorial that I put up in my mother's honour, above the lych-gate entrance into Pennal church, embodies the kind of religion that she would have me follow. Written in Welsh, the words are from the prophecy of Isaiah of the Outcasts. They read:

Gelwir fy nhy yn dy gweddi i'r holl bobloedd.

They come from Isaiah 56:7 and celebrate the fact that the Divine will and purpose is that 'My house will be a house of prayer for all peoples.' This sentiment has come to embody one of the main principles of beliefs of the Order of Sancta Sophia. One corner of the church sanctuary has been dedicated to the Divine Wisdom and is adorned with a traditional Russian Sophia icon and a five-pronged candelabrum. Members of the Order also financed a project in 1991 whereby a copy of all the main holy books of the world's religions were acquired and placed under the Wisdom icon. On some festivals additional candles are lit to represent the Wisdom that lies at the heart of each religion.

A Paris Pilgrimage

As 1993 drew to a close, I began to think of ways in which the Order and I could celebrate the fiftieth anniversary of Sergius Bulgakov's death. Fr Bulgakov's spiritual odyssey has come to embody the Sophianic quest for many of us. I wanted to honour the memory of his life and ministry in a special way. It was impossible for me to travel to Paris for 12 July, the anniversary of the day that he died, but my wife Ann and I decided to include a trip to Paris as part of our October half-term vacation and celebrations leading up to Samhain. The plan was to visit Fr Bulgakov's grave at the Russian cemetery of Ste Genevieve-des-Bois and also the Russian Theological Institute that was such a big part of his life in exile. The visit to St-Serge (the name of the college chapel) as it is affectionately known, did come about. The chapel itself was closed to visitors but we managed to spend a reflective half-hour walking around the gardens, surrounded by a rich diversity of trees, all in different stages of shedding their leaves. Sitting under one of them I offered a prayer of thanksgiving for the life of this Orthodox priest. A theologian in the most patriarchal of churches, Bulgakov has helped me to honour the Divine Feminine in my ministry. A Christian, born in Russia and exiled to the West, Bulgakov's Sophianic vision is a bridge capable of uniting many across Europe who are seeking to rediscover or renew their faith.

Ann and I never made it to Bulgakov's grave, but our pilgrimage to Russian Orthodox Paris was crowned in a most unexpected way. In the early nineties, I exchanged several letters with the Dean and Professor Emeritus at Saint Sergius, one Constantine Andronikof. Then in his late seventies, Constantine stayed in Paris after his retirement from the Institute. He died in September 1997. A sub-deacon in the Russian Church, Constantine was twenty-five years old when he first entered the Institute, and had the privilege of studying with Bulgakov during the last five years of his life. He translated all of Bulgakov's major writings into French, about twelve books in all, and was one of his foremost disciples. We had no way of knowing whether Constantine was at home, but Ann and I decided to visit him. Total strangers, he received us with much grace and courtesy. We talked non-stop for the best part of an hour. It is the only time that I have met with a follower of Fr Bulgakov, and, what's more, a person who, in different ways, has been involved with the Russian theological Institute for over fifty years. I will always treasure the correspondence that I shared with Constantine.

Since the Samhain pilgrimage to Paris, the Order of Sancta Sophia commenced its second seven-year period in some very interesting ways, especially in terms of her relationship with Russian Orthodox Christians both in Russia and in the USA. The Lady Wisdom continues to weave the Celtic-Russian strands of our work together in a creative manner. The Order accepted the challenge of celebrating the Sophianic vision of life, by preserving, developing and promoting, Celtic and Russian spiritual traditions.

One request on my part, at the beginning of Lent 1995, bore fruit in a way that has greatly enriched the work of the Order. In 1994, when the Fellowship of St Alban and St Sergius moved its headquarters from London to Oxford, St Basil's chapel was dismantled and various furnishings and fittings dispersed to different parts of the UK. On Ash Wednesday 1995 I learnt that the iconostasis could come to Pennal, to take pride of place in our Upper Room. The latter was eventually dedicated to the Divine Sophia as a memorial chapel to Fr Sergius Bulgakov. The altar and its holy vessels were dedicated in memory of my father, who died on Holy Monday 1995.

Sophia's Prophets

As the twentieth century dawned in the West, two important figures, one a Celt, the other a Russian, shared the prophetic vision that lies at the heart of Sophianic spirituality. Both were seeking for ways to revive the spirit of the Church, and, as prophets, it was with eyes towards the future that they encountered, in different ways, the Divine Feminine. As a new millennium dawns the West needs to listen, with much urgency, to what these prophets and their followers have to say. One of them, Vladimir Soloviev, we shall hear more about in a later chapter. For now, suffice it to say that he was the founder of the Russian Sophianic movement. A brilliant philosopher and poet, he combined deep mystical intuitions with a sharp speculative mind. A four-line verse from Soloviev is his annunciation of Sophia's appearance on earth. It reads:

> Let it be known that today the Eternal Feminine
> Is descending on earth in an incorruptible body.
> In the unfailing light of the New Goddess
> The heavens have become united with the deeps.

The other person was the Scotsman, William Sharpe (1855-1905) who, although educated in Glasgow, spent a great deal of his youth among the native fishermen and shepherds of the Western Highlands. For the last decade of his life, he wrote under the pseudonym Fiona Macleod, thus honouring the wisdom which helped him reconnect with his other, more feminine self. He immersed himself in the mysteries of his native land, and like Soloviev and Bulgakov, became an apostle of a very distinctive kind of Christianity. In Iona, published in 1910, he writes of the old Celtic prophecy that

> 'The Holy Spirit shall come again which once was mortally born among us as the Son of
> God, but, then, shall be the Daughter of God.' All will be aware of the 'descending of the
> Divine Womanhood upon the human heart as a universal spirit descending upon awaiting
> souls'. I believe,' wrote Macleod, 'that though the Reign of Peace may be yet a long way off,
> it is drawing near; and that Who shall save us anew shall come divinely as a Woman.'

The prophecy concludes with these deeply feminine sentiments —

> 'I have learned, and do see, that not only prophecies and hopes, and desires unclothed yet in
> word or thought, foretell her coming, but already a multitude of spirits are in the gardens of
> the soul, and are sowing seed and calling upon the winds of the south; and that everywhere
> are watching eyes and uplifted hands, and signs which cannot be mistaken, in many lands, in
> many peoples, in many minds; and in the heaven itself that the soul sees, the surpassing
> signature.' (pp. 20-22)

Gates of Mystery

The sanctuary at Pennal Church has been the location of many an episode in the Divine-human drama that is unfolding in our midst, a sanctuary that is forever on the move since Sophia came among us. 'Travel light' seems to be one of Her favourite watchwords! It was the removal of the reredos, many years ago, that helped set in motion a whole series of exciting events. Among them, we witnessed the loving embrace of earth deities and angelic beings, both united again. There was no holding back the joy that prevailed when the Green Man adorned Sophia with garlands at the Wedding feast. Barrier after barrier disappeared in our lives, the more Sophia unveiled Herself. Different gateways appeared into the mystery of creation. Or maybe it was one gateway but with many different aspects? It was the arrival of the iconostasis at the Spring equinox that crowned the first period in the work of the Order. It also inaugurated a new episode in our history. We had exchanged one barrier for another. The screen is not symbolic of the partition or divide between heaven and earth. On the contrary, it celebrates the link between the two, for in the Sophianic vision, heaven and earth are conjoined in a unique way. The passage or entrance between the two is symbolized by the 'royal doors', as they are called in the Orthodox tradition. The gates of mystery, guarded in this case by the four living creatures, first mentioned in chapter one of Ezekiel and again in the Apocalypse of St John:

> 'And the first beast was like a lion, and the second beast like a calf, the third had a face as
> a man, and the fourth beast was like a flying eagle.' (4:7)

Back to the Future
There was nothing sentimental about my pilgrimage to Saint-Sergius. It was not a journey to some romantic past but an affirmation of what is yet to come. It was also the celebration of a Movement that not only goes back millennia to the time of King Solomon but also comes to us from a future brimming with life and vitality. That future is now, and the teaching of the Russian Sophianist is on hand to help give meaning to it. My visit to Paris also brought to completion an important stage in my spiritual journey. In preparation for it, I retraced some important steps in my early life, especially Halfway House and the slate graveyards that have since become a monument to all that is dead and decaying in my life.

I have said my farewells. I will not be returning to that Halfway House again. It is time to move on. New challenges are beckoning.

Footnote:
Following a brief visit by the general Secretary of the Fellowship of St Alban and St Sergius to the Chapel of Holy Wisdom at Pennal, its governing council decided that it was not appropriate for the fellowship to be associated with an 'unorthodox' presentation of Christianity. Fr Bulgakov's memorial iconostasis was consequently returned to the fellowship's headquarters in Oxford during Advent 1997. A new iconostasis has been erected in its place, this time in a native Celtic style, and dedicated in memory of Fr Sergius Bulgakov and Sister Johanna Reitlinger.

NOTES FOR CHAPTER ONE

S. Bulgakov, *The Wisdom of God*, Williams & Norgate, London 1937
Adam Fox, *Dean Inge*, John Murray, London 1960
John A.T. Robinson, *Honest to God*, SCM Press, London1963
Hymns Ancient and Modern (Standard Edition), London 1924
Isidore Epstein, *Judaism*, 'Hymn of Glory', p. 231, Penguin Books 1980
Y Beibl Cymraeg Newydd, Cymdeithas Y Beibl 1988
Samuel D. Cioran, *Vladimir Soloviev and the Knights of the Divine Sophia*, Wilfrid Laurier University Press, Ontario 1977
Fiona Macleod, *Iona*, Floris Books 1991

2. Sophia and the Bible

I came upon a child of God
He was walking upon the road,
I asked him where he was going,
This he told me…

'Got to get back to the land
Set my soul free…
We are star dust…
And we've got to get ourselves back
To the Garden.'   (*Woodstock*: Joni Mitchell, 1970)

'In the Beginning'

There are two stories of creation in the Book of Genesis. The one in Genesis 1 opens with the well-known phrase 'In the Beginning'. This can also be translated as 'With the Beginning', i.e. 'With Wisdom, the Principle of all things, the Divine One created the heavens and the earth'. The story echoes the sentiments of Psalm 104, which declares:

> How many are your works, O Lord!
> In Wisdom you made them all.   (v. 24).

This story is not meant to be a scientific account of creation, in the modern sense of the word, but celebrates the fact that the whole created order issues forth from the desire and creativity of the Divine One, the Source of all.

Three times the story-teller affirms that Divinity looked with satisfaction upon the goodness (in the Slavonic language the word is 'beautiful') of what had been created. This does not mean perfect or sinless. 'Wholesome' is probably a better translation. The story breathes an awareness of a calm and ordered world. The pinnacle of this world and of this Goodness was the creation of homo sapiens —

> So the Divine One created homo sapiens
>   in its own image;
> Male and female they were created
>   in the Divine image.   (v. 27)

All human beings were created in this Divine image — created to imitate or to become like the Divine One, destined to exercise responsible stewardship over the whole of creation, exercising this honour in partnership with the Divine. And the Divine One blessed them (v. 28), a humanity created as being fit to exercise royal or sovereign rule. In the words of Psalm 8, a humanity 'crowned with glory and honour' (v. 5), the very image of the Divine One. But which one? Divinity has many aspects, just as there are many ways of experiencing and then talking about the Divine. El Elyon is, for example, an ancient title for 'God'. It is not a proper name but more of a description, since the actual Name of The Divine One is unknown. El Elyon was the Divine One as revealed to the Patriarchs and Matriarchs of old. The hymn by T. Olivers, written in 1770, claims to sing the praises of 'The God of Abraham', El Elyon, but proceeds to address him as 'Yhwh' — The Great I am. But Abraham's 'God' is not Yhwh. Abraham knew the divine as El Elyon.

The Elohim

The second verse in the Bible goes on to speak of the Spirit of the Divine One hovering 'upon the waters', as if covering the whole earth like a mist. The original Hebrew speaks of 'the Spirit of Elohim' covering the earth. The great commandment in Deuteronomy 6:4 informs us that 'Yhwh our Elohim is one Yhwh', while in chapter 19 of Exodus, Moses is described as going up to the Mount of the Elohim, where one of the Elohim spoke to him. The second creation story even speaks of 'Yhwh Elohim' when it speaks of the divine.

'El-lohim' is a feminine word (as in 'El') with a masculine plural. It means 'the divine powers' at work in creation, the gods and goddesses, the heavenly beings who, in different ways, manifest the Divine. The second verse in the Bible refers, therefore, to all the powers of creation, gathered together in perfect unity. It was a world where Harmony reigned. 'El-lohim' also means 'the shining ones'. Many ancient words for the Divine share this root meaning. *Ellu* is Old Welsh for El (Radiant One), from which we get the feminine name Ellen or Eli, the goddess of Light. In Old Irish the word is Aillil which means shining. The Babylonian word for El is Ellu, as in the Welsh. But it isn't only the Near Eastern and Western cultures that speak of the shining or shining ones. In Tibet, they are referred to as 'the luminous sons', one of whom 'shines forth as the sun', the blazing divine dragon-serpent of Wisdom. Following his face to face encounter with the Elohim on the holy mount, Moses himself was transformed and his face radiated with the divine light (Exodus 34:29).

The other creation story in Genesis has probably had more of an influence on western culture and religion — or at least a particular interpretation of it has. I refer to the story commonly known as the Garden of Eden (2:4-3:24) and subtitled 'The Fall'. It is the story or drama whose cast includes Adam and Eve, the Serpent, plenty of trees, which include the Tree of Knowledge and the Tree of Life, the Divine One, Yhwh (as it is called in this version), and the Elohim.

In most translations of the Bible the 'Elohim' are not mentioned by name, although some translators use an alternative word, mostly 'angel', which means 'messenger', which somehow sounds more respectable, and certainly more Christian, than gods or goddesses!

The appearance of the Elohim in the Eden narrative makes them part of one of the great mysteries in the Bible. In the Older Testament, there are two statements of fundamental importance that totally contradict each other. One is in Genesis and the other in 2 Samuel, known as the Court History. The latter is almost 3000 years old and is among the oldest material in the Bible.

In 2 Samuel, the author describes the much loved and heroic King David as being so wise and powerful that he was 'like the Elohim' (14:20). It is a phrase meant as the greatest compliment he could pay his monarch. Psalm 82, in fact, goes on to refer to the monarchs of the earth as being not only Elohim (gods and goddesses) but also 'Sons or Offspring of El Elyon' (v. 6). High praise indeed!

But according to the Eden story of creation, Yhwh did not want Adam and Eve to eat of the Tree of Knowledge, lest they become 'like the Elohim, knowing good and evil'. What is more, when they do partake of the fruit, both Adam and Eve are cursed and banished from Eden. So what happened between the time when these two stories were written, to change not only the status of the Elohim and their power and wisdom (two of their chief attributes, according to the Bible), but also the perception of what it means to be human? To answer this question fully we need to discover what happened to Sophia and Her Garden.

We go back to 'The Beginning', or at least 3000 years ago, to Jerusalem and the days of the first Temple built by King Solomon, back to an ancient spiritual heritage that is as dynamic and fresh today as it ever was. It is a tradition that is forever growing and developing, a tradition that still attracts the opposition of a certain type of religious person and threatens the *status quo* that they seem hell bent on preserving. Central to this heritage is the figure of Wisdom, Sophia, whose rejection by some, and corruption by others, is the Key that can help us to understand the dynamics of biblical spirituality.

Even when She was despised, rejected and efforts undertaken to deny Her very existence, Sophia remains the leading protagonist in the drama. The books in the Bible that claim She never really existed are, paradoxically, tributes to Her endurance, creativity and all-pervasiveness. Those who deliberately set out to extinguish all mention of Sophia, have helped to veil, and thus protect, Her Presence, until a time when She can reveal Herself, once more, in all Her Glory. Traditions within the Scriptures, which display a deep hostility towards Sophia and everything connected with Wisdom, have ended up, unwittingly, confirming the important place She once occupied in the lives of those who remained true to the Ancient Way. In the Wisdom Movement it is Sophia who lies at the heart of Genesis. It is Sophia who is The Beginning.

Sophia and Yhwh?

The prophet whom we know today as Isaiah of the Exile (Isaiah 40-55), sings the praises of Yhwh as Creator (40:12-13) — originally a Hymn of Praise to El Elyon — with whom no one and nothing can compare. It was Yhwh who was responsible for stretching out the heavens like a canopy and bringing out the starry host one by one. In the book of Jeremiah, in a fairly low-keyed way, reference is made to the Divine One (not Yhwh) who founded the world by his Sophia (10:12) i.e. by its power and understanding.

In the Wisdom tradition, however, we see a different theological view of the Genesis event. In Ben Sirach, it is Sophia herself who speaks :

> I emerged from the mouth of El Elyon
> And I covered the earth like a mist;
> I dwelt upon high, and
> In a pillar of cloud was my throne.
> Alone I journeyed through the heavens
> And I have walked in the bottom of the abyss   (24:3-5)

The same sentiment is expressed in the Book of Proverbs — part of which goes back to the time of King Solomon. But the text as we have it in the Bible bears witness to the time when Sophia was neutralized and nationalized, and Yhwh was substituted for El Elyon, e.g. I was there when Yhwh set the deep (v. 27) and again — 'I was the darling by his side' (v. 30). But Yhwh was self-sufficient. He needed no one's help, but his followers were eager, nevertheless, to adopt Sophia to their cause. For followers of El Elyon, however, it was Sophia who formed or fashioned everything that existed. She was the Mother of all things, although She Herself was created before all things began. Before the act of Creation, 'I was there', She declares. She was given birth before the great oceans existed. Fashioned from Eternity, She will exist for Eternity. She is the creativity of The Most High, pouring forth into the whole of creation, sustaining, pervading and penetrating all things. It is Sophia who controls and orders the universe, and maintains the Harmony of Nature.

Sophia is the Knowledge of the way things work, an initiate in Divine Knowledge, as the Wisdom of Solomon describes it (8:4). She is the Mystery at the heart of creation, the Divine Treasure House. Planted in Jerusalem, Sophia had no equal in beauty and height. From this ancient holy place, Sophia's instruction shone forth into the world, filling all who desired Her with knowledge and understanding. The Tree of Life and Knowledge, Sophia's branches spread out in all directions, glorious and fruitful. The Wisdom books in the Bible celebrate Her presence in Eden, a tradition that has more in common with the first creation story in Genesis than the second. It was Sophia who

> protected the first formed father of the world
> When he alone had been created;
> She delivered him from his transgressions
> And gave him strength to rule all things.   (*Wisdom of Solomon* 10:1-2)

What a complete contrast to Yhwh's actions in the second creation story in Genesis, with its curses and expulsion. Chapter 17 of ben Sirach also has an account of homo sapiens' creation out of the earth, the red clay or *adamah*, as the Hebrew calls it:

> The Lord [a deity other than Yhwh] created
>
> them out of the earth,
>
> He filled them with knowledge and understanding,
>
> And showed them good and evil,
>
> He bestowed knowledge upon them....
>
> Their eyes saw his Glorious Majesty.   (vv. 1,7,11,13)

Adam and Eve were 'endowed with strength' like the strength of the Divine One (17.3). This type of spirituality has also more in common with the tradition of 2 Samuel. Knowledge is a gift that can be exercised and used in a responsible manner. The Wisdom tradition, however, is not blind to the fact that creation is far from being perfect or truly harmonious, but its outlook is far more optimistic and it has a positive view of the human condition.

> Even if we sin we are Thine [i.e. El Elyon's]
>
> Knowing Thy power;
>
> But we will not sin, because we
>
> Know we are accounted Thine.   (*Wisdom of Solomon* 15:2)

The Apostle Paul could not improve on this sentiment. All he could do was remind us of this Wisdom teaching. Ben Sirach adds, in the same vein:

> Whoever obeys me will not be put to shame, and those who work with my [i.e. Sophia's]
>
> help will not sin. (24:22)

At the heart of the Cult of Sovereignty was Sophia. It was She who communicated the Divine will via an array of intermediaries, both human and angelic. She guided, instructed and initiated Her servants in the Truth. Ever since Jacob's vision at Beth-El, there had been a regular intercourse between heaven and earth. The gap was always being bridged by representatives or emissaries from the Heavenly Court, all of them with a role or task to fulfil. In ancient times not everyone experienced the heavenly ascent into the Divine Presence, only the elect few were granted the privilege: e.g. 'I have exalted a young man from among the people, David my Servant' (Psalm 80). He was allowed to join the Elohim in the Divine Assembly. But Sophia never appeared Herself, never revealed Herself. Her place was in Heaven. Hence Solomon's longing for Her to appear in person.

> Send Her forth from the Holy Heavens
>
> and from the Throne of Thy glory send Her
>
> that She may be with me and toil,
>
> And that I may learn what is pleasing to Thee.   (*Wisdom of Solomon* 9:10-11)

It is Sophia who reveals El Elyon. It is She who reveals the things that lie hidden, the secrets of the universe, the mysteries of the Divine. It is Sophia who is the Key to Eden, the meaning of creation. In Her, before time began, lay the Christic seed, the Hope of Glory. In the verse in Ben Sirach (24), where we read of Sophia emerging from the Mouth of El Elyon, we also read of Her opening Her mouth 'in the Assembly of The Most High,' in the presence of the Elohim, the Host of Heaven, Her people.

At the heart of Eden is Sophia's personal and wholesome invitation:

> Come to me, you who desire me
>
> And eat your fill of my produce.
>
> For the remembrance of me is sweeter than honey

And my inheritance sweeter than the honeycomb.

Those who eat me will hunger for more

And those who drink me will thirst for more.   (*ben Sirach* 24:19-21)

Her thought is 'more abundant than the Sea, and Her Counsel deeper than the Great Abyss.' She declares:

I went forth like a canal from a river

And like a water channel into a garden.

I said, 'I will water my orchard

And drench my garden plot.'

And lo, my canal became a river,

And my river became a sea.   (vv. 29-31)

By discovering more about Sophia and the dynamics of the Divine Assembly, we will find out more about what the Older Testament has to say about El Elyon's blueprint for the universe, and hence, the role of homo sapiens, as well as the Elohim.

The Divine Assembly

The cosmos and its ideal Harmony was focused on the Holy Mountain in Jerusalem, the centre of the earth. Established by The Most High, Jerusalem was Queen among the provinces. She was the Divine Mother Goddess, like a fruitful vine, conspicuous for Her height and many strong branches. She nourished Her children, who drank deeply of, and delighted in, her bountiful breasts. Her sisters were the nations round about. Samaria, for example, was an older sister, Edom a younger sister. Lebanon was particularly favoured, a little Eden in herself. The prophet Ezekiel said of her: 'Which of the trees of Eden can be compared with you in splendour and majesty?' (31.18) Every sister had a holy mount of her own. Edom's holy mountain was Mount Seir. Samaria's holy mountain is called Mount Gerizim, the focus of worship to this day. The princes or kings of the earth (the rulers of 'the nations', such as Ammon and Egypt, Tyre and Sidon) were looked upon as lovers of Jerusalem, the Divine Bride, the Virgin Mother. Every nation was apportioned a share of Eden, the Beautiful Land. In the Greek version of the Hebrew Bible (known as the Septuagint or LXX), we read in Deuteronomy that

When The Most High gave the nations their inheritance,

When he divided all humanity, he set up boundaries for the peoples

according to the number of the sons of God. [i.e. El Elyon].   (32:8)

These sons were the kings of the earth and they were divine. Jacob, for example, was allotted his inheritance, as the Deuteronomy passage reminds us. But this eighth verse was changed in the Hebrew version, so that 'sons of El Elyon' became 'sons of Israel', thus changing the complete meaning of the sacred text. The other sons were therefore excluded. But all the sons of The Most High were apportioned a share of the Glory, or the Majesty of El Elyon, from the very beginning. The Kings who represented the people of El Elyon, the 'nobles of the nations', took their place in the Temple that was situated on the Holy Mount, also called The Heavenly Court, The Assembly of the Holy Ones. On the Divine Throne, in Heaven, sat El Elyon with Sophia, the Mother Goddess, surrounded by the Elohim, the holy ones, each with their counterparts on earth, the princes of the people. It was an ancient belief that every nation, as indeed each individual, had its guardian deity or heavenly patron. In Job 38, for example, in a passage that praises the work of the Creator, we read of the morning stars singing together, as creation was in progress, while all the sons of El shouted for joy (v. 7).

The King of Zion eventually came to be regarded, by some, as El Elyon's viceroy on earth, one King, who governed all the Kings of Eden. In Psalm 45 we read of the Daughter of the King of Tyre, 'glorious... and beautifully robed', being led to the King of Zion (v. 12). This was a royal visit or a gift from the King of Tyre.

A poem or hymn in Ezekiel 16 probably records an ancient tradition where the union of El Elyon and Jerusalem, the Bride, The Divine Mother, was virtually enacted in the marriage of the King and Queen as Sovereignty's representatives, a sacred fertility rite that took place in Eden, the Holy Mountain.

Each King had his own throne, booth or sanctuary (possibly one of twelve or twenty-four) representing his royal house, he being its 'guardian angel'. The soul of each nation was believed to abide in the person of the King. It was from him that strength and inspiration flowed out to the whole nation, like sap bringing life to the branches of a tree. He was the vine and they were the branches.

The King was a special link between heaven and earth, a channel for Wisdom's power and knowledge. The monarch was the one who 'trusted in Elyon and who loved him. He rejoiced in Elyon, who gave him victory and strength. He wore a crown of pure gold and had splendour and majesty bestowed upon him' (Psalm 21). Another psalm (45) spoke of the King as 'the most blessed of men', blessed by El Elyon for ever. The King was he who rode forth on 'behalf of truth, humility and righteousness'. Ezekiel describes the sovereign as a model of perfection, full of wisdom and perfect in beauty. He was the anointed cherub guardian, 'for so it was ordained' by El Elyon. He was 'blameless in [his] ways from the day [he] was created' (Ezekiel 28:15). The goal of this royal, sacred cult, embodied in the person of the King, and supported by his court, was the maintaining and thus restoring, if need be, of harmony between heaven and earth. Justice in the heavens meant that right (or righteous) order would be maintained in the natural order of things on earth. Heavenly knowledge had therefore to be discovered and then transmitted to earth where it would be handled responsibly in maintaining order and harmony. Christians still pray: 'Thy will be done, on earth as it is in heaven'.

The Wise Ones: Sophia's Servants

The monarch and his 'wise ones' (e.g. diviners, magicians, enchanters and prophets) had acquired, or were granted, this knowledge. They were adept at handling the dynamics of the Otherworld, a knowledge which the Elohim helped to impart, the very secrets of creation. Mortals and heavenly beings shared this divine knowledge or wisdom lore for the common good. Both were privy to the sacred names or words which were essential to maintain cosmic harmony. Both co-operated in the task. This knowledge included the natural sciences of the day, metal work, the interpretation of dreams (a special way of discovering the Divine Will), as well as ways of interpreting history and consequently the ability of predicting the future. In Exodus 31 Bezalel ben Uri ben Hur, who worked on the Ark of the Covenant, was one 'full of the Divine Spirit' [i.e. Wisdom], a prerequisite for 'skill, ability and knowledge in all kinds of craftsmanship' (vv.3-5).

Sophia was the root of this knowledge, the source of all understanding, the power of creation.

The wise ones had a special relationship with Sophia. They were empowered to see into the heart of the universe. In order to uphold the cosmic order or harmony, they faced and confronted the elements that had gone astray and had thus become alienated from the whole. The wise ones were instrumental in healing the fragmentation that ensued. Daniel, the legendary wise man of Israel, acknowledged in prayer to El Elyon —

Praise be to the name of God for ever and ever...

He gives wisdom to the wise
and knowledge to the discerning,

He reveals deep and hidden things....

I thank and praise you, O God of my fathers,

You have given me wisdom and power.   (Daniel 2:20-23)

The author of the Wisdom of Solomon could confidently declare — 'I learnt both what is secret and what is manifest, for wisdom the fashioner of all things, taught me' (7:21-22).

The Cult of Sovereignty

The Cult of Sovereignty is at the heart of this ancient form of spirituality — a distinctive relationship or communion with the Divine — and at the heart of this experience was the vision of the Glory and Majesty of El Elyon. Isaiah of Jerusalem, for example, was rooted in this tradition, and became a severe critic of its corruption. He received his call or commission in the Temple, on the Holy Mountain, in the presence of the Elohim and the Hosts of Heaven. Surrounded by the Seraphs, he saw the Divine One and returned to the world as an envoy of heaven. Isaiah knew of the conflicts which corrupted Sophia. He saw in the affairs of earth a reflection of hostilities in the heavenly world. He even mocked the Elohim who abused the heavenly secrets, but never denied their existence. Compared to Yhwh, his god, who was supreme, they, however were as nothing.

Something very dramatic took place to change Sophia's status in Israel and the gifts which She had to bestow on those who sought Her. Sophia was ultimately judged by the behaviour and standards of those who professed to love and serve Her. In the early history of Israel and her neighbours, this meant the King and his wise ones. Royalty mirrored the cosmic blueprint, since the King was a copy or image of El Elyon. So what went wrong? What happened to the harmony ordained by El Elyon on the Holy Mountain? What would result in some traditions in the Older Testament going out of their way to ignore, belittle or even maintain that Sophia and the Elohim had never existed? Part of the answer lies in the fact that the institution of monarchy failed.

Paramount in the Ancient Faith was the importance of honouring and acknowledging the presence and supremacy of El Elyon. The temptation was to put oneself in El Elyon's place; to set oneself up against The Most High. It is the eternal temptation to self-exaltation and self-aggrandizement. El Elyon was defied, envied and challenged. But envy, says the Wisdom of Solomon, does not associate with Sophia (6:23). In the prophecy of Isaiah of Jerusalem we hear a King declare, 'I will make myself like The Most High' (Isaiah 4:15). We read earlier of the splendour and majesty of the King of Lebanon, 'but you too will be brought down with the trees of Eden [i.e. his fellow kings] to the earth below. 'The Cedar of Lebanon', as he was known, had exalted and magnified himself above the other kings and above El Elyon. The kings had misused their power. They did as they pleased. They ignored the pre-ordained harmony of Eden that they were anointed to uphold and defend. They did violence, opposed the alien, ill-treated the fatherless and widowed and traded dishonestly — to name but a few of their of their failures. They denied justice and thus 'corrupted their wisdom' (Ezekiel 28:20). They misused their sovereignty and thus caused disharmony on earth. They brought about The Wasteland.

Given the capacity to transcend themselves, Kings were enabled to become as the Elohim, an integral part of the Divine Assembly. But in being able to look beyond themselves, they imagined themselves to be supreme, the centre of the universe. They foolishly imagined themselves to be the whole instead of an integral part of it. Sons of El Elyon, they rebelled against their Heavenly Father. The Book of Isaiah takes its title and theme from the 'fall' of the kings, namely 'Sons I have reared and brought up, but they have rebelled against me' (Isaiah1:2). The kings became proud, boastful and arrogant, and were consequently deposed and stripped of glory, and driven in disgrace from the Mount of the Elohim. Expelled, they were cast aside and made a spectacle of before their peers. The words of Isaiah of Jerusalem (Isaiah 14:12) are among the most tragic in the whole of Scripture:

> How you have fallen from heaven
> O 'Morning Star', 'Son of the Dawn' —
> the sacred titles of the King of Tyre.

In the ninth and eighth centuries, there were prophets who were continually on hand to censure the behaviour of the kings and to challenge both them and their people with their strict ethical demands. These included among their ranks the likes of Elijah (*c.* 850 BC) and Amos (*c.* 750 BC), the latter personifying the prophetic ideal with the words:

> Hate evil and love good
> and establish justice in the gate.
> Let Justice roll down like water,
> and righteousness like an ever flowing stream.   (Amos 5:14, 24)

The Edenic dynamics disintegrated, and with it the individual's assumptions about Sophia and the Elohim. In rejecting the Cult of Sovereignty some rejected Sophia and attempted to remould Her in their own image. It is in a very real sense that Jewish mystics in a later age came to speak of Sophia as being exiled from the Divine Presence.

Eden Revisited

Was there a way of getting back into the Heavenly Eden? And equally as important, Who would be allowed inside? Who was good or righteous enough to be included, if kings had failed? What steps needed to be taken to complete or 'make right' the work of creation, the work which Sophia was so eager to fashion? The answers which individuals furnish us within the Bible include not only their assumptions about human nature but also their opinions of Sophia and Her handiwork, the Elohim and the quest for knowledge.

The loss of sovereignty elicited an array of responses — solutions, in fact, to a series of 'falls' in Israel's history. Most biblical writers agreed that something new was needed, some even suggesting that the original Eden would have to be rebuilt. For Ezekiel all vestiges of a dynamic and holy life were gone for ever. Eden was littered with a pile of old dry bones. Yhwh would create a new people and make breath enter them again (11:5). But in order to look into, or prepare for, a new Eden, Ezekiel, a priest, looked back to the beginnings of Israel's history and in particular to Moses and the events of Mount Sinai when the Law was given. For Ezekiel, Yhwh was the true Sovereign, the once and future king. He had room for a prince — a Davidic one — but he was more of a tribal leader, as in the days of old. The ideal of Sovereignty on earth, however, now lay with the nation as a whole, a 'Kingdom of Priests' (Exodus 19:6), although the manifestation of this ideal was concentrated in one section of the community. Actual sovereignty or power lay in the hands of a priestly hierarchy, the Sons of Zadok, whose pedigree, it was claimed, went back to the days of the first temple of Solomon.

The vacuum left by the demise of the royal cult was filled by ancient heroes, who took on 'kingly' qualities, such as Abraham, Ezekiel, and in particular, Moses. But even in the days of the Exile, the priest-prophet Ezekiel still lived out his spirituality in terms of the ancient cult of kings, El Elyon's cosmic blueprint. Approximately a third of his book concerns itself with heavenly visions and the Temple cult, both old and new; A third focuses on Jerusalem and the failure of her princes; while the final section is concerned with the nations and the plight of their princes.

In chapter twenty-nine of Isaiah, Isaiah of Jerusalem proclaims that the wisdom of the wise will perish (v. 14), but in the next chapter, he confidently proclaims rather mysteriously that

> Your teachers will be hidden no more,
> with your own eyes you will see them;
> your ears will hear a voice behind you saying,
> 'This is The Way, walk it.'   (30:21)

Isaiah prophesied that 'the powers in the heavens above, and the kings on the earth below' would be punished (24:2). And yet for all his disillusionment with the Way of Wisdom, Isaiah never stopped looking to the day when an ideal king would emerge, rooted in 'justice and righteousness'. Filled with 'wisdom and understanding, counsel and power, knowledge and humility (11:2), nations would rally to him' (12:10). With a righteous King reigning in Jerusalem, Sophia would return and the 'mind of the rash will know and understand' (32:4). In fact, Jerusalem would be filled with 'a rich store of wisdom and knowledge' (33:6).

In contrast, Daniel's vision of Sovereignty was much more Otherworldly. He looked 'beyond the clouds' to a new Eden, a new heaven and earth, where the righteous, the saints, would receive the true Kingdom, and govern it for ever. The power and greatness of all the kingdoms of the earth would be handed over to the Sons of El Elyon. As the enlightened ones, they would shine brightly in the heavens, like stars for ever (12:3). A similar sentiment is expressed in the Book of Job, when it declares that 'the righteous will be enthroned with Kings and be exalted forever' (36:7).

So deeply ingrained in the national psyche was the ideal of sovereignty that in spite of the split of the United Kingdom in 922 BC, the later fall of the Northern Kingdom (Israel) and its monarchy, and the continual failure of most monarchs, both in the North and in the South, to 'uphold justice', the monarchy continued to be supported by the majority. But the events of a few decades at the end of the seventh century BC changed all this, virtually for ever, because the monarchy did not exist in a vacuum. It was part of a complex religious and social system. In the space of a generation the whole system came to an end, with serious repercussions for the subsequent development of religion in Israel, namely the emergence of Judaism and later on the emergence of a re-interpreted Sovereignty Cult, whose followers came to be regarded as heretics and were eventually called 'Christians'. As for Sophia and the Elohim, both were expelled from Eden, along with Adam and Eve. Those who expelled them appeared to take a great delight in doing so.

Let's take a closer look at what happened during those fateful years in Judah and thereby discover the other major reason for Sophia's change of status.

The Deuteronomists

The Southern Kingdom of Judah experienced a new wave of patriotism as the seventh century approached its last decades. It displayed a new pride and fervour in its cultural and religious identity, as it struggled to deal with alien influences, especially the possibility of foreign rule. Nationalistic hopes were at fever pitch. A United Kingdom — last seen at the end of the tenth century — appeared to be a serious possibility. The focal point of this renewal was the boy King Josiah (640-609 BC), and the reform programme which he initiated in 629 BC. A project that soon went hand in hand with a revival of the Mosaic religion of the past. This was known as the Deuteronomic Reformation, a Puritanical religion that was to become a major influence on the religion of Israel and, later, on the development of Christianity and Islam.

Its followers were obsessed with the purity of 'the Faith' as they perceived it. Fanatical reformers who were also passionate nationalists, they would make sure that 'the Faith' became, and would remain, pure. Almost on cue in 621 BC an event took place (or maybe it was orchestrated?), that was seen as a sign of Yhwh's approval. An ancient manuscript was found, a copy of the sacred Law. Here was a second chance (*deutero* means 'second' and *nomos* means 'law') to get things right with Yhwh (2 Chronicles 34:21), an ideal opportunity to get back in favour with Him, by creating the perfect religious person. There were to be no excuses this time round if they were to remain Yhwh's elect. Unlike their ancestors, they would obey Yhwh's commands to the letter.

The Deuteronomists' theological tradition originated in the Northern Kingdom of Israel, whose shrine was at Samaria. But Israel had failed to keep the law and was defeated in 722 BC, a century or so earlier. Its population was deported and the land resettled with colonialists from Babylon and Syria. If Yhwh's commandments were violated a second time, He would bring evil upon Jerusalem, making it a desolation and a curse. The 'Second Chancers' would not abandon their sacred calling. Some of the Exiles came to regard themselves as the true heirs of the Second Chancers, who would provide the basis for the New Age of Yhwh's people. Religious exclusivism reigned. An insular type of spirituality developed, a religious community that was safe, secure and 'small-minded', Yhwh's elect. Every step was taken to ensure that their distinctive and religious purity would prevail. Contamination would be avoided at all costs. They would not mix with the unclean and the wicked. They alone were the 'holy ones', and they would keep themselves separate.

In 538 BC, the Exiles returned to Jerusalem, with the Deuteronomist blueprint in their hands, further inspired by the message of Isaiah of the Exile. Jerusalem would be restored. They repossessed the land and clashed head on with the 'poor of the land', the common folk, who had remained and had continued to practise the Ancient Faith in spite of the disappearance of the Temple and the religious status quo. They had never forgotten the spirituality of their ancestors, rooted in the religion of the Patriarchs and Matriarchs. In terms of the Deuteronomists' own religious logic, however, the common folk were the rightful heirs of the land, because they had not been dispossessed. Dispossession was a sign of Yhwh's disfavour. The Promised Land belonged to the unclean, the unholy, and not to the religious and moral elite. This was the dilemma that faced the heirs of the Deuteronomists.

So what was the Second Chancers' blueprint for the New Eden? The way they reacted to the crisis that brought an end to their nationalistic and religious dreams had serious implications for Wisdom and Her way. They drew in on themselves and blamed everyone and everything for their predicament. They could not re-write history to such an extent that King Solomon, for example, could be spirited away, but being a king he too was apportioned some of the blame for what had happened or came to a head in the events that opened the sixth century.

It was Sovereignty that was to blame. It was Wisdom's way of doing things that had resulted in calamity after calamity. Maybe Solomon was not a total failure — after all he had built the Temple — but he had serious weaknesses, especially the fact that 'his wives turned his heart after other gods' (1 Kings 11:4) — echoes of Genesis 2-3!

Solomon was too broadminded and tolerant of the spirituality of others, especially of his wives. This diluted and perverted the 'true faith', at least in the light of the Second Chancers' way of interpreting history. It is no surprise that Yhwh even became angry with Solomon the Wise! And doubt is expressed in 1 Samuel of the suitability of the institution of monarchy since Yhwh was Israel's true king.

Obedience became the leading characteristic of Deuteronomic spirituality: obey, or else! Wisdom was tied down and 'contained'. There was no need for speculation and questing in far off lands to discover the Truth (Deuteronomy 30:14). The Law was there for all to see. Obey it and all would be well. Time and again we hear the same words — 'Be careful… take care…. and watch yourselves closely. Go carefully… or you will perish,' for Yhwh was an angry deity, a jealous Elohim, a 'consuming-fire-kind-of-Elohim' that destroys the unfaithful.

With strict obedience came an intensive programme of indoctrination, starting with the children. Yhwh's laws were to be impressed on the very young:

> Talk about them [with your children] when you sit at home and when you walk along the
> road, when you lie down and when you get up. Tie them as symbols on your hands and bind
> them on your foreheads. Write them on the doorframes of your houses and on your gates.
>
> (Deuteronomy 6:7-9)

From the young, the Deuteronomists proceeded to make all who dwelt in Israel serve Yhwh, their Elohim. Then came the Destruction! 'Destroy' is the watchword heard over and over. 'Destroy them totally' (7:2). There was to be no contact or treaty with foreign kings. They were to be eliminated and their names wiped out. No pity or mercy was to be shown to foreigners. There was to be no inter-marriage. Wise ones, such as the interpreters of dreams, were to be put to death. If a member of one's close family enticed another to follow foreign gods, they were to be shown no pity and killed. Whole communities who followed such gods were to be burnt down and exterminated. Nothing was to be left standing. Yhwh's punishment knew no limits.

The 'true faith' was purged or purified of all aberrations — or at least as interpreted by the Second

Chancers. In fact, the basis of the Ancient Way of Wisdom was abolished. Every sign and symbol was destroyed, whether on the high mountains, the hills or under every spreading tree. Altars were broken down, the sacred stones smashed, the Asherah or Goddess poles cut down and the idols burnt in the fire. In 2 Kings we read that King Josiah was so fanatical in his purging that he took the Asherah pole from the temple to the Kidron Valley, where he burnt it, ground it to powder and scattered the dust over the graves of the common folk who worshipped the Goddess. This was the way of the new Puritanical spirituality. A religion of fear on every level became the norm, an obsessive fear of not pleasing Yhwh, a fear of divine disapproval, a fear of failing to keep the law. Instead of a spirituality of heavenly visions with the attendant orders of Elohim, each with their different ways serving Sophia and Her Knowledge, we see a new religion where of central importance is the concept of an imageless, invisible deity, far removed from 'His' people but present in The Law, which had to be obeyed at all cost.

This was the Deuteronomic way back to an Eden of its own making, and with it went a view of homo sapiens that encouraged men and women to remain dependent infants for ever — and not only dependent but subhuman also.

Wisdom and Sovereignty Democratized
The demise of the monarchy as an institution led to a gradual democratization of the ideal of Sovereignty, and therefore of Wisdom. The King had been the earthly image of the Divine Harmony. Because of historical calamities or 'falls', some began to think in a new way about the harmony ordained by El Elyon — or 'Righteousness' to give it its biblical name. This refers to the 'right way' or conduct necessary to maintain harmony in heaven and earth. Originally, it had been only the King who could ascend the Holy Mount to be endowed with Wisdom, only he could enter the Divine Presence and dwell upon the Holy Hill. But Psalm 15 declares that this is now the privilege of anyone who 'does what is right, speaks the truth from his or her heart and keeps an oath, even when it hurts!' The twenty-fourth psalm is even more succinct: the true sovereign is the one who has 'clean hands and a pure heart' (v. 4).

Jeremiah's experiences of Israel's unfaithfulness over the centuries led him to conceive of the first sacred covenant of Sinai being totally scrapped and a new one being formed, this time not written on stone but written on the human heart of every man, woman and child. There was no need for one chosen individual to climb the holy mountain to receive Wisdom. She would be given to everyone in a new loving covenant or partnership of 'the heart'. This was radical theology to say the least —

> I will put my law in their minds
> and write it on their hearts.
> I will be their Deity and they
> will be my people.
> They will all know me, from the
> least of them to the greatest.   (Jeremiah 31:33-34)

A new relationship was now available to all, without distinction. Sophia would speak personally and intimately with everyone, regardless of their religious, theological or national background. All could belong to the Divine Assembly, all could enter the New Eden. This promise received its final, and finest, expression in the prophecy of Isaiah of the Outcasts (Isaiah 55-66), who lived in Jerusalem after the Exiles had returned to Palestine. He clashed head on with the insular and separatist policies of the Deuteronomic School because he championed the Outsiders, who were deemed unworthy and unclean to belong to the New Community, the Eden of the Second Chancers. Isaiah of the Outcasts' vision of the new creation was also focused on Jerusalem, but a different Jerusalem to that of his opponents. His was a universal vision that celebrated a new partnership between Heaven and Earth, a new kind of union between El Elyon and 'His' people. Isaiah speaks of an Eternal Marriage from which a new universal community would emerge and from which the Divine Glory would radiate in a more glorious way. The Virgin Goddess Jerusalem awaits her long awaited Bridegroom:

> I delight greatly in the Lord, my Soul rejoiceth,
> For he has clothed me with garments of salvation
> and arrayed me with a robe of righteousness,
> As a Bridegroom adorns his head like a priest
> And a Bride adorns herself with her jewels.

The Divine Bridegroom is so pleased that he calls his Bride, *Hephzibah*, meaning 'My delight is in Her'. The Land he calls *Beulah* which means 'Married'. So unexpected and surprising is the union that the new community, the fruit of the union, emerges without the waiting of pregnancy and the pain of the birthpangs. A new land and a new people emerge in a day, in the twinkling of an eye. It is a marriage manifested in the bestowal of sovereignty upon everyone — especially the 'poor of the land', barred for so long from entering Eden. The 'scum of the earth', as they were also called by the religious elite, were also sons and daughters of Sovereignty, Children of Sophia, who can also become monarchs. Kings and Queens, each one of them —

> bestowed with a crown of beauty
> anointed with the oil of gladness
> adorned with beautiful garments.   (Isaiah 61:3.)

We have come a long way from the time of King Solomon, when Sovereignty was limited to the few. El Elyon declares

> This is what the High and Lofty One says, 'I live in a high and holy place but also with him
> or her who is contrite in heart and lowly in spirit. To revive the spirit of the lowly and to
> revive the heart of the contrite.'   (Isaiah 57:15)

Psalm 113 in a similar fashion speaks of The One Enthroned on High who 'raises the poor from the dust [and] seats them with the princes of their people.' Where? On the Holy Mount, in The Assembly of the Elohim.

So fired is Isaiah with the Beauty of Righteousness that all will be satisfied by Jerusalem, the Divine Mother —

> You will nurse and be satisfied at Her
>   comforting breasts:
> You will drink deeply and delight in Her
>   bountiful breasts.   (66:11)

Because of the Beauty of Her Glory, all the Kings of the earth will be drawn to Jerusalem. All will see Her glory, and power will be redefined, the power of holiness. 'Peace will be Her Governor, righteousness Her Ruler,' and the Temple will become 'A House of Prayer for all Nations' (Isaiah 56:7). She will be a city constantly preparing not for the coming of Yhwh as King (Isaiah 40:3), but for the coming of the people of the nations, foreigners and aliens.

> I revealed myself to those who did not ask for me,
> I was found by those who did not seek me.
> To a nation that did not call on my Name
> I said, 'Here am I, Here am I.'   (65:1)

The Book of Job

Sophia was not dismissed en bloc by everyone in Israel. The universality of Her invitation reached a climax in the message of Isaiah of the Outcasts. Long after prophecy had been silent for centuries, some were still singing the praises of Sophia, especially outside Israel. The Wisdom of Solomon was written in Greek during the latter part of the first century BC, by a cosmopolitan Jew living in Alexandria, Egypt. As the millennium came to a close, the author still had not given up on the ideal of Kingship. In the fifth chapter we are actually taken back to the time when the first kings failed to honour the Divine, because of their arrogance, their 'boasted wealth', their 'straying away from the Truth', having their 'fill of the paths of lawlessness' (5:7-8). The author places his message in the mouth of Solomon and begins his treatise by addressing the pagan kings of his own day.

It was the abuse of Wisdom that the enlightened addressed and not Sophia herself. The prophets were uncompromising in their criticism of Her abuse. Isaiah of Jerusalem addressed his people with these words — 'When men tell you to consult mediums and spiritists, who whisper and mutter, should not a people enquire of their God?' (Isaiah 8:19). Good advice, but it still begs the question of how the individual should seek for knowledge and, more importantly, of whom?

While Daniel was also critical of the religious establishment of his day, he too bears witness to the fact that El Elyon did have wise ones who interpreted dreams and had knowledge and power to discern the meaning of life. These were the ones who were grounded in genuine humility (5:22), the very quality that most kings failed to display. They also acknowledged and honoured El Elyon. Like Daniel himself, they were the ones who did set their minds on gaining understanding and walking humbly before The Most High. Similarly, what Ezekiel condemned was not visions as such but 'false visions and lying divinations' (Ezekiel 13:9,23), superstitious practices (13.18), and those who declared a false peace (13:16).

The Way of Wisdom is a path of tremendous responsibility. The possibility of misusing the Knowledge and power that Sophia imparts is very great. The Wisdom movement was its own severest critic, fully aware of the excesses that can arise, forever conscious of its limitations. We see this awareness *par excellence* in the Book of Job. One of the purposes of Job is to address not only the kings and their failures but also the 'men of understanding', who claim to know so much in the Name of Sophia. In a few verses in chapter twelve, Job confronts the religious establishment of his day, by reminding it that true Wisdom and power belongs only to the Divine. Consequently, counsellors and priests are stripped of their office, judges are mocked, trusted elders and advisers are silenced while kings and princes are treated with contempt and even deprived of the gift of reason.

With sarcasm at times [e.g. 'What great insights you have displayed' 26:3] Job proceeds, first of all, to de-mystify much of the traditional wisdom. He treats as common knowledge a great deal of what the wise men claim to know, for instance, 'What you know I also know' (13:2),' I have a mind as well as you, I am not inferior to you.' Who does not know all these things? In fact, wisdom is found among 'the aged, for long life brings understanding'(12:12). Secondly, Job admits that to understand the secrets of nature (the source of a river, the movement of the stars) is quite an achievement but 'these are but the outer fringes of God's work' (26:14). Finally, Job points out that there is a deeper knowledge, beyond the natural or the immediately apparent and observable, a knowledge before which one remains speechless and in awe. Human wisdom can no longer give immediate answers about, or automatic access to, the secrets of Sophia. There is a knowledge that no one individual or tradition, however hallowed, can contain or manipulate.

The powers of creation can say little or nothing on the matter when asked to divulge where Sophia dwells
> The Deep says, 'It is not in me,'
> The Sea says, 'It is not with me.'
> Destruction and Death say,
> 'Only a rumour of it has reached our ears.'   (Job 28:14, 22)

Job is part of the movement that sought to restore the dignity and honour of each human individual. He admits how he longs to see the Divine disclosing again the true secrets of Sophia (11.5b), for it alone knows where She dwells (28:23). The Most High, alone, can fathom Her mysteries, which are profound and vast, and probe Her limits. In Job, we see a veiling of Wisdom and therefore, a new way of experiencing Her Knowledge and creativity. We see the beginnings of a new way of thinking about or reflecting on theological issues. We see a change in the individual's perception of the divine and human. We see the re-emergence of Sovereignty, this time the Sovereignty of each individual. We discern the rudiments of a spirituality that can ask with conviction and freshness, once again, 'Where is Wisdom?' — a question that is the fruit of a deep and genuine longing, a mystery that has to be explored, a Mystery that has to be lived, and not an abstraction to be explained. It is a spirituality that begins to celebrate the Sovereignty of each individual, by enabling him or her to stand up to and confront caricatures of The Divine. It gave dignity to human anguish and suffering (31:3) — yes, even the righteous suffer — by revealing a new awareness of a person's divinely granted powers:

> Let us discern for ourselves what is right:
> Let us learn together what is good.   (34:4)
> How? With 'a heart endowed with wisdom and the mind with understanding'   (38:36).

Sophia praised and pursued

The person(s) who edited the first five books of the Bible, long after the demise of the monarchy, still reminds his readers that since 'the beginning' homo sapiens is the crown of creation, the noblest of creatures, living representation of Divine Sovereignty and rule on earth, visible tokens of the Splendour and Majesty of The Most High. Each one sovereign in his or her own right, exercising dominion on earth, responsible stewards of the good earth.

> When I consider your heavens
> the work of your fingers,
> the moon and the stars,
> which you have set in place,
> What is man that you are mindful of him,
> the son of man that you care for him?
> You made him a little lower than the Elohim
> and crowned him with glory and honour.
> You made him ruler over the works of your hands,
> you put everything under his feet.   (Psalm 8:3-6)

Long after the voice of prophecy had been silent for centuries, the author of the Wisdom of Solomon was singing the praises of Sophia as the millennium came to a close and the first 'Christian' millennium was about to begin. In the seventh chapter we read that:

> Wisdom is more mobile than any motion;
> because of Her pureness She pervades and penetrates all things.
> She is a breath of the power of God [i.e. El Elyon]
> a pure emanation of the Glory of the All-Mighty…
> She is a reflection of Eternal Light
> and Image of His Goodness.
> Though She is but one, She can do all things,
> and while remaining in Herself, She renews all things;
> She is more beautiful than the sun
> and excels every constellation of the stars…
> She reaches mightily from one end of the earth to the other,
> She orders all things well.   (vv. 24-8:1)

But Sophia is not limited to the celestial heights as an impersonal power or principle. In the Wisdom Literature's own account of creation, She was as active in Israel's (Jacob's) history as She had been in Eden. In chapter ten of The Wisdom of Solomon, in relation to Jacob:

She guided him on straight paths;
She showed him the Kingdom of God,
and gave him knowledge of angels;
She prospered him in his labours,
and increased the fruit of his toil.
She stood by him. She protected him.
She kept him safe and gave him the victory.   (vv. 10-12)

By the time this Wisdom book was written, Sophia was also referred to as 'the Spirit of the Lord' (1:7) e.g. that fills the world, and as 'thy Holy Spirit' (9.17) i.e. the Sophia sent from on high. In another verse She is referred to as 'the Immortal Spirit' (12.1) which is in all things.

The Wisdom tradition never lost sight of a person's relationship with Sophia as being a passionate love affair, the Edenic quest for Knowledge which demanded total commitment. Sophia is there for everyone, but as She seeks the individual that She desires, so we are meant to seek Her out, to woo Her and court Her with our whole being. Sirach 51 bears witness to this search for the Beloved:

While I was still young, before I went on my travels,
I sought wisdom openly in my prayer.
Before the Temple I asked for her,
and I will search for her to the last. ...
My soul grappled with wisdom ...
I directed my soul to her ...
I gained understanding with her from the first ...
My heart was stirred to seek her.   (from verses 13-14, 19-20, 21)

Sovereignty

We have come full circle. We are back to where we started, in Eden, learning to handle the knowledge of good and evil, the freedom to distinguish right from wrong, the responsibility of fulfilling our part in maintaining the harmony that lies at the heart of the universe. We have all been given divine sovereignty and it is through the exercise of this sovereignty that the crowning glory of creation is celebrated and manifested. Only in this way can the meaning of Eden be brought to fruition or destroyed and therefore denied. This Sovereignty proclaims unequivocally in the New Testament that —

we can be filled with the knowledge of the Divine Will: we can receive spiritual
understanding and wisdom.   (Colossians 1:9)
by constant use, we are able to train ourselves to distinguish good and evil.   (Hebrews 5:14)
by becoming spiritual persons, we can make right judgement about all things ourselves
(1 Corinthians 2:15)

Homo sapiens can grow in Divinity — if it so chooses. We can be transformed into Divinity, become partakers of the divine nature (2 Peter 1:4) and share in the divine status of the Elohim. We are not meant to stay in a perpetual state of childhood dependence and its immature system of obedience-rewarded and disobedience-punished.

The Sovereignty granted by Sophia is central to the Ancient Wisdom. We have seen in this chapter how individuals in the Bible responded not only to the failure of the monarchs and the corruption of Sophia, but also to the total collapse of the complex structure that was the Royal Cult. Some did not lose sight of the cosmic order that El Elyon had ordained for creation and the Vision of The Most High reigning in harmony with His/Her heavenly and earthly sons and daughters, the Elohim, the wise ones. In spite of the tragedy that lies at the heart of the human condition (the continual failure of many to walk in humility with El Elyon) and the bad press that some biblical writers, and their heirs, have given the Elohim, the name of one of the greatest of their number is a sign and a reminder, that the seats, the empty thrones of the banished kings, are meant to be occupied again. The name is 'Micha-El' and Michael has always been closely linked with the Universal Christic power. One of Michael's titles is that of 'Defender of the Woman [i.e. Mary] and her seed'. High praise indeed. The name Micha-El is in fact a quest or a question meaning 'Who is like El?' It is Michael's role to discover those who are like El Elyon in order to fill the empty thrones — some would say the seats perilous! — with new champions. It is in and through the office of Archangel Michael that human beings are helped in their exaltation and glorification, that is, their transformation into one of the Elohim — true sons and daughters of El Elyon, brothers and sisters of Christ.

Michael serves the Christ in all of us, witnessing our coronation as we take our place in the Divine Assembly. In the ancient words of Proverbs 4, that reminds us that Sophia is Supreme and that we are created to love Her, we are told:

> Esteem Sophia and She will exalt you.
> Embrace Her and She will honour you;
> She will set a Garland of Grace on your head and
> Present you with a Crown of Splendour.   (vv. 8-9)

Notes for Chapter Two

Woodstock Polydor Records Ltd, 1970, Copyright MCPS

All biblical quotations, unless specified, are from the New International Version (NIV), copyright 1978 and 1981, by New York International Bible Society. Published by Hodder & Stoughton.

Quotations from The Apocrypha are from the Revised Standard Version (RSV), copyright 1957 by Division of Christian Education of the, National Council of the Churches of Christ in the USA. Published by William Collins Sons & Co Ltd.

Since the author uses the term *The Divine One, El Elyon* and *Sophia* in his own study and private liturgical practices, some of the biblical passages quoted are his own paraphrasing.

I am deeply grateful to the writings of Margaret Barker for helping me to look at the Bible in new and exciting ways. She is a wonderful teacher, whose scholarship has helped me make sense of some very profound mystical experiences. Needless to say, she may not agree with some of my conclusions.

The Older Testament (1987), sadly out of print, *The Lost Prophet* (1988), *The Gate of Heaven* (1991) and *The Great Angel* (1992), all published by SPCK, London.

3. Sophia and the Russians

I will tell you about Sophia and how She came into being. Hiding nothing from you,
I will tell you about Her from the beginning of creation. Her knowledge I will make clear.
The Truth I will not hide.   (Wisdom of Solomon 6.22)

Vladimir Soloviev

On the wall in my church vestry at Pennal is a framed black and white copy of an original painting in the Trekiakov Gallery, Moscow. Painted by M.V. Nesterov, it depicts the Russian Orthodox priest FrPaul Florensky, dressed in a white cassock, with skull cap and staff in his right hand. On his left is Sergius Bulgakov in tie and coat. The time is probably early in 1918, and Bulgakov, a professor of political economy at the University of Moscow, is soon to be ordained into Holy Orders. For many Russian Orthodox Christians, F. Florensky is a much loved saint and martyr of Holy Russia, while Fr Bulgakov is regarded, even by his critics, as one of the greatest theologians in the history of the Russian Church. After the Bolshevik Revolution, their lives were to follow totally different paths. Florensky ended up in the Gulag Archipelago, where he died in 1943, while Bulgakov died in exile the following year.

There are times when I look at this painting and imagine that I can see a third person walking behind or between the two companions, who, following a deep conversation, now appear to be in a more reflective mood. The 'missing person' in this Russian trinity is Vladimir Soloviev, the founder of one of the most fascinating, if not unique, movements in modern Russia. A philosopher-poet, he inspired Christians and nonbelievers alike, with his teaching about Sophia, the Divine or Eternal Feminine. Russian religious and moral philosophy, the history of ideas and metaphysics, theology and poetry, all bear witness to Soloviev's creativity. He is the representative of an entire epoch in nineteenth-century Russian and European thought, and yet it is only now that his work is beginning to receive the wider recognition that it deserves. By the time of the centenary of his death in AD 2000, members of Solovian societies in Russia and in the West hope to have erected a memorial to Soloviev close to the University of Moscow's Institute of Philosophy. The statue will replace a memorial to Friedrich Engels, the Marxist.

Soloviev's spiritual pilgrimage began in Moscow in 1862, when, as a nine-year-old boy, he received the first of three visions of Sophia, whom he came to know intimately as his Eternal Friend. It was on Ascension Day, during the celebration of the Holy Eucharist in the university chapel. Before his death in 1900, at the age of forty-seven, Soloviev recorded his encounters in a poem entitled 'Three Meetings'. This poem occupies an important place in our Sophianic liturgy. His next encounter with the Divine Lady of unsurpassable beauty took place in 1875 while Soloviev was working on his post-graduate thesis in the Reading Room of the British Museum. The following year he encountered Her while visiting the Egyptian desert, and it was during the latter that he was granted the crowning revelation of the Divine Wisdom in all Her beauty and glory. Of that encounter, he writes:

And in the purple of the heavenly glow
With eyes full of azure fire
Your gaze was like the first shining
Of universal and creative day.

What is, what was, and what ever will be were here
Embraced within that one fixed gaze...The seas
And rivers all turned blue beneath me, as did
The distant forest and the snow-capped mountain heights.

I saw all, and all of it was one,
One image there of Beauty.Feminine
The immeasurable was confined within that image.
Before me, in me, you alone were there.   *Vladimir Soloviev's Poems of Sophia*, p. 35

Soloviev's father, Sergei Mikhailovich, was an academic, a well-known and respected professor of history at the University of Moscow. His mother, Polixena, was a deeply mystical and religious person, and it was from her that Vladimir inherited his love of poetry. One of nine children, Soloviev's parents believed that he had been born to fulfil a special destiny. That destiny was inexorably bound to the reality of the Divine Sophia, whose prophet and herald Soloviev was to become, as well as to the soul of his native Russia and the impending catastrophe that he knew would soon befall her.

Soloviev was a solitary and an ascetic but he was no hermit. He placed the well-being of others before his own, often going without food and clothing for days on end. An academic (by the age of twenty-one he was a junior professor), he was deeply committed to social and civic affairs. He was hailed as a genius by his peers when he received his doctorate. A poet, he was also a respected literary critic. He became a close friend of the great Russian novelist Fyodor Dostoevsky. From early adulthood, Soloviev was viewed with suspicion by the Government and the Orthodox Church, especially for his views on freedom and the need actually to practise Christian forgiveness in civic life. He truly believed in forgiveness as a transforming power. In 1886 the Procurator of the Holy Synod placed Soloviev's writings under 'spiritual censure', and by the last decade of his life the State had forbidden him to give public lectures, to teach in the University and even to publish books within Russia. All this took place before the Bolsheviks came to power. Soloviev was also shunned by his ultra conservative Russian Orthodox friends.

Soloviev always felt a close affinity with the West although he was critical of its materialism and moral decadence. He preached Christianity at a time when European, and especially the Russian, intelligentsia, had no interest in religion or Idealist philosophy. He struggled to discover ways in which the truths of Christianity could become an integral part of human knowledge. For many it had become totally incomprehensible, a situation that has changed little throughout the twentieth century. As his life came to a close, Soloviev wrote to a friend: 'I myself become ever more a kind of monument to unfulfilled dreams and destroyed illusions.' And yet his despair was balanced by an unflinching trust in the power of the Divine Wisdom. Even when all seemed hopeless, like a true Grail Knight, he stood firm, clothed in Sophianic splendour and beauty:

Forever it remains unique. Though in the slumbering temple
The infernal gleam shines in darkness and thunder resounds in silence
Though all has fallen round — still the banner will tremble not,
And the shield will not be moved from the crumbled wall.

Only the emblem alone of an incorruptible testament
Between heaven and earth stood as once before,
As from heaven the same light illumined as of old
The Maiden of Nazareth and the serpent's vain poison before Her.

(*Vladimir Soloviev and The Knighthood of The Divine* Sophia, p. 46)

Over a century ago, Soloviev was championing causes that still occupy centre stage in Western cultural and religious life. He was a passionate believer in the reunification of all Christians, and thus of the need for a truly ecumenical or worldwide community of Christ's followers. Christ died for all humanity and not just for Christians! Since every human being bears the Divine image and likeness, it is everyone's duty and privilege to honour this profound likeness which already exists between all nations and peoples. He was, however, not only an apostle of the union of all churches but also deeply involved in the destiny of the Jewish people. He openly condemned Christian indifference to the suffering and persecution of Jews. The Russian government of his day condoned terrorism against its own subjects if they were Jews. Soloviev knew on an intuitive level of the great suffering that would engulf the Jewish people in the twentieth century. He never lost faith, however, in the belief that Israel's role in the future would be crucial in creating a new international community of justice. He ranks among the most noble Christian defenders of the Jewish people. He was also a spokesperson for Mother Nature. She must not be exploited and manipulated in order to serve selfish human ends. All must be made aware of the fact that Nature can be hurt and wounded. He once wrote:

Nature does not permit you to strip
The garment from Her beauty;
With machines you will not wrest from Her
What your Spirit cannot divine!   (*Vladimir Soloviev, Russian Mystic*, p. 238)

Soloviev preached oneness with ourselves, with Mother Earth and with the Divine. His was an interdependent cosmos, and the key to its harmony was Sophia. Every one of his beliefs and actions issued forth from his own experience of, and personal union with, the Divine Wisdom. She was the Mystery that lay at the core of things both human and divine. She was the link between heaven and earth. He believed that the Russian people had always known Her in an intuitive way. For example, when the Russian people dedicated its ancient churches to Sancta Sophia, it was giving expression to a reality that was unknown to the Greeks, who identified Sophia solely with the Logos, the Word, the second person of the Trinity. Soloviev believed it was his task to articulate the Sophianic reality in as coherent and rational a way as possible. What is more, Soloviev believed that the Sophianic reality and presence can only become truly incarnate in the world through Divine-human effort and co-operation. A concrete and organic union must take place if the redemption wrought by Christ is to be realized on earth. Only then can the world be renewed and transformed in Christ. This is a long and complex process that cannot be realized automatically, and involves all of one's faculties, both emotional and mental.

Sophia also embodies a new kind of Freedom, or rather is that Primordial or Divine Freedom which is already being revealed in the religion of the Holy Spirit. Soloviev preached and lived a Christianity that was not trapped in an outmoded ritual or rigid dogma but one fired by the social and universal message of Christ. This type of Christian spirituality is broader and more embracing in content than all individual religions. It is in reality an association or community of free human beings, at one with the Divine Wisdom, She who is One but whose names are many.

The pure lily among our thorns,
In the gloomy abyss the bright pearl,
In the evil flame the unburning bush,

In the general flood the ship secure,
The bright cloud in the evening gloom
Gleaming brilliant as God's elect,
The rainbow reconciling heaven with earth,
The faithful ark of divine promises
The precious phial of heavenly manna,
The unassailable height, the One who bears God!
Protect our world with your resplendent veil,
Blessed one from on high,
All illuminated
With light and the world!

(Vladimir Soloviev and The Knighthood of The Divine Sophia, p. 51)

Following Soloviev's death, no Sophianic School of Spirituality was established, at least not in the formal sense. But through the influence of two Russian Orthodox priests in particular, Soloviev's Sophiology not only survived but also continued to develop, eventually becoming a well thought out and radical alternative to traditional Christian Orthodoxy. The two priests in question were Fathers Paul Florensky and Sergius Bulgakov, who, along with Soloviev, may rightly be regarded as the Fathers of modern Sophianic Christianity.

Paul Florensky

Paul Florensky was born in 1882, in what is now Azerbaijan. He grew up to be one of the most talented individuals of his generation. Even as a youth he displayed a great thirst for knowledge and he was to become what many described as the Russian Leonardo da Vinci. His enormous creative energies were channelled into mathematics, astronomy, physics and electrical engineering, poetry, music, art history and languages. He was fluent in Greek, Latin, most of the modern European languages as well as those of the Caucasus, Iran and India. He had research papers published in fields of mathematics, applied science and linguistics. His genius was recognized in both secular and ecclesiastical circles.

In 1899 he underwent a spiritual crisis, which revealed to him the inadequacy of physical knowledge. Even physics, one of the great loves of his life, had its limitations. There was clearly a level of existence beyond which science could not reach. Nurtured in a home where religion was almost non-existent, Florensky reached the point where science, the new religion for many, ceased to be an object of faith for him. In 1904 he enrolled at the Moscow Theological Academy, and seriously considered taking monastic vows. By 1908 he had become a professor at the Academy's Faculty of the History of Philosophy. He became a colleague, friend and co-worker of most of the leading intellectuals of his day. He was ordained in 1911 and was married the following year. One of the greatest influences in his life was a Russian holy man called Abba Isidor. Florensky's spiritual classic, *Salt of the Earth*, is his account of Isidor's life and the simple yet profound spirituality that he radiated. He helped put Florensky in touch with this mystical reality and taught him to value the importance of his own religious experiences.

Florensky's greatest work is *The Pillar and Foundation of Truth*, his master's thesis amplified and expanded. It won him the highest academic recognition at the Moscow Academy. However, his chapter on Sophia was later omitted by church authorities. In what proved to be the most challenging chapter in the whole book, Florensky raised many more questions than he answered, for this is the essence of the Sophianic quest, to ask questions and to provoke awe and wonder. It was Sergius Bulgakov who continued with the bold speculations of his close friend and mentor, Paul Florensky, and developed modern Sophiology. Florensky was later to change some of his earlier conceptions and modify some of his teachings on Sophia. This in no way detracts from the originality of his contribution to Sophiology, and to the lasting influence that he had on the thought of Sergius Bulgakov. It was under Florensky's spiritual guidance and inspiration that Bulgakov returned to the Church and finally sought holy orders. Both became leading figures in the religious and spiritual renaissance in Russia during the decades preceding the First World War.

In the wake of the Bolshevik revolution of 1917, Florensky refused to take part in politics or to emigrate. Following the great banishment of 1922, when the likes of Sergius Bulgakov were expelled, Florensky stayed in his homeland. He was of too much practical value to the new government to be discarded. He continued to exercise his priestly ministry, even wearing his cassock, pectoral cross and hat while working for the Soviet government in an official capacity as a scientist. He continued his research work and became one of Russia's chief electrical engineers, namely Assistant Director of the All-Union Electrical Engineering Institute. He concentrated primarily on developing new materials from the home market for high voltage transmission over long distances, which meant that Russia did not have to rely on foreign imports. Florensky's inventions and discoveries in science and technology were crucial to national industrial growth, and these included the invention of a famous non-coagulating machine oil. Florensky's interest as a scientist was in working on the fundamentals of matter as it manifested itself in practical experience. For him there was no other way of getting closer to reality. He had little interest in developing theories worked out from a series of formal propositions. Even in captivity he kept up his research work, working on extraction of iodine and agar from marine algae. He anticipated the development of cybernetics and developed an interest in space physics.

Florensky saw and experienced the world as one organic whole, one single reality which could be viewed from different perspectives. Each plane or level of existence was different but nevertheless complemented and enriched each other. His search was for one common wisdom and for the essence that lay behind all things. Hence his interest in, and passion for, the Sophianic reality, which lies at the heart of all things, both human and divine. He believed that there was one transcendent reality and hence one transcendent Truth that lay at the foundation of all world religions and systems of thought. It thus followed that there was one religion at the root of all religions, although this was not the same as believing in the relativity of all religions. He longed to be moved and nourished by this Truth. It had to be something real in his life, something that he had experienced for himself in the depths of his being. It wasn't enough merely to go through the motions, as often happened in nominal church life.

Florensky was imprisoned several times but it was in vain that the authorities tried to get him to renounce his faith. He spoke out publicly against official church policy as represented by the Moscow Metropolitan, the government's 'Yes Man'. In 1933 he was finally silenced — condemned to a life in concentration camps for a decade, first in Solovetski, in Siberia, then in the harsher Slovki Islands, along with thousands of other priests and monks. Before the Revolution the latter was home to several thriving monasteries, and Florensky, as a youth, yearned to visit them on pilgrimage. Ironically, he was now its prisoner, cut off from the world. Alexander Solzhenitsyn says of him that he was perhaps one of the most remarkable men devoured by the Gulag Archipelago. He died in 1943, the year of his intended release. He was either deliberately killed or the inhuman conditions of the camps finally took their toll. Through all his trials he never lost faith in the intrinsic goodness of creation.

Sergius Bulgakov

Sergius Bulgakov was born on 16 July 1871 in the central Russian town of Livny. He traced his family history to a Tartar named Bulgak who was converted from Islam to Orthodox Christianity in the sixteenth century. Bulgakov was to become the seventh generation of priests and deacons in his family. His was a traditional upbringing, but by the age of fourteen he had turned his back on the Church, and by his late teens had become a Marxist. One of the main reasons for this was the lack of freedom that seemed to be the norm in everything connected with the Church, the subservient attitude to all forms of authority, especially among theological students and priests. Such an atmosphere stifled Bulgakov's spirit of free enquiry and self-expression. It was this period of his life that helped him to embrace the cause of intellectual freedom and truth. The Church, apparently, had no interest in such things. Following studies in Moscow, Berlin, Paris and London, Bulgakov published his first book, the topic being *The Role of the Market in Capitalist Production*, followed by *Capitalism and Agriculture*, published in two volumes in 1900. In a country where the majority of the population were peasants, this was a subject of crucial importance. Already an established teacher, scholar and writer, Bulgakov became one of the leading moderate Marxists of his day.

From 1901 to 1906 Bulgakov was Professor of Political Economy at Kiev Polytechnic, from where he moved to occupy the Chair of Political Economy and Statistics in the law faculty of Moscow University. He gradually became disillusioned with Marxism and the 'Religion of Progress', and turned instead towards Russian Spirituality and German Idealism. His book *From Marxism to Idealism* describes this stage in his spiritual odyssey. It was published in 1903 and marks an important stage in his return journey from atheism. At Moscow he continued to write numerous essays and articles on political theory. His 'History of Political and Economic Theory' serves as a good example of the breadth of his knowledge and ability as a theoretician, and he was also practically involved in political and social circles. For two years he was a member of the Second Russian Duma and campaigned vigorously against capital punishment. In 1909, along with six other leading members of the Russian intelligentsia, who included Nicolas Berdyaev, a close friend, Bulgakov published a journal called *Landmarks*. In this collection of essays they expressed serious reservations about the lack of vision among most of the intellectuals of the day, and in his own essay, Bulgakov shared his reflections on the religious ideals of the Russian intelligentsia. The publication became an important landmark in the renaissance of Russian Christianity.

Bulgakov was no ordinary political scientist. In 1912 he wrote a unique volume which carried the title *The Philosophy of Economics*, in which he gave his first systematic statement on Sophiology, which was to become the focal point of his philosophical and theological beliefs. In 1917, while still Professor at Moscow University, Bulgakov served as a delegate of the All-Russian Church Council, which set about restoring the freedom of the Moscow Patriarchate. The saintly Tikhon, to whom Bulgakov was a close adviser, became the first Russian bishop to occupy the office of Patriarch since the time of Peter the Great. What many regarded as the unholy alliance of Church and Monarchy was finally at an end. In 1917 Bulgakov also published his second book on Sophia, called *The Unfading Light: Contemplations and Speculations*. Part of the book had appeared in serial form during 1915-16.

Bulgakov kept his university post until ordination in 1918, by Bishop Volokolamsky, who had ordained Florensky, the latter being present along with many other friends, including Berdyaev and Prince E.N. Trubetskoy. Now a priest, Bulgakov was expelled from the university by the Communists. Following a brief period as a lecturer at Simferopol University in the Crimea, Bulgakov was exiled from the USSR on 1 January 1923. He took with him two manuscripts from the final period of his life on Russian soil, namely *The Tragedy of Philosophy*, published in Germany in 1927 (and in Russia as recently as 1993) and *Introduction to the Veneration of the Name of God*, which was published in France after his death. Bulgakov and his fellow refugees first made for Constantinople (Istanbul) and then travelled on to Prague, the recognized centre of the Russian émigré community. Many expected to return home to a liberated Russia in the near future, and consequently their outlook was hopeful and positive. While in Prague, Bulgakov played a key role in forming the Russian Student Christian Movement in exile, whose members were also keen supporters of the idea of setting up an Orthodox Theological Seminary in Western Europe. In Prague Bulgakov also lectured at the Russian Law Institute and continued with his theological writing.

In 1925 a Russian Theological Institute was finally established in Paris, due primarily to the vision, courage and sheer hard work of Metropolitan Evlogy, who acquired the property. It was he who invited Bulgakov to take up the post of Professor of Dogmatic Theology and Dean of the new Seminary. He lived there with his wife Elena and their three sons and one daughter. Bulgakov's involvement with the RSCM continued, and his passionate belief in the need for Church unity led him to be one of the founder members of the fellowship of St Alban and St Sergius at High Leigh, England, in 1928. The Fellowship continues to this day and aims at furthering mutual understanding and co-operation between the separated Christians of East and West, being a society of prayer, study and common work. Its aim is achieved by providing opportunity for personal contacts and the sharing of Eucharistic worship. My own membership of the Fellowship goes back to the early eighties. Bulgakov attended ecumenical conferences at Lausanne, Switzerland in 1927 (World Conference on Faith and Order) and at Oxford and Edinburgh in 1937. In 1934 and 1936 he made an extensive tour of the USA and Canada as a guest of the Protestant Episcopal Church. He was undoubtedly one of the great ecumenical pioneers of his day.

The focal point of Bulgakov's life in Paris — probably the most creative period of his life — was the daily pattern of prayer and worship centred on the college chapel. His day started every morning at 7 with the Divine Liturgy, and ended with Vespers late at night. In addition to his work as an academic, studying, teaching and writing, Bulgakov also fulfilled the responsibilities of administrator, preacher, father confessor, in addition to the general pastoral care of students.

In addition to the books already mentioned, Bulgakov wrote two great trilogies, embracing all Christian theology. It is the most ambitious programme undertaken by any Orthodox theologian in many centuries. Totalling eight hundred pages, the common theme of the lesser trilogy is the Divine Sophia in the created world. It consists of *The Burning Bush* (1927), which examines the nature of the Blessed Virgin Mary, *The Friend of the Bridegroom* (1928) i.e. John the Baptist, and *Jacob's Ladder* (1929) which examines the teaching about the Holy Angels. The second, larger trilogy occupied Bulgakov throughout the 1930s, and its overall theme is Divine-humanity. *The Lamb of God* was published in 1933 and looks at the person of Christ. *The Comforter* (1936) examines the teaching about the Holy Spirit, and finally *The Bride of the Lamb* (1945) is about the Church. *The Johannine Apocalypse* was added in 1948. In 1500 pages this second treatise contains Bulgakov's reasoned but openly speculative re-statement of major Christian teaching in terms of Sophia, the Divine All-Wisdom. It represents a theological system equal in importance to that of Thomas Aquinas in the Latin Western tradition.

The Sophianic Mystic

Sergius Bulgakov's return to Christianity at the age of 30 was sealed by three powerful mystical experiences, mediated through Nature, art and a personal encounter with a Russian holy man. In his Autobiographical Notes, Bulgakov describes the first experience of 1895 in these words:

> I was twenty-four years old. I had lived devoid of faith for a decade. After an early period of tempestuous doubts, a religious emptiness grasped my soul. It was evening. We were driving across Russia's southern steppes, and the strongly perfumed spring grass was adorned by the rays of a glorious sunset. In the far distance I saw the blue outlines of the Caucasus. It was my first sight of the mountains. I looked on enraptured at their rising slopes, drinking in the light and air of the steppes. I attuned myself to Nature's revelation. My soul had become accustomed to the pain of seeing Nature as nothing more than an arid desert, its manifested beauty merely a deceptive mask. Yet in opposition to all my intellectual beliefs, I saw no way of being reconciled to Nature without God. Suddenly, at that late hour, my soul was joyfully

stirred. I began to contemplate what would happen if the cosmos was not a desert, and its beauty not a deceptive illusion. I wondered if Nature itself may well be life instead of death. I even thought that if He existed, the merciful and loving Father, if Nature might not be the vestment of his love and glory. Then I remembered the devout feelings of my childhood, when lived in His presence, and loved Him. Because of my weakness, I trembled. If all this was true, then the tears and enthusiasm of adolescence, the sweetness of my prayers, my innocence and all the other emotions which I had discarded and ignored, would be vindicated, and my current view of things with its emptiness and sterility would appear as nothing more than blindness and lies. What a transformation it would bring me.

The second call to return to Christianity took place in a different setting and in a different part of the world. This is how Bulgakov describes it:

> A new surge of intoxication with the world came over me in 1898. I experienced personal happiness. For the first time I encountered the West. My admiration for its culture, its comfort and its social democracy was unlimited. One Autumn, while in Dresden, a memorable encounter with Raphael's Sistine Madonna took place. It was a foggy morning. Armed with little or no knowledge of European painting, I visited the Art Gallery. I was a tourist and had no idea what to expect. The eyes of the Heavenly Queen, the Mother who holds the Eternal Infant in her arms, pierced my soul. I cried joyful yet bitter tears, and with them the ice melted within my soul. Many psychological knots within me broke loose. It was without doubt an aesthetic emotion, but it was also a new knowledge. It was a miracle. I was at that time still a Marxist, but I was duty bound to call my contemplation of the Madonna a prayer. Early every morning I went to the Zwinger before anyone arrived, in order to pray and weep in front of the Virgin. Not many experiences in my life were more blessed than those unexpected tears.

The final act of reconciliation took place in a remote northern Russian hermitage, a far cry from the beauty of the Caucasian scenery and a masterpiece of Italian art. Bulgakov relates the story in these words, and they are worth quoting in full. He was seeking peace of mind.

> It was Autumn. In the forest I came across a solitary hermitage. It was a sunny day, and I was surrounded by all the familiar features of the northern landscape. I remained in the clutches of doubts and hesitations. I had journeyed there as the companion of a friend, hoping, somehow, to encounter God. But my conviction soon left me and at Vespers I remained frigid and without feeling. When the prayers of those who were preparing for confession began, I almost ran out of the church. In deep anguish I walked towards the guest-house, aware of nothing around me, when suddenly I found myself before the elder's cell. I had been led there. I had planned on going another way, but due to my absent-mindedness, I took the wrong turning. Clearly another sign of my distress.
>
> A miracle had taken place, of that I had no doubt. The father, seeing his prodigal son, ran to meet me. The elder told me that all human sins were like a drop of water when compared to the ocean of Divine Love. I left him, pardoned and reconciled, shaking and in tears, aware of myself redeemed, as on wings within the church precincts. At the entrance I met my surprised and delighted companion, who had previously seen me leave the church in a state of great anxiety. He was witness of his turning point in my life. Soon, it was evening again, another sunset, but this time a northern not as southern one. Bells were calling to prayer. I listened to them as if I was hearing them for the first time. I saw the world with new eyes.

Progressive Revelation

In order to understand fully Bulgakov's role in the Sophianic Controversy that engulfed the Russian Church in the early decades of the twentieth century, we need to know something of how he viewed Christian doctrine, in addition to the passionate way he defended the freedom that lay at the heart of the theologian's vocation. Since for Bulgakov the Christian life was vibrantly alive and dynamic, he believed that our understanding of it is never completed 'once and for all' but is forever developing. Revelation (at least from the human perspective) is a progressive thing. It follows, therefore, that doctrine develops in human history, with Christians being regularly challenged not only to look deeper into revealed truths but also to discover ways of interpreting and communicating these truths in a new way. There are times, argued Bulgakov, when the Church has to reinterpret key elements in its tradition. The Russian Sophianists believed that they lived in such a time. The Church was on the threshold of an era ripe for doctrinal development. At the heart of this development was the figure of Sophia, whose unfolding would have a profound bearing on the very essence of Christianity. Seeing the world through Sophianic eyes, Bulgakov called for a theological change of heart, a total renewal of human thought, so that a fresh interpretation of Christianity could occur. He wrote in *The Wisdom of God* (the only English-language summary of Bulgakov's Sophiology, published in 1937) that

all the dogmatic and practical problems of modern Christian dogmatics and ascetics seem

to form a kind of knot whose unravelling inevitably leads to Sophiology.   (p. 39)

Like Soloviev, Bulgakov could not abide a Christianity frozen within a rigid and outmoded traditionalism. For him, the Spirit demanded creative understanding and engagement with the Divine. It was the traditional approach that had contributed towards a stagnant and decaying Church.

Now if one is of the opinion that Christian doctrine, as formulated in the early centuries of the Church, is not to be tampered with, and changed, under any circumstances, then Bulgakov's pioneering work will be anathema. His theological daring was condemned at the outset. No open theological debate was allowed about the state of the Church and its teachings. This opposition to Bulgakov was nothing new. It was part of the same climate that had prevailed in Russia for decades, bordering on an ecclesiastical fascism, the theological dictatorship of an ultra conservative Church that had methodically been persecuting intellectuals like Soloviev since the last quarter of the nineteenth century. They were even prohibited from publishing works on religious topics by the church hierarchy, for fear that 'new' ideas would contaminate the faithful. This tension between traditional and new ideas was one of the many tensions that lay at the heart of Russian society in Bulgakov's day.

Knights of Sophia

At the beginning of the nineteenth century, the great liberal Tsar, Alexander I (grandson of Catherine the Great), initiated a cultural programme with the view to bringing together Western and Slavic spiritualities. Along with many other members of the Romanoff dynasty, Alexander had a strong mystical bent and his travels, both inside and especially outside Russia, brought him into contact with many fascinating and often strange esoteric traditions. Interest in unorthodox ideas and movements was a European phenomenon during the latter part of the eighteenth century and the beginning of the nineteenth. Magicians and seers became a common sight in the courts of many kings and princes. In an age of spiritual hunger, many people drew nourishment from both pagan and Russian Orthodox sources. (The story of the relationship of the Russian holy man, Gregory Rasputin, with Tsar Nicholas I and the Tsarina Alexandria, is well documented.) The movement set in motion by Alexander I was to have a profound effect on many Russian thinkers, especially in religious matters. It opened members of the conservative Russian Church to new ideas, in addition to challenging them to look at their own native spirituality in a fresh way. Vladimir Soloviev serves as a good example of the way that Russian spirituality had developed as a result of Alexander's initiative. Soloviev was able to embrace many diverse traditions into his Christianity and weave them into an integral whole. He was, in fact, the only thinker of distinction in the second half of the nineteenth century to create a new system of Christian philosophy. A system that Bulgakov was later to develop in his own unique way. A deep fear of all so-called 'new ideas', and especially the revolutionary spirit of the Russian Sophianists, caused the leaders of the Russian Church to retreat further into a rigid and uncompromising conservatism.

This attitude of the Russian hierarchy also clashed with Bulgakov's faithfulness to the historic freedom of Orthodoxy. In Russian spirituality *Sobornost* expresses the profound sense of unity that individuals share with one another. It is a wonderful sense of togetherness and oneness, unrestrained by any legal or intellectual barriers or coercion of any kind. It is that kind of unity which enables an individual still to be spontaneous and completely free to be oneself. Such a community knows nothing of authoritarianism, intolerence and compulsion of any kind. Bulgakov never claimed to be speaking for the whole Russian Church, least of all the whole of Christendom. He used his vocation as a theologian, nay, his right, to interpret Scripture and Tradition, in the light of his own experiences of, and reflection upon, the Divine. His commitment to the quest for Truth meant that he was not afraid, along with Florensky, to follow new lines of theological enquiry and teaching (what Bulgakov called *theologumena*) in order to serve that truth better. With great pride in his native Christian tradition, Bulgakov wrote in his classical introduction to *The Orthodox Church* that

> The predominance of *theologumena* over dogma is the special advantage of the Orthodox Church, which is a stranger to the legalistic spirit, even in matter of doctrine. Orthodoxy has felt no disadvantage resulting from this impractical attitude, even when some diversity of theological opinion exists.   (p. 100)

It wounded Bulgakov greatly to see the breadth and openness of the Orthodox spirit betrayed by some of the Russian hierarchs, primarily for political gain — a point I shall return to later. In his *Autobiographical Notes*, Bulgakov responded to the charges directed against him with these words:

> My faithfulness to the Church is the foundation of my life. I dedicated my entire being to its service after my return to Christianity. But my churchmanship is bound up with my recognition of the need of spiritual freedom. Where the Spirit of the Lord is, there also is freedom. Freedom is the greatest gift of God. Sins against freedom are sins against Orthodoxy and against the Church, and accordingly spiritual self-enslavement is the blasphemy against the Holy Spirit'.

Bulgakov also reiterated the importance of the experiential aspect of the Christian faith. Living religious experience was the sole legitimate method for understanding Christian doctrine. A Christianity devoid of such experience was an impossibility. The great themes of the Church could never be grasped in abstraction from the concrete situation of each individual, an individual's personal encounter and relationship with the Divine, sustained by prayer and study, worship and fellowship. This Divine-human adventure unfolds in a variety of ways, because, for the Russian Sophianists, the whole universe is a sacrament. Every aspect of creation is able to manifest the Divine purpose and will.

It was from their own experiences of the Divine that the Russian followers of Soloviev developed their special awareness of, and devotion to, Sophia. In stronger language than Soloviev, Florensky even argued that the very idea of Sophia determined Russian religious consciousness from the very beginning. He even stated that 'Russia' and 'Russian' without Sophia was a contradiction in terms. Both he and Bulgakov had no doubt that all contemporary philosophical and theological problems came from and return to the question of Sophia. The two companions did their theologizing, therefore, not only from studying Scriptural and other writings but also from studying the meaning that lay behind iconography, church liturgy, festivals and ecclesiastical architecture. According to legend, the most beautiful example of Byzantime architecture, the Church of Hagia or Sancta Sophia, in Constantinople, played an important part in the conversion of the Kievan Rus to Christianity in 988. At that time, Kiev's pagan prince was torn between Judaism, Islam and Roman Christianity. The messengers he sent to Constantinople brought back the news that in Hagia Sophia they felt as if they were in heaven. The prince became a Christian! Bulgakov's own visit to Hagia Sophia in January 1923 resulted in one of his quasi-personal encounters with Sophia. He found himself 'enriched by a new apprehension of the world in God, that is, of the Divine Sophia' (p. 13). He continues:

> This heavenly dome, which portrays heaven bending to earth to embrace it, gives expression
> in finite form to the infinite, to an all-embracing unity, to the stillness of eternity, in the form
> of a work of art which, though belonging to this world, is a miracle of harmony itself.
> (*The Wisdom of God*, p. 13).

Florensky and Bulgakov suggested that through these different mediums can be seen the presence of a Sophianic cult in Russian history, a cult related to and yet quite distinct from that of Christ and the Blessed Virgin Mary. Sophia, who is absent in Roman Christianity, has been part of the Eastern Orthodox tradition for centuries, even appearing in some icons as an extra Trinitarian figure — a woman of great heavenly beauty. The often mysterious and elusive Sophianic symbolism has never been fully articulated. In reverential tone, he states that

> All this wealth of symbolism has been preserved in the archives of ecclesiastical antiquities,
> but, covered by the dust of ages, it has been of no use to anyone. The time has come,
> however, for us to sweep away the dust of ages and decipher the sacred script…
> (This is) a call to creative understanding and development.   (*The Wisdom of God*, p. 18)

Sophianic Iconography

It was Florensky in particular who first became aware of the way in which different aspects of Sophia are reflected in a variety of icons. He discovered three main types, which can be classified in relation to the city in which the best examples are to be found. These icons, dedicated to Holy Sophia, are the Novgorod type, where Sophia is depicted as an angelic being seated on a throne; those which highlight the Sophianic nature of the Church (and sometimes the Logos), found at Yaroslavl, and finally the Kievan Sophia, where the Blessed Virgin Mary is prominent.

In the Novgorodian type a golden-yellow colour predominates. The church dates from the eleventh century and so, in all probability, does the icon. The angel, which is crowned, sits on a throne, supported by seven pillars. On the angel's right hand is Mary and on her left is St John the Baptist. Above the image of Sophia is the All-Compassionate Saviour. Her wings are symbolic of the heavenly world, their fiery colour indicative of perfection. Her imperial insignia represent the extent of Her universal rule, while cosmic power over the heavens is represented by the numerous star-filled concentric circles which encompass Sophia. While Christ occupies the highest place, it is Sophia who is in the very centre of the picture, subordinate to Christ but still of central importance for the whole of creation. She is its guardian angel. The second type of icon honouring the Holy Sophia dates from the sixteenth and eighteenth centuries. The scene is of the Crucifixion, where the cross is on an altar supported by six columns, the cross itself acting as a seventh column. The inscription in the top centre of the composition is from Proverbs 9: 'Wisdom has built her temple' This icon celebrates Sophia's tabernacling in the Church: the totality of the faithful, including the prophets and apostles, martyrs and evangelists, kings and bishops. Their rallying cry is three words, 'Rally the peoples.' Finally, in the Kievan Sophia, the focal point is Mary, the Mother of God. In this tradition She is pictured as the Woman Clothed in the Sun in the Apocalypse of St John, the last book in the Bible. She is the Virgin Mother, Sovereign over both the earthly and heavenly Church.

Having immersed himself in the Sophianic icons and their history, Florensky became aware of the fact that these icons also reflected the development in the Church's theological understanding of Sophia's nature and role. The oldest tradition is characteristic of Greek Christianity that celebrates the Sophianic nature of Christ. In fact Sophia is virtually identical with the second person of the Trinity. Early Slavic Christians, on the other hand, concentrated on the moral dimension of Sophia, especially as revealed in the person of Mary, who is honoured as the most pure and perfect vessel of Divine Grace. Finally, it was Russian Christianity, argues Florensky, from the eighteenth century onwards, that focused in particular on the cosmological dimension of Sophia, rooted as it was in a deep awareness of the joy of the unity of the whole of creation.

Florensky never claimed to offer a complete account of Sophianic ikons. His task was to point out patterns in order to understand better the Sophianic dynamics in the history of Christian thought. The truth is that the more one meditates on these icons, the more one discovers that they contain many layers of meaning. Sophianic reality can never be fully explained and neatly packaged — nothing that is truly divine ever can be. But this doesn't mean that there isn't a place for a fairly systematic account of divine things, such as the nature of Christ, the role of the Holy Spirit and the meaning of the Trinity. Such an account must always be rooted in a dynamic life of prayer and worship, study and fellowship, contemplation and creativity. Sophianic spirituality is concerned with the whole person and it draws upon the insights of the poet and philosopher. Its wisdom nourishes the heart as well as the mind.

Church Controversy

With such a radical theological programme, it's little wonder that Bulgakov's writings were eventually denounced as 'new, idiosyncratic, arbitrary',and of course, 'heretical', by church leaders. By 1935, the attack on Bulgakov came to a head, with two formal condemnations issued within six weeks of each other by two church bodies. This move had no practical effect, since Bulgakov was not under the authority of the senior clerics involved. He did, nevertheless, reply formally to the charges against him. The condemnations were more to do with church politics than the search for Christian truth, at a time of crisis and great social change. A bitter storm of controversy ensued, and although their impact was alleviated, the charge of heresy against Bulgakov has not been withdrawn to this day. The Russian Church of the 1920s and '30s was a Church at war, at least in theological and ecclesiastical terms. Charges and counter charges became a regular feature in Russian émigré journals and church publications.

Instead of being given a fair hearing, Sophiology became an excuse for some sections of the Russian Church to attack and vilify another. Three factions eventually appeared, and to understand the fate that awaited Sophia, we need to look briefly at what happened to the Russian Church in 1917, following the Bolshevik Revolution. The Holy Synod of the Bishops of the Russian Émigré Church, received permission from the Serbian Orthodox Patriarch, to make its base in Yugoslavia. The Holy Synod regarded itself as the legitimate head of Russian Orthodoxy abroad and demanded the allegiance of all provinces outside the Soviet Union. But Metropolitan Evlogy, the head of the Diocese of Western Europe (based in Paris), strongly resisted the demands of the Holy Synod. He disliked its highly authoritarian character. Any degree of independence from the Synod was seen as a threat — the very independence that Evlogy himself had been granted by the Byzantine or Ecumenical Patriarch, who had given him the status of Exarchate. To this day the Russian Church in the West comes under the jurisdiction of the Byzantine Patriarch of Constantinople. What made matters worse in the 1920s was the fact that Evlogy had become head of the newly founded Russian Theological Seminary in Paris, whose professorial staff included some of the most liberal and modern émigré theologians of their day, including Fr Bulgakov. The Holy Synod, led by Metropolitan Anthony, claimed that it alone had jurisdiction over the Seminary, that it alone could appoint its staff. It duly refused to recognize the Seminary and set about investigating its professors. In 1927 it denounced the Seminary as modernist, accused it of behaving like a Secret Society, and decided that the Seminary needed purging: the lax leadership of Metropolitan Evlogy was also condemned; it was foolish to suggest that the Russian Church was in need of renewal; and the modernism, which had become synonymous with Russian Orthodoxy in the West, would have to be stamped out. The Holy Synod even called in Archbishop Anastasius of Jerusalem to mediate between the two bodies, but the Western Metropolitan continued to assert his independence. Evlogy never wavered from supporting his followers, including Fr Bulgakov and his work as a theologian.

The Sophianic Controversy came to a head in 1935-37, when Metropolitan Sergei of Moscow decided to enter the affair. He played what he believed to be his political trump card, by claiming that he and he alone was the legitimate leader of the Russian Orthodox Church, and that both the Western branch of Orthodoxy and the Holy Synod had to recognize his authority. He set out to discredit the entire church jurisdiction to which Bulgakov belonged. He appointed the Lithuanian Metropolitan to supply him with a written report on the Paris-based Russian theologians, and in particular Bulgakov, and he came to the conclusion that Bulgakov was clearly unorthodox in his beliefs and consequently not in communion with the true Soviet Church, of which he was head. Bulgakov was to be deprived of his students and parishioners, while all the lay people who supported him were called to repent of their errors and to submit to the Moscow Patriarchate for 'healthy cleansing'. Bulgakov confirmed his belief in Orthodox doctrine and his Metropolitan declared unequivocally that Bulgakov was not guilty of any heresy.

Ironically, much of the criticism levelled against Bulgakov was drawn from his book *The Unfading Light*. When it was published in 1917 nothing was said against it. In fact, Bulgakov was allowed to take holy orders, under the patronage of the Moscow Patriarch! Florensky was even promoted within the Soviet Church for his epoch-making book, *The Pillar and Foundation of Truth*, chapter nine of which is devoted to Sophia. Both Sophianists were accepted as Orthodox; neither was condemned for his views. Metropolitan Anthony had attacked Bulgakov for heresy in 1924, but this accusation was withdrawn, and the Moscow Metropolitan had reasserted his full confidence in Bulgakov's integrity and ability as a scholar.

Early in 1939 Bulgakov was diagnosed as having cancer of the throat. Two operations helped conquer the disease, but he was left with no vocal cords. However, he learnt to speak in a whisper and was able to resume most of his duties at the Seminary. He continued with his scholarly work and wrote many sermons. Sister Johanna Reitlinger, a spiritual daughter of Bulgakov, helped nurse him during his last years. In her 'Reminiscences' she writes poignantly of this period in his life:

> Because of the loss of his voice and the virtual impossibility of his being able to participate in the great Sunday Liturgy, Fr Sergius was allowed to perform daily early liturgies [i.e. Holy Eucharist], about which he had dreamed all his life. Previously, we had to fight for his being allowed to perform such liturgies. But now these liturgies became 'natural', for those who had previously hindered Father Sergius now felt too great a pity for him to continue obstructing him.   (*The Final Days of Father Sergius Bulgakov*, p. 37)

(Because of his Sophianic views, Bulgakov's celebration of the Blessed Sacrament was limited until his operation for cancer.)

Bulgakov remained active until May 1944 when he suffered a cerebal haemorrhage. He died on 12 June and was buried three days later in the Russian Cemetery of Ste Genevieve-des-Bois in Paris. With the outset of World War Two, in addition to Bulgakov's illness, the Sophianic debate lost much of its impetus and has remained in the background ever since. Bulgakov's Sophiology has been largely ignored by mainstream Russian Orthodoxy, and almost totally neglected by English-speaking theologians and scholars.

Philosophy:the love of Wisdom

One of the charges most often levelled against the Russian Sophianists and other so-called 'modernist theologians' [e.g.Nicholas Berdyaev 1874-1948], by the ultra conservative wing of Orthodoxy, is that they had betrayed and polluted true Christian Orthodoxy — which the conservatives claim to be in their possession! Like the Deuteronomists of old, these traditionalists elected themselves to defend this genuine biblical faith, a faith they want to keep pure, in comparison to the 'new' Christianity, which is basically 'pagan', 'syncretistic', and highly 'speculative' — all words employed in a derogatory manner. Furthermore, the assumption is always made that, where non-Christian influences (initially Greek philosophy) have been grafted on to biblical truth, they can be removed. But philosophical language and concepts have always played an important role in Christianity, and pagan belief systems have served the Church for centuries. Christianity is in fact a highly creative merging of Judaism and Greek thought. The latter also played an important part in the Judaism that developed outside Jerusalem, especially in Alexandria, where Jews soon adapted to the cultural life of a non-Jewish society. Greek became their mother tongue and eventually the Hebrew Scriptures were translated into Greek (known as the Septuagint or simply as LXX) to serve Jewish devotional needs. In the process some key Hebrew words were not always translated accurately, and approximate meanings had to be found. Jewish concepts took on a new or extra meaning. For example, *Torah*, the Divine Law given to Israel, became *nomos*, a standard Greek word for law. The divine law existed, therefore, for all humanity and not just for the Chosen People. The Greek Old Testament was shaped to appeal to a cosmopolitan religious consciousness and awareness, and Judaism was eventually to grow into a universal missionary religion on the basis of the Septuagint. This was the context in which the early Christian missionaries soon found themselves preaching to Greek Jews. Many of the early Christian evangelists and teachers (themselves mostly Jewish) continued to make full use of Greek philosophy to communicate the meaning of the Christ event. St Paul, in his famous speech on the Areopagus (Acts 17:16f.) is the first written record of a Christian encounter with pagan philosophy. He made use of the pagan idea of the 'unknown god' to get his message over. He talked in non-Christian terms of The Divine One 'in whom we live and move and have our being' (v. 28). Paul even quoted the Greek poet Aratus (c.315-240 BC) who said of the Supreme Deity that 'we are all of his family'. Pagan philosophy continued to be utilized by Christian scholars for many centuries.

In the prologue to chapter one of the Fourth Gospel, a major motif from pagan religion was used to convey the universality of Jesus Christ. He is equated with the figure of the Cosmic Logos or Word, the Divine Reason or Order that generates, permeates and governs all of creation. It was the Logos that dwelt with prophets and all genuine teachers of the Truth, whatever their religion. The Fourth Gospel declared that the Logos became fully incarnate in Christ. Eventually, Logos theology gave way to Christology, because some of the Christian teachers argued that Christ was more than a created mediator or link between the Divine and creation. In some mysterious way Jesus Christ had a unique relationship with His Heavenly Father. Justin Martyr (writing in the middle of the second century AD) even regarded Christianity as the 'absolute philosophy', a phrase that Bulgakov would be quite at home with. Greek culture and learning was regarded by many as as divinely inspired as Jewish law and prophecy. It was through the work of these early theologians that Christianity became the heir to all that was good and worth preserving in Greek pagan thought.

Neoplatonism

One pagan philosophical school in particular has had a major influence on Christian spirituality down the centuries. I refer to Plotinus (205-270) and the movement known as the New Platonism (or Neoplatonism), although its followers would have regarded themselves simply as Platonists, disciples of Plato, the classical Greek philosopher born in 428 BC. The writings of Plotinus are one of the major guiding forces in Western culture, important in theology, philosophy and mysticism, having influenced Christian theology more than any other thinker since St Paul. Remove them and a vital part of the structure of Christian theology and spirituality would disappear.

One of the reasons why this major influence on Christian spirituality has been neglected, and even belittled, is the reluctance of some to acknowledge the influence of a pagan and what's more, a pagan whose pupil, Porphory (c.233-305) became a passionate anti-Christian writer. It was Porphory who published Plotinus' writings just when Christianity was about to become the official religion of the Empire. The new religion was settling into European culture and soon discovered that it had a natural affinity with Neoplatonism. For example, St Paul's doctrine of Christ as Divine wisdom and power; the reality of temporal things that are visible, and the Eternal which is invisible; a theory of the resurrection which stresses that the physical cannot inherit the Kingdom of Heaven, and finally a psychology of body, soul and spirit, where the soul occupies the mediating role between matter and spirit. All these points would have rung true to a Neoplatonist. The two faiths were major rivals, because this example of refined pagan spirituality also preached a religious and moral idealism, stressed the primacy of the Spirit, the path of the human soul on its journey to the One and the offer of salvation as the culmination of its Quest.

Theological pioneers

Christian spirituality has always been enriched and challenged by a certain type of Christian thinker, of whom Sergius Bulgakov is probably one of the most original in recent years. A kindred spirit to Bulgakov lived in the fifth century AD, this time in Syria. In all probability a Syrian monk (he may even have been a bishop), who belonged to a Christian tradition known for daring and audacious speculative theology, he was a member of a very distinct mystical movement. In addition to drawing from the pagan mysteries, this anonymous author also made use of the writings of one Proclus, a Neoplatonic teacher who lived in Athens in the fifth century and was head of The Academy, Plato's recognized successor. This Syrian holy man took the pseudonym Dionysius (or Denys) the Areopagite, thus locating himself firmly in a Christian tradition that went back to the Acts of the Apostles (17.16f). He clearly regarded St Paul as his spiritual father and the Christian encounter with Plato as the stage upon which he would develop his Christian spirituality. One of his spiritual guides was a visionary, Stephen bar Sudaill.

A mystic, we are told that he actually 'felt the things of God' . His book on the hidden mysteries of the Divinity was only discovered in the early part of this century. Utilizing, adapting and even sometimes reversing the meaning of the Neoplatonic concepts that he had been taught, Dionysius developed a daring Christian mystical theology and accompanying techniques of contemplation. Dionysius believed that the truths Plato and his successor knew belonged to Christ and did not have to be abandoned when one embraced Christianity. In being given a Christian interpretation, pagan truths were themselves raised to a higher level and consecrated to serve biblical revelation. Dionysius's new, speculative writings were fully accepted by the Church, and soon acquired a great reputation after their appearance in the early part of the sixth century, first of all in the Greek original, by the Eastern Church, where they were widely used, and then via the Latin translation of the Celtic sage, Eriugena, in the ninth century, when they became well known and revered in the West. They were practically welcomed as having the same authority as holy writ. Almost a Third Testament, in fact!

It was primarily through the writings of the Aeropagite that Neoplatonism was incorporated into Christianity. To this day the mystical tradition of the Church owes a great deal to the Syrian monk whose real identity will for ever remain a mystery. A dynamic and growing Christianity has never feared being open to the truth, wherever it may be found. Bulgakov, and the movement to which he belonged, teaches us to embrace Athens as well as Jersualem. Standing under the dome of Hagia Sophia in Constantinople, Bulgakov, declared in awe that 'here Plato is baptized into Christianity' (*The Wisdom of God*, p. 13).

> As Plato's pagan Sophia gazes upon herself She learns to recognize herself in the Divine Sophia and, indeed, this Church is an artistic proof of her existence and of her reality, spread like a protecting canopy over the world. It represents the last, silent revelation of the Greek genius, bequeathed to the ages, concerning Sophia, the Wisdom of God.
>
> (*The Wisdom of God*, p. 14)

The encounter between theology and philosophy is an integral part of the Christian ethos. The relationship between the two is never easy, but is unavoidable in a Christianity that is committed to serving the Truth, as well as to discovering different aspects of that Truth in other disciplines and sciences. While the distinction between the two must never be blurred, it is imperative that theology and philosophy remain in dialogue. This way they can continue to challenge each other to think and reflect, passionately and creatively, about their special insights into human and divine realities. While no one philosophical tradition can offer a belief system that explains everything about life, a Christianity is needed that can weave the different aspects of life into as meaningful a whole as is possible. This is what the Russian Sophianic tradition endeavoured to do, particularly aware as it was of the fragmented nature of modern life, and thus of the need for synthesis, harmony and unity. Bulgakov rooted this unity in the figure of the Divine Sophia.

NOTES ON CHAPTER THREE

Vladimir Soloviev's Poems of Sophia, Translated by Boris Jakim and Laury Magnus, The Variable Press, New Haven, Conn. 1996

Samuel D. Cioran, *Vladimir Soloviev* and the Knights of the Divine Sophia, Wilfrid Laurier University Press, Ontario, Canada 1977

Paul Marshall Allen, *Vladimir Soloviev, Russian Mystic*, Rudolf Steiner Publications 1978

Sergius Bulgakov, *The Wisdom of God*, William and Norgate, London 1937

Sergius Bulgakov, *The Orthodox Church*, St Vladimir's Seminary Press, Crestwood, New York 1988

'The Final Days of Father Sergius Bulgakov: A Memoir' by Sister Joanna Reitlinger taken from Sergius Bulgakov: Apocatatsasis and Transfiguration, Variable Readings in Russian Philosophy No 2), translated, edited and with an introduction by Boris Jakim, Variable Press, New Haven, Conn. 1995.

4. Sophia Unveiled

I gazed upon it all, and all was fair,
In form of Womanhood,
embracing all in one;
The infinite encircled there,
yet limitless,
Before me and within me — You alone!

O radiant Countenance,
you have not deceived me!
Your fullest glory I beheld
amid the desert waste;
Ever will your heavenly roses
bloom within me
Where'er my stream of life may flow.
(from Soloviev's *Three Meetings*, quoted in *Vladimir Soloviev, Russian Mystic*)

The Lady in Waiting

'The Lady' came into our lives out of the blue. None of us can point to the day or even the month when She appeared, but by Lent 1987, She had become an important part of our common spirituality. I cannot imagine a time when She was not present in our lives. She tabernacled within us and among us, stretching her tent curtains wide to embrace the whole Valley. No aspect of life was out of bounds to Her indwelling. Her Sovereignty was all-embracing.

A year or so passed by before we started to question amongst ourselves as to Her identity. It was enough to enjoy the intimate togetherness that seemed to embody Her very being. Like lovers, we were content 'just to be together. Words were largely superfluous. When some of us did attempt to put our experiences on paper, it was mostly 'love poetry' and prayers that emerged…

Oh Lady	Sweet Lady
But grant me	but Grant me
The Eye to	The right to
Behold Thee,	Adore Thee
My Spirit	For I would
Desires Thee…	Draw near Thee
This night.	This night.
My servitor	My Servitor
I grant thee	I grant thee
The Eye to	The right to
Behold me	Draw near me
With love thou	In love I
Shalt see me	Embrace thee
This night.	This night. (AMH)

The moment came when we had to leave the intimacy of Her embrace in order to contemplate and reflect upon Her identity. This was no cold and clinical exercise but an opportunity to discover in all its fullness the meaning that She embodied. I knew intuitively that if my communion with Her was to continue to grow, then it would engage, not only my heart but my intellect as well, and weave the two into one harmonious whole. Knowledge is an integral part of any relationship, especially one built on love.

In my confirmation class I was taught, as an Anglican, to apply a threefold test to any religious or mystical experiences. This proved to be a most useful tool over the coming months, namely:

What does Holy Scripture teach about it?

Does it have a place in the tradition of the Church?

How does it relate to, and compare with, the experiences

of one's contemporaries?

Over many years I had built up a detailed library of Russian Sophianic literature, at least in the English language, gathering together almost everything available by, or about, the Russian Sophianists. I was able to follow Sophia's emergence, as it were, from Soloviev's initial intuitions and scholarly research, in the latter part of the nineteenth century, to Bulgakov's efforts at developing a fully-fledged Sophiology, as it came to be called, in the 1930s. Both came to represent the tensions in my own experiences and understanding of Sophianic reality. On the one hand, reading Soloviev gave me the confidence to follow Sophia wherever She led me, often beyond the confines of traditional Christianity. Although his work is scholarly, there is nothing dry about it. In fact it was he who helped set me on my own Sophianic quest, a journey as exciting and fascinating as any medieval tale of knights and their search for the Holy Grail. Bulgakov's approach helped me to channel my passions for Sophia and brought more theological discipline into my Quest. He challenged me to relate my Sophianic encounters to Christian dogma.

In addition to all this I had a wealth of material on hand from a wide variety of sources. These included Jewish and Christian mystical teaching, world myths and legends, the place of the goddess in religious experiences, and the insights of modern transpersonal psychology, especially the pioneering work of the Swiss psychiatrist, Carl Gustav Jung (1875-1961). But all these were of a secondary nature. Primary was our continued encounters with The Lady, in prayer and meditation, in worship and Bible study, and in dreams and visions. She had become an integral part of our Christianity. None of us doubted that Her presence was genuine and transformative, even when we were uncertain as to Her identity. We proceeded to explore every possibility, not in a cold and clinical fashion, but in an atmosphere of reverence and awe.

The first Jewish Christians regarded the Divine Spirit as a personal feminine reality or presence and not as an impersonal cosmic force or power. She was revered as the true mother of Christ and was known as 'The Lady' or simply as 'Mother'. An early Hebrew gospel even has Jesus speak of 'My Mother the Spirit', and many of these early Christians prayed to her as the main revelation of Divinity. A prophetic and visionary movement in second-century Asia Minor, known as Montanism, even believed that the Divine Spirit would incarnate as a woman. Its followers also spoke of Christ appearing in the likeness of a woman and planting the seed of wisdom within them. *The Shepherd of Hermas* is a series of revelations to Hermas, written in the early part of the first century, which for a while was included in the New Testament. In this gospel it is the Church that appears in the shape of a woman or a shepherd angel:

And as I was praying, the heaven was opened and I saw the woman which I had coveted,

saluting me from heaven, and saying, 'Hermas, hail'. And I looking upon her answered,

'Lady, what dost thou do here?'   (The Apocryphal New Testament, 1:5)

In the last book of the New Testament, The Revelation of St John, or The Apocalypse, as it is also called, many scholars believe that the 'Woman clothed with the Sun' in the twelfth chapter is also a personification of the Church or the Heavenly Jerusalem. For others she is the Blessed Virgin Mary or at least a prefigurement of her. Others believe her to be Sophia in her cosmic aspect. Whoever she is, there is no denying her all-pervading presence

> A great and wondrous sign appeared in heaven, a woman
> clothed with the Sun, with the moon under her feet and
> a crown of twelve stars on her head. She was pregnant
> and cried out in pain as She was about to give birth.   (vv. 1-2)

This and many similar images are so powerful and endurable, that they have been interpreted in various ways at different periods in history. No doubt they will continue to be so interpreted, especially if one believes the age-old tradition that Scripture has different levels of meaning, from the most basic and historical to the most mystical and esoteric. The Book of Lamentations in the Older Testament is a lament over the fall of Jerusalem during the Babylonian exile. Who cannot fail to be moved by its opening verse?

> She who was Queen among the provinces
>   has now become a slave.

Her beauty and splendour long since departed, 'bitterly she weeps at night, tears upon her cheeks' (v. 2). For Origen (c.185-253), one of the greatest of all Christian theologians, this book was an allegory for the soul's plight in the world. It tells of the soul's slavery to the passions and hence of her inability to reach the Truth through wisdom. Although he paints a bleak picture of the soul's predicament, Origen holds out the hope that through suffering the soul will be purged of all that is unworthy, and will finally reach salvation.

The idea of the soul as feminine has continued down the centuries, especially through the teachings of the mystics. In the writings of the thirteenth-century Flemish mystic Hadewijch, the mother of European 'love mysticism' it is not only the soul that is feminine but also the essence that lies at the heart of the Divine, personified as 'Minne' or Lady Love, a passionate female presence that pervades her whole life. She is also known as The Noble Maiden, Queen, Mother of the Virtues or Fertility herself. Drawing upon the imagery of medieval courtly love, Hadewijch describes the service of love to The Lady, as an example or fore-shadowing of the love offered by the soul to the divine. Having experienced the Divine indwelling herself, Hadewijch sings the praises of a deity that allows itself to be possessed in the most intimate of ways. Having been penetrated herself by Lady Love, Hadewijch throws herself headlong into the Mystery of Divine love:

> To sublime love
> I have given away all that I am.
>   Whether I lose or win, let all
> That is owed Her be Hers without diminution.
>   What has happened now?
>   I am not mine:
> She has engulfed the substance of my spirit
>   Her fine being
>   Gives me the assurance
> That the pain of love is all profit.
>
>   If anyone wishes to content Love
> I counsel him to spare himself in nothing.
>   He shall give himself totally
> So as to live in the performance of the noblest deeds,
>   For lovers secret,

To aliens, unknown,
For they do not understand the essence of Love.
That sweet attendance
In the school of Love
Is unknown to him who never enters there.   *(Hadewijch, The Complete Works 3,* 16:8,10)

The Return of the Goddess

Followers of Jungian psychology, and a plethora of Transpersonal ones, may not speak of the union of the soul with the Divine, but they are equally as passionate about the need for balance and harmony, in their case manifested in the coming together of unconscious and conscious aspects of the psyche. Crucial to this is the release of the long repressed Eternal Feminine, or Goddess, as she is more commonly known, in all Her different guises. This is facilitated by paying close attention to dreams and the spontaneous images that emerge from an individual's depths (or heights!). Also important is the use of rituals, both inner and outer, personal and collective, that help to channel or focus long ignored aspects of the human personality. While an array of 'sub-personalities', gods and goddesses or archetypes, as they are also called, have re-emerged into Western consciousness over the last thirty years or so, it is the return of The Goddess and Her entourage that has occupied the centre stage for many. In a real sense, of course, She has never been away, even if a Christian Orthodoxy banished Her to the fringes of Western cultural life.

As we grew in Her presence, we began to see things in a totally new way. It was as though we were being prepared to see the complete picture for the first time. Take, for example, the fifth episode of Michelangelo's (1475-1564) *Creation of Adam* on the ceiling of the Sistine Chapel in Rome. I refer to the scene where the male deity, who is on the right, reaches out with one arm extended to make contact with Adam, who reciprocates the gesture.

Many of us have looked at this painting for years but never fully awakened to the truth that it contains. Michelangelo knew his Wisdom literature! The left arm of the male deity embraces the female figure of Sophia, in celebration of the passage in chapter 8 of the Book of Proverbs, where Sophia speaks for herself:

I was there when he set the heavens in place,
  when he marked out the horizon on the
    face of the deep....
I was the craftsman at his side.
  I was filled with delight day after day
    rejoicing always in his presence,
  rejoicing in his whole world,
    and delighting in mankind.   (vv. 27,30)

The Elizabethan poet Edmund Spenser (1552-1599), gives little information about Sophia, but he sings her praises in his 'Hymn of Heavenly Beauty. (Sapience, in the poem, is the Latin for Sophia.) Spenser may have been inspired by one of the many Orthodox icons of Sophia. There is little doubt that he too was inspired by the teaching of Proverbs, when he wrote:

There in his bosom Sapience doth sit,
The Sovereign darling of the Deity,
Clad like a Queen in royal robes, most fit
For so great power and peerless majesty,
And all with gems and jewels gorgeously

Adorned, that brighter than the stars appear
And make her native brightness seem more clear.

And on her head a crown of purest gold
Is set, in sign of highest Sovereignty;
And in her hand a sceptre she doth hold,
With which She rules the house of God on high
And manageth the ever-moving sky,
And in the same these lower creatures all
Subjected to her power imperial.   (*Via: The Way of Life,* p. 85)

We were astonished to discover that the Eternal Feminine is present, not only in some of the greatest works of European art but also in literature as well. The German poet Goethe (1749-1832), the last great pagan, as he is known, describes in Faust the development of the human soul to ultimate fulfilment and salvation, following its search for Wisdom. As the soul rises heavenward, guided by three female figures, visible is the Heavenly Queen and Virgin, 'the Mother throned supernal, Godhead's peer eternal'. This epic poem comes to a climax with words that some of us have appropriated to our use in prayer and worship. These words by Goethe draw together in a profound way, the whole spectrum of the Eternal Feminine which we encountered on our Sophianic quest:

O contrite hearts, seek with your eyes
The visage of Salvation;
Blissful in that gaze, arise,
Through glad regeneration.
Now may every pulse of good
Seek to serve before thy face
Virgin, Queen of motherhood,
Keep us, Goddess, in Thy Grace.
              (in prostrate adoration)
All things corruptible
Are but a parable;
Earth's insufficiency
Here finds fulfilment;
Here the ineffable
Winds life through love;
Eternal Womanhood
Lead us above.   (*Faust Part Two,* p. 288)

The Wisdom Tradition

Our quest gradually revealed to us that the reality which some of us had come to know as 'The Lady', or simply as 'Sophia', was something more than a feminine way of talking about the Divine, the Church, the human soul or a long repressed aspect of the unconscious. From Holy Scripture we discovered that The Lady was the Divine Wisdom which had been an integral part of the Divine-human drama since before the creation of the world. In the Older Testament, King Solomon is Sophia's patron par excellence, and the movement which he encouraged nearly three millennia ago continues to this day. Although a fully-fledged Sophiology only emerged with the Russians, a Wisdom tradition has flourished, at different times, within the Church's long history.

Vladimir Soloviev was a rare combination of poet and systematic thinker. Such a combination is reflected to a certain degree in Florensky and Bulgakov, although in the former the poet predominates while the latter was primarily fired by the need to present as ordered a picture of the Sophianic vision as possible. In a similar way, different Wisdom traditions and individuals have focused their attention on specific manifestations of Sophia, and have done so very often by leaning more towards the affective or rational, as the case may be. Take for example the Victorine School in Paris in the early part of the twelfth century, based at the Abbey of St Victor. It was served by some of the most brilliant thinkers of the day, including Hugh, Richard and the philosopher-poet Godfrey. It was an open school where students of all ages attended in their droves to study, and thus grow in, the Christian life. Education was for salvation, with every branch of knowledge playing its part in an ordered programme that lead eventually to spiritual perfection. Every discipline was a sacred tool that would assist the individual into deeper union with the Divine Wisdom — especially as revealed in the person of Christ. Along with other schools, such as the one at Chartres, the Victorines were also preoccupied with Sophia's role in creation and the wider question of the relationship between the human and the divine. But this played a secondary role to the Victorines' chief concern, which was Wisdom's role in the inner processes of the individual personality or the human mind. They shared with non-Christian philosophers the desire for Wisdom, but whereas the pagans saw this Wisdom at work in nature, the Victorines stressed the Wisdom that transcends all created things and resides in each individual. It was this wisdom that was synonymous with right knowledge — the divine knowledge that enables one to grow in understanding and thus be able to penetrate the secrets of heaven and earth. It also helps one to probe the inner deeper meaning in the words of Scripture. The more, through knowledge, an individual understands of divine things, the more one is able to comprehend one's divine origin and destiny. Self-knowledge and divine knowledge are always interconnected, the knowledge that leads to virtue, to right living and hence to holiness. The source of this knowledge is the Sophianic Christ, and Wisdom is always on hand, not only to summon one to pursue Enlightenment but also to guide one along the spiritual path.

Many of the early Church Fathers were devoted to the Divine Wisdom, although it remained for the Russian Sophianists to draw out and develop the Sophianic teachings of the Church, as recorded in Scriptures and in church tradition. For them no earthly or heavenly beauty can be compared with the beauty, inspiration and pleasure of Sophia. Her love and knowledge is to be sought above all else. St Basil the Great, one of the Cappadocians, sought to remove Sophia's veil of secrecy when he taught that the soul follows its instinct when it meets Sophia and embraces Her like a passionate lover. In this embrace, the soul is filled with all goodness and made pregnant with holiness. But for Vladimir Soloviev it wasn't enough simply to contemplate Wisdom in a heavenly vision or in the depth of the human soul. Sophia was more than an object of pious contemplation. Sophia is the divine reality or essence that needs to be incarnated in the world through Divine-human effort and co-operation. It is only in this way that the world can be transfigured, and the whole person, not just his or her intellect or soul, be saved. The spiritual must be realized in the material. Heaven must actually become one with the earth, as happened in the person of Christ, the perfect Divine-human.

Henry Suso: Servitor of Eternal Wisdom

Soloviev's personal devotion to Sophia can only be matched in the Middle Ages by the Dominican ascetic, poet and preacher, the Swabian-born Henry Suso (1295-1365). Suso was one of the best known and admired pupils of another Dominican, Meister Eckhart (1260-1328), who produced a masterly interpretation or restatement of Neoplatonism for a Northern European culture that was evolving its own distinctive kind of Christianity. From this spirituality grew what is known today as German Idealism. So bold and courageous were Eckhart's mystical teachings (he too, like Bulgakov, explored the unknown regions of the Divine Mystery) that he was put on trial and condemned as a heretic by papal decree in 1329. His teachings were described variously as 'blasphemous and insane', 'worthy of laughter among all intelligent persons' and as 'wrong and heretical'. Sadly Eckhart's contemporaries never really made the effort to understand what the Master had to say. There is also no doubt that he was used as a scapegoat in ecclesiastical power games. In 1980 (six hundred and fifty years after he was condemned) representatives of the Dominican Order initiated official procedures to reopen Eckhart's case. Although Suso was also reprimanded once for publishing heretical doctrine, and was for a while deprived of his teaching post, he did not continue his Master's philosophical and theological pursuits. Suso leaned more towards affairs of the heart. He stressed the importance of personal religion and the daily discipline of an ordered and devout life. The turning point in his spiritual life came when he began to immerse himself in the Bible's Wisdom books. They formed the basis of his daily study and prayers. Like Bulgakov, Suso's experience of Sophia was rooted in the revealed word of the Scriptures. Like Soloviev, Suso was granted intimate, personal visions of Sophia, sometimes without form but more often than not in the lovely guise of a gracious and beautiful mistress. He referred to Her as 'The All-Lovely One', 'My Queen', 'My Empress', but mostly as 'Eternal Wisdom'. She sought Her lovers, wooing them with Her exalted love and then drawing them into Her. Suso became Her Servitor. His life was dedicated to her service, his prayers and songs offered continually in adoration to Her. In his Autobiography, we hear one of these love songs:

> She shone like the morning star
> and Her radiance was dazzling as the Rising Sun.
> Her Crown was Eternity;
> Her vesture bliss;
> Her words sweetness;
> Her embrace the fullness of every delight;
> She was far, yet near; High, yet lowly;
> She was present, yet hidden;
> She reaches above the summit of the heavens
> and touches the depths of the abyss....
> Sometimes She showed Herself as one rich in wisdom,
> at other times as overflowing with love.   (*The Life of Blessed Henry Suso*, pp. 14-15)

Jacob Boehme: The Mystic Cobbler

Devotion to Sophia transcends all Christian traditions and churches. She is equally at home within Medieval Catholicism as She is today in certain sections of the Russian Church. As some have been surprised to see Sophia honoured within the very patriarchal structures of Orthodoxy, so others are equally surprised to learn of Her presence in Protestantism. Within the first century of the Reformation, a radical Lutheran called Jacob Boehme (1575-1624), a master shoemaker by trade, was reminding his contemporaries of the Feminine principle within the Judeo-Christian heritage. Boehme is regarded as the last of the great European mystics, the Father of Protestant spirituality. Having challenged Medieval Catholic Orthodoxy, Lutheranism soon became a rigid Orthodoxy in its own right. For some it was Popery in a new guise! Groups of disenchanted Protestants became widespread, radicals who lived their Christianity on the fringe or even outside mainstream Lutheran life. Early in his own life, Boehme was supported by a Lutheran pastor who shared his broad learning and mystical leanings. Boehme was a member of his mystical-meditative parish group. But Pastor Moeller was replaced by the narrow-minded and bigoted Pastor Richter, who was fearful of anything that did not adhere to strict Lutheran teachings. Boehme was eventually banished from his hometown for publishing accounts of his spiritual visions, and condemned as a heretic.

Disenchanted with institutional Christianity of all kinds, radical Protestants began to teach that the true

Church is the spiritual Church, whose members, of whatever external persuasion, are united freely in loving fellowship and mutual tolerance, a secret temple hidden from the world. This invisible Church is Sophia, the Divine Mother, who nourishes all true Christians. Because they draw from the same maternal source, tolerance and simplicity of faith prevail. There is no strife or conflict about one's religion, since every Christian carries this true Church within. Every believer is a temple of the Divine Spirit, where Christ dwells within the human soul or heart. And even if one becomes a member of a sect, for the sake of worship and fellowship, one remains ultimately detached from these sects.

We also see in Boehme the search for that Unity which not only draws Christians together but also explains all the different aspects of creation. This All-Embracing Original Unity is Sophia, the Breath of Divine Power from which issues, as with the Victorines, all knowledge, virtue and holiness. She is the Great Mystery which is the Source of all, the Divine Understanding which underlies everything. Guided by this Wisdom, Boehme was able to penetrate not only the secret workings of Nature but also the dynamics of the human soul and the process whereby one becomes Christ-like in nature. The core of this process lay in the spiritual or mystical marriage between the human soul and the Virgin Sophia. In his prayers to Sophia, Boehme, the explorer of Nature, becomes the mystic intoxicated with the 'Noble Sophia', 'The Flower of Sharon', 'The Precious Garland'. All who will obtain the royal garland of Christ from Sophia must woo Her for it in great desire of love. Boehme's prayers, which are part of our Sophianic liturgy, sing the wonders of the Sophianic love between the human soul and Christ. These, like many other prayers and hymns by devotees of Sophia, bear witness to the truth that Sophianic awareness does not detract from or diminish other aspects of the Divine economy. Soloviev and Suso, Bulgakov and Boehme, remained profoundly Trinitarian in their understanding of the Divine.

The same is true of many of the English Sophianists of the late seventeenth and the eighteenth centuries. One of their leaders was the Revd Dr John Pordage (1607-1681), one-time Rector of the parish of Bradfield in Berkshire, and a follower of Jakob Boehme. He belonged to a movement for religious renewal through the cultivation of mystical experience and devotion to Sophia. The main inspiration for this movement was an Englishwoman named Jane Leade (1620-1704), a close friend and spiritual companion of John Pordage. Her remarkable life was one of direct communion with the spiritual world. Three times the Virgin Sophia appeared to her, once with a face shining with the brightness of a crystal. Sophia granted Jane privileged access to Divine secrets, and the Sophianic spring of wisdom and understanding never ran dry throughout Jane Leade's eighty-one years on earth. In collaboration with her colleagues and students, Jane established in London a group of mystics called the Philadelphia Society. Her mystical experiences are recorded in a charming diary entitled *A Fountain of Gardens*. Here is an extract quoted in *Vladimir Soloviev, Russian Mystic*: —

> There came upon me an overshadowing bright cloud, and in the midst of it a Figure of a
> Woman, most richly adorned with transparent gold, her hair hanging down, and her face as
> terrible as crystal for brightness, but her countenance was sweet and mild. At this sight I was
> somewhat amazed, but immediately a Voice came saying, 'Behold, I am God's Eternal Virgin,
> Wisdom, whom thou hast been enquiring after. I am to unseal the Treasures of God's deep
> Wisdom unto thee.'   (p.59)

Sergius Bulgakov and Sophiology

Our quest led us from a feminine presence relegated by many to the fringes of Western culture, to the biblical Wisdom or Sapience tradition, and eventually to the fully-fledged Sophiology of Sergius Bulgakov. Occupying a unique place in the Judeo-Christian heritage, Sophia is clearly no 'optional extra' in the Divine-human drama, even if for centuries She has been The Lady waiting in the wings. Church history, in addition to the

Bible, bears witness to Sophia's continued presence. It was the genius of Fr Bulgakov that helped unveil Her presence at the heart of Christian doctrine. It is in the Creeds, of all places, that Sophia's sovereignty is ultimately revealed! With great sensitivity and scholarly insight, Bulgakov led his students and followers deeper into the Divine Mystery towards which the Creeds point. Although only one book by Bulgakov was translated into English during his lifetime (*The Wisdom of God*, published in 1937) it is a relatively complete exposition of Bulgakov's mature thought on Sophia. Subtitled 'A Brief Summary of Sophiology', this book presents a panoramic view of Sophia and Her relevance to every aspect of Christian dogma. It is an epic as awe inspiring as any of the great European works of art, literature and music.

The Wisdom of the Creeds

The Creeds that finally emerged, at the end of a series of theological debates spanning many centuries, were the result of much discussion, heated arguments and plenty of political conniving. It was a complex process, as much the result of political pressure as theological necessity. Theologians from different traditions and cultures had their own native creeds questioned and challenged, many of them eager to see their own doctrinal formulas become the norm for a summary of the Christian Faith. Bulgakov never pretended that his theory concerning the relationship between the Divine and human, i.e. the Sophianic quest, was the only way of looking at the issue. What he wanted to do was stimulate others, after centuries of neglect, to look creatively at the issues which he raised. Doctrinal debates have been a feature of Christianity from the very beginning. People's spiritual experiences were passionately questioned and discussed in order to discover whether they were authentic or not. The New Testament itself contains different ways of looking at the person of Christ.

Who is Christ? The challenge of answering this question was already under way well before the bulk of the New Testament was finally drawn together. Even before St Paul began to develop his theology, the tradition enshrined in the Letter to the Philippians understood Jesus not as a Jewish prophet or an enthroned Messiah but as a divine being, who in heaven was 'equal to the Divine One' and as being in 'the form of the Divine', before he took on the likeness of homo sapiens (2:6-11). St Peter and the Apostolic Community parted company with the Christian Community represented by the theology and spirituality of the Fourth Gospel, because they had no comprehension of Christ's pre-existent divine origin, unlike the 'Johannine Christians' who proclaimed Christ as the Son 'who is at the father's side' (John 1:18).

I wonder what the first Jewish Christians would have made of the Church Council that in 325 AD declared Christ to be 'not only of the nature of the Father', but in 385 to have been 'born of the Father before all time'?

Jewish spirituality abounds with tales of earthly persons who journey up into heaven to receive Divine revelations, most of them returning to earth with them. A similar tradition describes the descent of angelic beings who came to earth to fulfil certain Divinely appointed tasks. At the heart of this intercourse between heaven and earth was Wisdom, the Ladder between the Creator and creation. The 'Wisdom pattern' is always the same. Human beings ascend-descend while angels descend-ascend. By the time of the Fourth Gospel (whether it was written early or later in the first century), we see that a total reversal of the traditional pattern had taken place. Christ is first of all described as having descended from heaven, although He clearly was no angel. A tradition was already developing which brought together two well established beliefs and formulas for the first time, namely the heavenly-angelic and the earthly-mystical. It is difficult for us to appreciate how earth-shattering this new doctrine was. No one before had ever thought of linking the Archangel Michael, for example, with an Abraham, in one individual, but one or more members of an alternative and radical Jewish sect did just that! In the person of Christ, the angel and the seer were seen as one and the same, the heavenly and the earthly united in a unique way, the Sophianic aspect of Divinity. This was one of the great discoveries in the history of Christian thought.

A radical re-assessment followed in relation to the question of Messiahship, and it was Wisdom that provided the background. Although Jesus was called Messiah or Christ ('the Anointed One'), His early followers turned the traditional meaning of Messiah on its head. The expected Messiah was to be a worldly king: Jesus clearly was not. He would establish the perfect age of an earthly kingdom of peace: Christ spoke of another Kingdom 'not of this world'. Jesus died a common criminal, a failure and rejected. He had more in common with Isaiah of the Exile's 'Suffering Servant', than with the success story normally associated with a hero-warrior like King David. What's more, Jesus was believed to be Divine while the Messiah would be a human person. Jesus was a unique Divine Messenger sent to proclaim justice and establish righteousness for all. The figure of Sophia had never been linked to the Messiah, and, like Jesus, She too possessed Divine qualities and partook of Divinity in a special way. Like Jesus, She too failed in Her Divinely appointed mission (or at least appeared to by worldly standards) and, rejected, returned to Heaven. Within an already existing Sophiology, we can see how Christology was developing. Sophia was traditionally regarded as:

> a Divine heavenly being, loved of the father
> the Image of Divine Goodness
> the Beginning of creation and Firstborn
> an Intermediary between Creator and creation
> the Agent of creation
> the principle of order in the world

Christ, in Colossians and Hebrews, respectively, was

Beloved Son	Son
Image of the Invisible One	Reflects the Divine Glory
Firstborn of all creation	Mediator of a New Order
Acts as Heavenly High Priest	
All things created through Him	World created through Him
and held together	and upholds the universe

Christ did not replace Sophia, He became Sophia manifested to the world. In the Fourth Gospel Sophia is embodied or enfleshed in Christ, and it is within the mystery of Sophianic reality that we see unfold the drama of the Word's unique relationship with the Father. Sophia was not forgotten. She was not pushed out by male theologians. She became the matrix of a radical theological development within a first-century Palestinian Jewish sect.

The more theologians struggled with reality of 'the Word made flesh', the more they had to begin to face up to the role played by the Divine Spirit, the study of which goes by the name of Pneumatology — pneuma being the Greek word for wind or breath, as in 'pneumatic tyres'. Belief in the unitarian nature of the Divine One grew to a binitarian theology, as the Son or the Word's relationship with the Father began to be taken seriously. Gradually the Church teased out the esoteric truth about the trinitarian nature of the Divine one, the mystery of the One-in-three. The word 'trinity' does not appear in the Bible, and yet the reality to which it points is there, albeit veiled. It is ironic that the word Wisdom (in whatever language) does appear in the Bible, yet it has taken nearly 2000 years for the Church to develop a mature Sophiology!

In developing its Creeds, the Church has turned, therefore, to every major figure in the Divine-human drama, except Sophia! There were, eventually, discussions about the status of the Blessed Virgin Mary, which came to be known as Mariology. It is instructive to look briefly at what happened to Mary, to see the role played by Sophia in this debate as well. By the fifth century a Marian cult had become a key part in the life of many churches. Theologians could not keep out speculations about her role in the divine plan of things, a situation similar to the Russian theologians in relation to Sophia. Mary was eventually more closely associated with Sophia than was Christ, filling the gap between heaven and earth that for many Christians even the Divine Trinity could not bridge. From being the Mother of Christ, Mary soon became *Theotokos*, the Mother of God, a title that many deemed heretical, smacking as it did of the pagan myths. It was the fourth-century Cappadocian Fathers (named after a region in present-day Turkey, where they lived) who successfully campaigned, following a bitter controversy, to make *Theotokos* a test of Christian Orthodoxy. They boldly declared that if anyone did not accept the Holy Mary as Mother of God he was without the Godhead. Wisdom texts from the Bible and the Apocrypha were also applied to Mary instead of Sophia, and used in liturgy on Marian holy days. For example, Mary became the Creator's Beloved in Proverbs 8 and the key passage (vv. 22-31) adopted as the lesson for the Festival of the Immaculate Conception. A passage from the Wisdom of Jesus ben Sirach, where it tells of Sophia being 'established in Zion' (24:3), was adapted to celebrate Mary's Assumption into heaven, although the ninth verse. which refers to Sophia's pre-existence, was wisely left out:

from Eternity, in the beginning, he created me, and for Eternity, I shall not cease to exist .

There were already boundaries beyond which speculations about Mary could not go. In a similar vein, the Creeds set the parameters within which the debate about Sophia could take place, although her presence in the early Christian centuries remained veiled from a doctrinal viewpoint. After centuries of neglect, the doctrinal debate which Bulgakov initiated placed the Sophianic quest back at the heart of the theological agenda.

In challenging us to look again at the teaching contained in the Credal confessions of the Church, Bulgakov reminds his audience of the radical nature of the Christian 'Good News' about the Divine-human condition. In the process he spells out clearly the alternative beliefs that seek one's allegiance, or at least the philosophy behind them. These can be reduced to two diametrically opposed ways of looking at life. On the one hand is the belief, whether it be in religious or secular garb, that there is only one ultimate reality, the Creator or creation. Whether one follows a mystical path or an atheistic, humanistic creed, both are, paradoxically, variations on the same theme. If the Divine Creator is the 'All', and all that really exists is the Creator, then creation and every aspect of it, in particular homo sapiens, is subordinate to it and is eventually swallowed up by it. If, on the other hand, the world of creation is considered to be sufficient unto itself, then the Creator becomes superfluous. In both cases the sovereignty of each individual person is obscured as it becomes indistinguishable from a reality greater than itself, be it divine or human.

The alternative belief system regards the Creator and creation as being mutually exclusive and in perpetual opposition to each other. The universe is conceived as a battleground between good heavenly powers, represented by the Divine, and earthly powers which, to all intent and purpose, are evil or at least in the perpetual grip of evil forces. Even should heaven be regarded as the stage for both good and evil forces, earth is rarely seen in a good and positive light, except when 'God is on our side'. The drama between Good and Evil is eventually played out on earth between a whole series of polarities, such as the spiritual against the material, body against soul, male against female, light against dark. In this creed, whether the ultimate reality is envisaged as a Supreme being dwelling in a transcendent realm or as a Heavenly Judge who rewards the faithful and punishes the sinful, the result is always the same, namely a superior being or power, pitted against an inferior creature, who has all the cards stacked against it.

Sophiology presents a third way of looking at the relationship between the Creator and creation or the Divine and human. It not only honours both but also joyfully celebrates the marriage between them. A marriage revealed in all its glory in the Christ Event, Divine-humanity perfected. Sophia lies at the heart of this mysterious union, as Bulgakov demonstrated in his prayerful study of the Creeds.

Sophia: The Divine Essence

The fifth-century Creed of Athanasius contains teaching about the Divine Trinity recognized by the churches of East and West. It affirms the tri-personal character and unity of the Divine One, while sharing one nature, substance or essence. The Church, however, has not developed its understanding of what it means by essence and hence its implication for Christian doctrine in general. In other words, it has developed teaching about the 'persons' of the Trinity but it has overlooked the nature of the common unity that they share. The Council of Chalcedon (AD 451) acknowledged the reality of this common unity or essence in relation to the person of Christ. Having stated that He is 'at once complete in Divinity and complete in humanity, truly Divine and truly human' it goes on to state that He is also

> Of one essence with the Father as regards His Divinity, and at the same time of one essence with us as regards His humanity.

The word 'essence' is therefore of central importance to our understanding of Divine reality, this time in relation to something that the Divine and human have in common. This certain 'something' which is the common unity underlying the Trinity is the same principle that unites the Divine and the human in Christ. Surely this 'something' merits our attention? It was not until the work of Fr Bulgakov that the question of the nature of this principle returned to its central place within Christian spirituality. He dared to speculate as to the nature of the Divine Essence itself.

Meister Eckhart (1260-1328) speaks of the 'Godhead' and 'God' or of the Divine One as 'Divinity and Trinity'. He taught that the path of divine knowledge leads the individual beyond the knowledge of the Trinity, which describes the personal nature of the Divine, into that which underlines the Trinity. This is the Ground from which all divine and human attributes originate, which Eckhart calls the Divine Darkness, because it is unknowable. In penetrating this Mystery the individual becomes one with the Divine Essence. It is not surprising that this bold assertion made Eckhart very unpopular with the religious establishment of his day. Here was one of the greatest masters of European spirituality teaching that an aspect of Divinity existed other than the Trinity. The danger in taking this teaching out of context is that one can end up believing that the Divine Essence is so far removed from creation that only the elect few can participate within it — the very opposite of what Bulgakov believed to be the truth.

In the Eastern Church St Gregory of Palamas (1296-1359) also endeavoured to penetrate the mystery of the Divine Essence, this time in relation to creation. His teaching is accepted as the norm in Eastern Orthodoxy to this day. Since the Divine Essence, even within the Trinity, remains hidden and inaccessible, Gregory distinguished between the Divine Essence and the Energies (or 'rays of divinity') which permeate creation. They are in fact the power of being which not only created the world but sustain it also. It is through these energies that the Divine One goes forth from itself in order to give itself to the world. These energies are limitless but include qualities such as Goodness, Justice, Knowledge and Holiness. The Divine one is totally and wholly present in each energy, and union with it is possible through them. The energies mediate between the Creator and creation and as such have both a divine and a creaturely mode of existence. The Divine Essence itself still remains unknowable, dwelling as it does beyond the world of time and space. Bulgakov disagreed, however, and he did so on biblical grounds. He shared with Eckhart the belief that there existed an aspect of The Divine One that was other than the Trinity. He also agreed with St Gregory that there was a link or a way in which the Divine is wholly present in creation. The 'energies' were only part of the answer. For Bulgakov the Divine Ground of Eckhart and the energies of St Gregory are one and the same, namely the Sophianic aspect of Divine life, the Divine nature or essence itself.

The Bible does not use the word substance or essence, but it does have its own terminology to describe non-trinitarian aspects of Divinity. They are Wisdom and Glory. Both are distinct aspects of the Divine but that does not imply that they are separate from it, which would be an impossibility, since the Divine possesses only one Essence. Both Wisdom and Glory are one in their essence. Wisdom is the power at work in creation as well as the principle which sustains it. Glory is the visible manifestation of Divinity, not 'personal' in the trinitarian sense and yet intimately related to the Divine. Wisdom and Glory represent the creative dynamics of Divine self-revelation.

Bulgakov reveals the way in which biblical teaching about Wisdom and Glory prevents the Divine nature from being thought of as an empty, abstract and purely metaphysical concept or reality. It is Wisdom and Glory, The Divine Sophia, that manifests the depth of Divinity. She gives it real substance. She is the Divine Essence, the link between the Creator and creation. Sophia is the Mystery at the heart of Divinity itself, which embraces both the Divine and human in a unique way. Bulgakov writes:

> The doctrine of Divine Sophia has nothing to do with putting forth any new dogma and
> certainly cannot be described as a new heresy within Christianity, although such is the attitude
> adopted by certain 'guardians of the faith', who see in complete stagnation the only guarantee of
> a true faith and accordingly dread all new ideas.   (*A Bulgakov Anthology*, p. 149)

Finally, Bulgakov points to the great truth of Holy Scripture, that this Sophianic essence is Love, the pure, unconditional love which is the core of Divinity and not one property or quality among others. In the words of the First Johannine Letter —

> Whoever lives in love lives within the Divine One and the Divine One lives in them. (4:16)

Sophianic knowledge celebrates the intimacy of Divine love and friendship. The Christian Good News declares that this love which lies at the heart of The Divine One can be comprehended, not as an intellectual exercise but as the dynamics of a love affair which involves a person's whole being, a love affair that enables the individual to participate in, and partake of, Divinity. The unveiling of the Divine Essence in this way does not mean that one can thereby sum it up in concepts, lay claim to it, or manipulate it for one's own end. The Mystery is not reduced in any way whatsoever. On the contrary, one is initiated into its infinite and unfathomable nature. Infinite, however, does not mean incomprehensible, neither does unfathomable mean unknowable. The more one enters the Mystery the more one becomes part of it. The more one partakes of the Mystery, the more one grows in love and begins to understand the dynamics and power of this love.

The Garden of the Lover and the Beloved

Sophianic reality lies at the heart of Divinity. The mysterious and loving union between the Divine and human is eternally celebrated within the Divine mysteries. The mystery prefigured millennia ago in ancient fertility rites, where the marriage of El Elyon, The Most High One and His Bride, Jerusalem, was celebrated on the Holy Mountain, the garden where the passionate embrace of lovers' bodies becomes a celebration of the coming together, the sacred union, of heaven and earth. This union reached its most perfect expression in the lush erotic imagery of Solomon's Song of Songs. The loveliest of love poems, not only in the Wisdom tradition, but also, if Rabbi Akiba (AD 100) is to be believed, in the whole of Scripture. He once declared that the entire world is unworthy of the day the Song of Songs was given to Israel, for all of Scripture is holy, but the Song of Solomon is the Holy of Holies.

> I slept but my heart was awake.
> Listen! My lover is knocking:
> 'Open to me, my sister, my darling
>   my dove, my flawless one'...
> I arose to open for my lover.   (5:2,5)

This beautiful evocation of loving desire is part of the supreme beauty that suffuses the whole of creation, the Sophianic goodness that shines forth not only in the celestial heights but also in the rhythmic patterns of nature. The pattern which Bulgakov, at his most poetic, describes in these words, as he sings the praises of Sophia who is revealed as the beauty which is the sacramentality of the world:

> The spring flowers emerge from the gloomy bed of Demeter; the beautiful young Persephone, creature of wisdom, makes her appearance in the world as she leaves the dark nothingness of Hades' arms. For whom do they grow, these flowers, adorned with a beauty which man, more often than not, never sees? Why are the tiger and leopard so beautiful in their awe-inspiring grace? Why does the beauty of young girls blossom on earth? Is it not the glory of Sophia illuminating the inert flesh of matter from within? And the erotic impulse of the creature intoxicated with beauty, how can we describe it otherwise than as cosmic love? These wings of eros bear it to the foot of the altar of Wisdom.   (*The Unfading Light*)

It is Sophia who seeks the free and loving response of every individual being into intimate union with the Divine. As we seek Her out, so She in turn courts us.

> My Noble Bridegroom, my strength and power, thou art a thousand times welcome… O Kiss me with thy desire, and then I will show thee all of my beauty. I have indeed broken into thee through the deep gates of God and have graciously bestowed my love upon thee. I have betrothed thee to me in my highest love. I will be with thee and in thee always, to the end of the world. Thou shalt drink of my fountain, for now I am thine, my dear love. Do not turn thy face away from me any more. Work thou thy wonders in my love, for which purpose God hath created thee and brought thee into being.   (*The Way to Christ*, Jakob Boehme, pp. 47-52)

In the Sophianic vision the Feminine presence is clearly the prominent one. It is the Feminine voice that can be heard above all others. It is She who invites, it is She who initiates, it is She who is in charge. The bridegroom does not initiate the desire for union as in normal practice. Age-long traditions are reversed. The Bride anticipates the coming of her companion without shame, openly making her love and passion known. She is eager to enjoy her lover's kiss. There is nothing passive about her. Not only does She speak openly and honestly about her heart's desire but she also invites the listener to become part of her intimacy. The veil is pulled aside. Everyone is to share the consummation and thus become part of the mystery of love. It is this Mystery that the Russian Sophianists endeavoured to elucidate and celebrate. Courageous companions of the Divine Wisdom, let us follow them.

Notes on Chapter Four

Paul Marshall Allen, *Vladimir Soloviev, Russian Mystic* , Rudolf Steiner Publications 1978

The Apocryphal New Testament, W. Reeves, London (date unknown)

Hadewijch: The Complete Works (Classics of Western Spirituality Library), translation and introduction by Mother Columba Hart, O.S.B., SPCK, London 1981

Roger Hodgson, *VIA: The Way of Life*, Churchman Publishing, Worthing, 1987, expanded as *The Way of Wisdom* and published by VIA, Arundel, Sussex in 1997.

Faust Part Two, translated with an introduction by Philip Wayne, Penguin Books, 1982

The Life of Blessed Henry Suso, translated by Thomas Francis Knox, Methuen & Co. Ltd, London 1913

Paul Marshall Allen, *Vladimir Soloviev, Russian Mystic*, Rudolf Steiner Publications 1978

A Bulgakov Anthology, edited by James Pain and Nicolas Zernov, SPCK, London 1976

The Unfading Light — source of English translation unknown to author

Jakob Boehme, *The Way to Christ*, John M. Watkins, London 1964

A Sophianic Meditation on Divine Love

This meditation is the heart of *Honest to Goddess*.
It is offered to you as a Gift of Love.
Please take your time to enter its own special rhythm and intimacy.
My hope is that you approach it in a contemplative manner.
Do not try to understand all of it at once.
Use a section or two, for example, as a theme for your daily prayer and meditation for a week or more.

A Sophianic Meditation on Divine Love

The essence of the Divine Nature is Love.
It is through this love that the Divine knows itself.

Sophia is the Divine Nature,
    the love of the Divine Trinity for itself:
The love existing among the persons of the Divine Trinity
    is consequently Sophianic in its essence.
Sophia is the living unity of the tri-personal or triune One.

The self-sufficiency of the Divine nature is completely realized in the loving
dynamics of the Divine Trinity. Nothing else can add to it or give it further
fulfilment. But Divine love cannot remain self-contained in itself. It cannot but give
itself to another, not out of any compulsion or necessity but out of a superabundance
of love. Divine love is always relational, hence the tripersonal aspect of The One.
It contains the mystery of the 'I', 'The Other', as well as the 'We'.
The dynamics of true love is seen in the Divine Trinity.

It is a love so amazing in its nature that it leads the Divine One
    to transcend even the limit of its own absolute nature.
For the sake of love,
    the Absolute sacrifices its own absoluteness!
A love that reveals its perfection
    by showing that it can relate unconditionally to 'the other'.
A love that has the power to extend beyond the Trinity
    to the creation of something other than itself.
There is no limit to Divine Love.
At the depth of the Divine

is a passionate longing for 'the other'.
A yearning whereby 'the other' is transformed into the Beloved.
It is a love so profound that it grants the Beloved
    the highest dignity and worth.
It is the love that crowns the Beloved with Sovereignty.

Divine love is the total giving and going out-of-oneself
    for the sake of the other.
It is a self-emptying love that draws no attention to itself
    but is a continual focusing on the other.
A transparent kind of love that enables and empowers the other
    to openly receive and then return this love
        in all its purity.
In the act of creation,
    the Father empties himself of his own nature
        by granting it existence in itself
            apart from his own person.
This is how the world came into being:
    a mysterious outbirth from Divinity;
        the Father acknowledging his Motherhood.
Without the instrumentality of Motherhood,
    the work of the Father could never take place.

But prior to the creation of the world,
    the Father emptied himself in bringing his Son into being.
His own Glory becomes translucent in the Son, the Divine Word.
The Father sacrifices himself for 'the other' within the Divine,
    fully aware of the pain involved in such a self-giving.
This gift, made in Eternity, is the Father's self-negation
    for the sake of love, the love of 'the other'.

The Son, with equally sacrificial love, empties himself,
    content to be the Father's Word,
        the Voice of the transcendent Source of all things.
The Son humbles his own will to that of the Father,
    fully aware of the suffering inherent
        in such self-renouncing humility.

There is no true love without suffering.
    Herein lies the tragedy of love.

The Spirit is the Father's Daughter, the Divine Comforter.
She it is who transforms eternally sacrificed love
    into the fullness of mutually jubilant love.

She is the fulfilled union of 'the One' and 'the other'.
The Divine Spirit is
    the triumphant life which emerges out of self-giving love;
    the resurrection after the crucifixion and dying of the self,
    the absolute transforming power of vivifying and redeeming love.

The Daughter has Her own self-emptying.
In Her procession from the Father,
    She surrenders Herself as She does when She rests in the Son.
She is the power that Eternally returns love
    to its source in the Father.

The Word and Spirit are the revealed masculine and feminine poles,
    respectively, of the Divine Trinity.
        manifesting Sophia, the Divine Nature, to creation.
The 'All' within Sophia is revealed by the Word:
He comes to us as the ideal, giving rational content to the ideas;
    He is the Thought and Memory of Divine Truth.
The Spirit, in turn, makes real what is there in potential.
She perfects and brings to completion by giving life to 'the idea',
    in order to realize, and make concrete, the Truth.
She glorifies each aspect of creation in the process,
    empowering them to be themselves,
        enabling them to shine with Sophianic beauty,

Sophia is the Matter of Glory,
    Glory the form of Sophia in the world.

Sophia is possessed and loved in a different way
    by each person of the Divine Trinity.
She is the life and foundation of each,
    although She does not take part in the intra-divine life.
Herein lies the mystery of her own self-emptying.
Sophia belongs to each one in a unique way…
As receiving the Essence from the Father,
    Sophia is the Creature and Daughter of the Divine One;
as knowing the Word and being known by Him,
    Sophia is the bride of the Son, the Spouse of the Lamb;
as receiving the outpouring of the gifts of the Spirit,
    Sophia is Mother Church, Mary and restored Humanity.

Sophia is the celebration of love at the heart of Divinity.
    the mysterious dynamics of super-abundant love,
        with all its inherent risks and vulnerabilities.

In the act of creation the Father chooses and wills
    to make a gift of Himself to the world.
Creation is consequently a continued celebration and extension
    of voluntary Divine self-emptying and self-abandonment,
    this time 'outside' the tri-personal Divine life.
This is the sacrificial renouncing
    of the Father's possession of Sophia for Himself.
It is the loving and creative act whereby He leaves Sophia
    to Her own existence 'outside' of Himself.
In this act the Father possesses Divine Sophia in a new way,
    as Terrestrial or Cosmic Sophia.
The more spontaneously Sophia answers the Father's invitation,
    the more She manifests him:
The more She manifests Him the more He surrenders to Her.
Once the Father became Creator
    He initiated a love affair with the Cosmos.
Because of this loving act the Divine One
    chooses to be bonded to creation in a unique way and thereby
        establishes the Sophianic quality of His own created being.
This Eternal relationship means that the Divine
    will always share in the destiny of creation.
This in no way ties the Creator to creation,
    neither does it divest the Transcendent One of its majesty.
On the contrary,
    herein lies the awesome power and majesty of Transcendence

The Creator and creation belong eternally together:
    Sophia is this Togetherness.

Creation is not the making of a second reality outside the Creator.
The created world is distinct and different from the Creator,
    but not separate. It originates within the Divine
        and is sustained by it.
It was created in order that everything could be its Divine self
    and thus shine forth with Sophianic beauty and glory.

The supreme manifestation of this creative act is homo sapiens,
    who is challenged and empowered to respond freely, and in
        loving gratitude, to the Creator for the gift of life.
Humanity is a cosmic 'Thanksgiving'.
The life-blood of this Thanksgiving,
    is the possibility of common-union, of a love affair,
        with the Divine.
We can enter the Divine Life

because the Divine One loves us and sacrifices itself
　　to allow us knowledge and experience of itself.
An incredible ecstasy and intimacy is created
　　through self-surrender, especially when it is the Divine
　　　　which is offering itself to us.
This is an ecstasy which is multiplied when we reciprocate
　　by giving and offering ourselves in return.
In this ecstasy is knowledge,
　　a salvific and transforming knowledge…
　　　　the divinization of humanity.

In the act of creation, the total absence of being,
　　or pure nothingness, is transformed by the Father into
　　　　potential being, as yet completely indefinite.
Nothingness springs towards being, or non-being, as the case may be,
　　ignited by the spark of Divine love and longing for 'the other',
　　　　which energizes it into a constant state of becoming.
This potential being is the 'higgledy-piggledy' of chaos,
　　the total freedom of Cosmic Sophia
　　　　awaiting Her myriad forms of life.
In creating the world through Sophia
　　The Father separated Sophia from her Eternal Essence
　　　　for the sake of the potential becoming of all things in Her.
This is another aspect of the continuing unfolding
　　of the mystery of Divine Love.
Not only is Sophia the object of Divine love:
　　She also gives of Herself to each person of the Trinity.
　　　　In creation She gives Herself for the creation of the world.
This is Her sacrifice,
　　Her own self-yielding movement,
　　　　continually offering Herself up to the Divine purpose.

Sophia is released from the Trinity,
　　where She is Divine,
and in allowing Herself to be poured out or emptied
　　She becomes Cosmic,
　　　　lovingly conceiving everything in Herself.
Sophia thus becomes the foundation of the world.

Remaining One, Sophia exists in two modes.

As Divine, Sophia is the Fullness
　　in which all the divine qualities or energies meet as one.
　　　　She is the sum and unity of them all.

Sophia also contains the divine prototypes of all species
    which have existed in embryo prior to the world's creation.
In Her womb abid the destinies of all creatures.
This 'ALL' is known to the Divine One,
    and is part of its self-revelation.

As Divine, Sophia is the Wisdom and Principle of Divinity.
    As Creaturely, Sophia is the root and substance of creation,
        Our Mother Earth.
The Father entrusts this 'ALL' to His creatures,
    holding nothing back and granting the world the capacity
        to sustain its own Sophianic existence through the Spirit.
In the act of creation the Divine Spirit
    penetrated Sophia's terrestrial manifestation
        giving shape and life to all things, endowing them with
        their own Sophianic beauty and glory.

Sophia is One in Divinity and Many in creation.

So intense and superabundant is the Divine Love,
    that the climax of creation is the Divine One becoming human
        and incarnating in the person of Jesus Christ.
The Word is the Incarnate, Sophia the Incarnator.
It is She who brings forth from Her substance the Child
    that reveals itself to be the perfect 'Divine-human'.
This unique act extends to complete the divinization of creation
    and the union of heaven and earth in Christ.
In this supreme act of creative love,
    we see the Creator's ultimate condescension
        for the sake of the creature's exaltation.
The union of the two natures in Christ
    is more than the mere mechanical conjunction
        of two alien principles, as traditionally taught.
Not only would this be a metaphysical impossibility
    but it also makes a mockery of the intimate and loving
        relationship between the Divine and human.
This union presupposes their original conformity in Sophia:
We cannot fully understand the meaning of the Incarnation
    without first grasping the significance of Sophianic reality.
The basis of the marriage of the two natures in Christ
    lies in Sophia and in the mutual relationship between
        Her celestial and terrestrial self.
Christ, who possesses the fullness of Divine Sophia in His heavenly
    nature, in his physical person assumes the fullness of human

nature in its pure, Sophianic state, from Mary, His mother,
and so reunites Sophia's two aspects in Himself.

Mary also represents Sophia in a double sense;
As the bearer of Christ and the Temple of the Divine Spirit,
    Mary manifests Sophia's Divine nature,
and by being totally open and transparent to the Divine,
    Mary is the perfect image of Sophia's terrestrial nature,
        which attains fulfilment in her.

In Christ is realized the Sophianic idea of the 'Divine-human':
    the unity and complete harmony of the Creator and creation,
        brought about by the operation of the Divine Spirit.
Nothing can be divinized which has not the capacity,
    and power of being, to receive such a divine gift.
Divinization cannot result from some mechanical impulse or
    intrusion from 'without', any more than the incarnation can.
Consequently, human nature must bear within itself some intimate
    and personal token of such an end or goal.
There must be something in each creature
    which has a profound and intimate affinity with the Creator,
        a bond of some sort.
Sophia is the original and intimate relation
    between the divine and human; the mysterious bond which
        does not blur or destroy the difference between the two...
Sophia does not destroy or diminish one or the other,
    but honours and celebrates both in an eternal loving union.

5. Sophia and Human History

Alone I have made the circuit of the vault of heaven
and I have walked in the depths of the abyss.
In the waves of the sea, in the whole earth,
and in every people and nation I have gotten a possession.
 Among all these I sought a resting place,
I sought in whose territory I might lodge.
Then the Creator of all things gave me a commandment.
And he said, 'Make your dwelling in Jacob.'
In the Holy Tabernacle I ministered before him.
and so I was established in Zion.   (The Wisdom of Jesus ben Sirach 24:5-8)

The Wisdom of Jesus ben Sirach, in these few verses, celebrates the whole sweep of Sophia's influence, from divine and celestial heights to the rhythm of nature and the historical drama of Israel. Sophia earthed Herself in a special way in Zion. The Hebrew word for the Divine One in 'the act of dwelling on earth' is the feminine word *Shekhinah* or *Shekhinah* El. Although it does not appear in the Scriptures, the notion of the Divine lodging or tabernacling in the world, is a common one. The term was used to describe the Feminine presence of the Divine from the first century BC onwards. In ben Sirach, Sophia earths Herself, but in another spiritual tradition, the Book Of Enoch (late first century), we discover that Sophia went forth to make Her dwelling among humanity but found no home. She returned to Her place in heaven and took Her seat among the angels. The Apostle Paul's experiences of the Divine, and in particular his profound awareness of the ongoing work of creation, in and through human history, bears witness to an experience of Sophia that is the very opposite of Enoch's. Instead of retreating to the heavens, Sophia descends to the depths of creation to fulfil Her work. Paul sees the whole of creation involved in the Divine refashioning.

We see something similar going on in the experiences of Isaiah of the Exile. He was aware of Yhwh, his God, in the throes of childbirth. The deity who had created Israel and formed him in his womb (proof that Yhwh embraces masculine and feminine qualities), breathing life into His chosen people, is now in the process of creating something brand new. Isaiah saw Yhwh giving birth,'like a woman in childbirth, I cry out, I gasp and I pant'(Isaiah 42:14c), Yhwh, struggling to form a new people, a righteous community, that would be instrumental in restoring harmony to all things. It was to be a totally new creation and not an adaptation of something that had been before.

The writings of St Paul are suffused with the presence of Sophia or Shekhinah-El. Paul could not have spoken of her as he did, unless he had had an intimate experience of Her. Sophia lay at the core of his experience of the Divine. It was only through Her earthing that the work of creation, the Edenic adventure, would come to its fulfilment. In the first creation story in Genesis, we read that the Creator rested on the seventh day, but a more accurate translation speaks of the beginning of the work of creating, an undertaking requiring the co-operation of the Divine and human. The clay from which homo sapiens was first fashioned is still fresh and pliable, destined for a noble purpose. Every human being has a part to play in its fashioning. Paul, in one of his most Otherworldly moods, could still pay a compliment to *adamah*, the red clay of the earth, by describing human beings as 'jars of clay', primordial clay vessels, worthy to contain Sophia, the Heavenly Treasure, the Divine Glory.

But there is nothing Otherworldly about Paul's core vision of creation. Genesis 2 speaks in a childlike manner of the deity forming Adam from the earth, a very matter-of-fact masculine way of doing things. But in the Letter to the Romans, we are thrown into a different world altogether. There are no onlookers here. Everyone becomes part of the cosmic process. The pregnancy is at an end. The waters have broken and one is immediately in the throes of childbirth. Everyone involved is either giving birth or being born. The groaning is audible throughout the whole universe. Mother Earth, or Creaturely Sophia, as Sophianists refer to her, is in labour pains, waiting in anticipation for the sons and daughters of El Elyon to be born and revealed to the world. She awaits in eager longing to see exercised and realized the glorious freedom which all of Her creation will eventually share, the Freedom of Eden. What is more, every human being is groaning inwardly in solidarity with the Spirit of Sophia, as he or she awaits their manifestation as sons and daughters of El Elyon, their birth into the New Eden. This, too, is part of an all-embracing birthing which celebrates the intimate union of heaven and earth in a new way. Creation is clearly not over yet!

In this incredible Cosmic vision, Paul is taken into the heart of Divine activity and becomes aware of El Elyon not 'afar off' but present as Shekhinah-El, dwelling intimately in creation, overshadowing everything with Her presence. She is also in the pain of birth, crying out in moans beyond human comprehension, Sophia struggling to bring forth Her divine offspring, expressing their inarticulate longings in Her own deeply felt groans. It saddens me that the word 'Spirit' in English or *Ysbryd* in Welsh, makes this intimate cosmic reality sound so intellectual and 'proper', as if Paul is simply talking about a concept in the human mind. Paul had been part of a real Divine-human birthing event. In fact, every time I read and meditated upon this passage in Romans, I am left breathless and elated!

In another of his letters (Galatians) we see Paul himself groaning in labour pains, as he too becomes part of this cosmic birthing, the birthing where he sees Christ being formed inside those under His care, the process whereby individuals become bearers of the Christic seed, the result of Sophia's impregnation. The hidden process of Sophia in all things is the foundation of Paul's understanding of the new creation, the fulfilment of the Edenic plan. The arena for this fulfilment is human history, where the Divine gift of freedom is exercised and where it must ultimately triumph.

The Hebrew and Pagan Windows on the World

The Hebrew and Pagan viewed life in totally different ways. For the Christian, who draws from both traditions, Hebrew and pagan beliefs are not mutually exclusive, however, but complementary aspects of the Western spiritual heritage. From a Christian perspective they are concerned with different levels or dimensions of cosmic life. True, both together create a tension, but it is a tension that lies at the heart of being human, a tension that cannot be ignored or explained away. The Eternal and temporal poles of life will remain in continual tension for the duration of human history.

The pagan lives in a universe of set laws, governed by the regular cycle of Nature's rhythms of death and rebirth, growth and decay. It is a pattern which continues, mechanically, season after season, year after year. Part of what it means to be human entails becoming conscious of this cyclical movement and honouring it by living in harmony with it. At the heart of this world is the principle of universal or cosmic law, an impersonal soul of the world, which governs and upholds everything. This principle is manifested in and to the human intellect. It is this god-like power of reason to know and understand the nature of the universe, which gives dignity and worth to each individual human being. Fixed cosmic laws can therefore be discovered and studied and patterns developed in order further to elucidate the meaning of life. In principle, anyone committed to the task can work out their place in a rationally ordered universe. Eventually, in the pagan world, the forces of Nature became too much for some to bear, and mystery cults developed which enabled individuals to escape the often meaningless and brutal round of Mother Nature. This they did by seeking an abstract timeless dimension, which provided temporary liberation from the demands of every-day life. Myths of redemption proliferated. Salvation was possible, if only for a while, and for a few! The idea developed that there was an invisible or non-material aspect of the human personality (e.g. reason or consciousness) which was not only independent to the rest of one's humanity but could somehow be extricated from the wholeness which is homo sapiens. This 'something' could be freed from the temporal and consequently be saved or redeemed. This invisible reality eventually came to be thought of as being higher or more superior to the material, which was now regarded as being of secondary importance. But consciousness and reason are part of human nature. If there is something within a human being which is in touch with the Divine, then it must somehow embrace both. The instincts are potentially no less Divine than the rational processes. For the pagan, however, there was no getting away from Nature. It was the ultimate reality, a closed and self-contained cosmos.

The Hebrew shared with the pagan the belief that everything in creation is ordered and set within a hierarchy, the sacred order of things which makes possible right knowledge and action. It means that everything can work as divinely ordained and thus remain in harmony or in perfect union with the Divine. The Biblical word for this order is 'Righteousness', the right balance between the Creator and creation, the correct way of doing things. Conformity to the established pattern of things entails following certain standards or laws which must be adhered to if the integrity of creation is to be maintained and honoured. Since creation is an ordered structure of inter-relationships, to cause disorder among different aspects of creation is to harm the Divine order. It means breaking up the Divine Harmony, setting parts or aspects of the Whole in opposition to each other. This breeds alienation which leads to the disintegration of the Whole. In biblical terms this is 'Sin' or alienation. Sin is separation. The person responsible for an act which harms the integrity of creation is judged or measured by the set standard. In other words, to commit or cause such an act will produce a certain effect on the part as well as the Whole. The way that the universe and its laws are structured, makes this inevitable. For the pagan the ultimate standard was either Nature or reason. For the Hebrew it was Divinity, which lay beyond the rhythm of Nature, and had, in fact, brought Nature into being.

The Hebrew, while inhabiting the same universe, came to perceive it in a totally different way, since for him the ultimate reality lay beyond a rational universe. The Hebrew's was an open, infinite universe, consisting of historical as well as natural dynamics, from which there was no real escape. If one of Paganism's gifts to Western culture is a deeper understanding of Nature and the workings of reason, it was the Hebrew insight which gave birth to history in the true sense of the word. The pagan world was cyclical, the Hebrew linear and open-ended. The transitory, every-day world was no accident of Nature but an integral part of human life, within which meaning has to be worked out. Such a meaning, however, cannot be neatly wrapped-up and totally explained, since reason is not the ultimate source and meaning of life. The Divinity which created the world, and is therefore superior to the world, does not however, diminish the individual but gives it much dignity and worth. Every person is a sovereign 'I' which must discover and create meaning for itself through constant questioning and struggle. A part of Nature, the Hebrew, with its strong awareness of the Divine Other, became conscious of the fact that it was also set apart from Her.

This distancing from Nature resulted in greater and greater detachment from her power and influence. The individual could stand apart from the gods and goddesses. In depotentizing the deities, the cultus that had developed to please and placate them was rendered obsolete. Fate no longer had the last word. Human events were no longer at the mercy of good or bad deities but were the result of good and bad strivings within each individual. Evil could no longer be projected on to causes outside one's control but had to be embraced as originating within each individual or group of individuals. The newly discovered 'I' became responsible and self-determining. For the Hebrew, meaning is not given by Nature and her deterministic dynamics. Meaning comes from the choices and decisions of each new moment, pregnant with numerous possibilities, and always demanding to be realized in the sight of the Divine One.

The meaning of Nature and history lies, paradoxically, outside both, although it has to be discovered and actualized within the temporal realm. This meaning, uniquely revealed to each individual, does not yield itself up exclusively to a person's power of thought, but invites each individual to enter into its mystery as a goal to be aimed for, a journey to be undertaken and a reality that gradually unfolds, in freedom. For the pagan, classically revealed in the Greek psyche, reason works at producing a good, ordered and beautiful world. Perfect form triumphs and anything that stands in the way of this vision is regarded as being accidental and irrational. History is full of both! The Greeks had no concept of history as a power that fulfils itself. It was alien to their mentality to think of a process that had a beginning which was gradually progressing towards a definite goal. But the Hebrew consciousness was always striving towards a future, full of endless possibilities. Life was rooted in an intense expectation of a great and definite event some time in the future. What lay at the root of such a contrasting view of life was the fact that Greek thought had no authentic experience of Freedom and consequently of the irrational principle of life. It had no idea of the capacity to create history and hence of the ability to change, re-order and transmute the mechanical ordering of Nature. For the Hebrew the ultimate harmony and beauty is that which arises out of the free play of human endeavour and creativity. Only this goodness has true and lasting value and worth, the goodness which is fulfilled in history through the creative actions of free individuals, the truth revealed, not in the eternal pattern of nature but in history, a much more tempestuous and messy affair.

The basic flaw or weakness in a combination of the Hebrew and pagan view of life is the belief that the growth of knowledge, the conquest of Nature and a passionate belief in human progress towards greater understanding of life does not guarantee triumph over chaos. Every human invention or 'step forward' can be instrumental in producing as much chaos as order. The tragedy of history is that human creativity carries within itself the seed of its own destruction. Human development is not synonymous with advancement in the Good, the True and the Beautiful.

Joachim of Fiore: Prophet of History

One person who best exemplifies the tension within the classical Christian view of the world, as it attempted creatively to weave Hebrew and Pagan insights together, is the twelfth-century Sicilian Abbot and Christian revolutionary, Joachim of Fiore (c.1135-1202). Rooted within the passionate biblical belief that the Divine One is actively involved in human history, his teaching helped ensure that Medieval Christianity did not develop as simply an 'Otherworldly' philosophy. Belief in the soul's immortality (essentially a pagan idea) had been linked in Christianity with the role of the individual person or society in an ongoing historical process. This implies some degree of control and influence over the cosmos, present and future. A Christian prophet could not only forth-tell the future but also help to create it.

Joachim was born during a time of great spiritual energy that was allied with a new interest in the dynamics of human history. It was an age that witnessed many experiments to discover the perfect type of spiritual life. Joachim himself lived as a hermit, for a while, on Mount Etna, before becoming a travelling preacher in his native Calabria. He was eventually ordained and took the Benedictine habit. As Abbot he campaigned to bring his own House under the jurisdiction of the more austere Cistercian Order. Deeply committed to monastic reform, in 1188, Joachim, accompanied by a band of his followers, finally set up his own monastery at San Giovanni da Fiore. Although denounced as a renegade by the General Chapter of the Cistercian Order, Joachim was to become one of the most famous religious leaders of the Middle Ages. In just over a decade after his death, the Order he founded was celebrated as one of the four pillars on which the Church was built. The same cannot be said for his views on the Divine Trinity, which were condemned as heretical.

He himself was never formally denounced as a heretic, probably due to his great sanctity and the fact that he was courted by kings and queens and patronized by three popes. Joachim met King Richard the Lionheart en route to the Third Crusade in 1190, an episode which shows him at the heart of one of the major European political preoccupations of the day.

Joachim received two visions that revealed to him the true meaning of the Divine Trinity. He never thought of himself as a prophet in the biblical sense but as one who had been given the spiritual understanding to grasp all the mysteries of sacred Scripture through the wisdom of the Divine Spirit. He did not produce a new revelation but like Fr Bulgakov was given the divine intelligence as a gift to interpret the truth already present in the Bible. Joachim was enabled to read the signs, pagan as well as biblical, placed by the Divine within history. While deeply pessimistic about the state of the world and the coming trials that the Church would soon have to face, Joachim never gave up on the hope that a faithful remnant of believers would remain true to the Gospel. Unlike many reformers who kept on looking back to a golden age long past, and to the apostolic model of Christ and His disciples, Joachim looked to the future for a renewal and to a new explosion of Divine power in history. He became one of the most influential prophets in the history of the Church to announce the coming New Age of the Spirit.

Joachim took over and developed an embryonic idea from the Cappadocian Fathers, that spoke of different periods and modes of revelation conferred by the 'persons' of the Divine Trinity. Following long and disciplined study, prayer and meditation, on the words of Scripture, Joachim developed new ways of thinking and meditating about the total meaning of history and the mysterious activity of the Trinity within it, a mystery not so much grasped intellectually as entered into through profound spiritual experiences, a mystery that takes one to to the very heart of Divinity and the Wisdom that holds the whole universe together. In Joachim mystical experiences and historical studies were totally interlinked, spiritual exaltation and concrete earthly events went hand in hand.

St Augustine (354-430) had produced the first philosophy of history worthy of the name. He lived during one of the most traumatic moments in the history of the Western world, namely the collapse of the ancient classical world and the fall of Rome, which coloured his way of looking at life and especially human history. Something similar happened to many theologians after the First World War, when their faith in human progress was almost totally extinguished. Others never recovered their faith after the Second World War and the horrors of the Holocaust. The collapse of Soviet Communism has helped to restore confidence, for some, in humanity's ability to shape its own destiny. For Augustine and his followers history had come to an end. The Incarnation of the Divine Word therefore became history's pinnacle and fulfilment. The only salvation left was that of the individual soul, since the only perfect society now possible was the one to come in the blessed state in Eternity. There was little hope for human history except in so far as individuals could discipline themselves to watch and wait for The End. Joachim broke with this pessimistic view. Before the End Time, he argued, having been purged by countless trials, some individuals in history could reach a new level of spiritual illumination in the coming Age of the Divine Spirit. There is no denying that Joachim's spirituality did offer comfort and nourishment to individual souls but it also prepared the community of the faithful for the painful transition into a new historical Era, an era that would be characterized by the human growth towards greater and greater Freedom.

The Three Ages of the Trinity
In Joachim's opinion, the Grand Plan of both Testaments in the Judeo-Christian heritage, is a scheme based on three periods of time, or states of awareness into the workings of the Trinity. One aspect of the Trinity

consequently takes on a particular shape or form in history corresponding to the unique nature of the Trinitarian persons. The changing and inter-changing faces of the Divine One are consequently revealed in history. This does not mean that when one 'person' is sovereign the other two are excluded. One state or Age is pregnant with the others.

The Age of the Father is concerned with power and the rule of power, the creation and preservation of the world by the almighty workings of the Creator. Joachim coloured it green, because in this Age individuals first become aware not only of the Creator but also of Mother Nature in all her beauty and glory. It is the material or physical promise of Glory, full of the signs of the greater Beauty yet to come. In this Age is revealed the whole spectrum of responses towards the power of the Creator and Nature, from stark fear to an ecstatic childlike awe, such as the psalmists'

> How many are your works, O Lord! [i.e. not Yhwh]
> In wisdom you made them all;
> the earth is full of your creatures.
> There is the sea, vast and spacious,
> teeming with creatures beyond number —
> living things both large and small.   (Psalm 104:24-25)

The Father's Age is the time when followers of all religions begin to come to terms with the forces of Nature, the various gods and goddesses honoured by native spiritualities the world over. Integral to this status is the need for laws and regulations, no matter how basic or sophisticated their nature. The Letter to the Colossians refers to them as the 'basic principles of this world' (2:8,20) that regulate human religious and cultural behaviour: what one eats and drinks, dietary practices, the festivals that one observes, including New Moon celebrations, the Sabbath rest and various ascetic practices, or not, as the case may be. The negative side of any law, however, is that by refusing to grow up, one can so easily become enslaved to it. Jesus summed up this predicament succinctly with the words that the individual has pre-eminence even over the Sabbath (Mark 2:27). Rules and regulations are ultimately only valid in so far as they serve one's spiritual growth and development. In the Letter to the Galatians when Paul, on one occasion, refers to these natural principles as being 'weak and miserable'(4:9) he is actually celebrating the fact that Christ has set human beings free from the forces of Nature and therefore free for Freedom! This is because the creation that the Father sets in motion is an ongoing adventure, a world kept open for its true destiny which is forever unfolding in history. This is possible because of the gift of time, which prevents creation, and especially the creature, from turning in on itself and thus shutting itself away from 'the Other'.

Another characteristic of the Age of the Father is the Divine Order of things or the Righteousness referred to earlier. The human perception of Righteousness deepens as the Trinitarian Ages unfold. One incident in the Abrahamic cycle of stories (in Genesis) reveals the heart of this ultimate harmony, the mystery that lies at the centre of, and even beyond, the law of cause and effect, which most in the Primary Age take to be the ultimate standard. For them the law is rigid and uncompromising. The people of Sodom, for example, had become so sinful, that in harming the integrity of creation they inevitably brought punishment upon themselves. In biblical terms they had incurred the wrath of Yhwh. The right order of things had to be upheld. Human sin would be punished. But Abraham argues against this standard of justice represented by Yhwh and the law. He makes a significant move towards the eventual unveiling of the deeper meaning or core of righteousness. The law of cause and effect, the mechanical ordering of things, is transcended for the sake of only ten individuals, who did embody that which was true and right. Abraham champions the cause of this righteousness although the majority, in the eyes of the law, deserved to be punished. An automatic cosmic and legal process, already set in motion, was halted. In other words, the mechanical operation of cause and effect does not fully explain the way that creation works. Something more special lies beyond the realm of necessity. It was in the Second Age of the Son that the Divine Righteousness, or the loving way of ordering the cosmos, was fully revealed, a righteousness based on the self-sacrifice which alone can bring lasting peace and harmony out of disorder. It is the true Freedom that keeps every aspect of the Whole in a harmony that lies beyond necessity or compulsion.

Jesus was so saturated in this reality that He knew only of forgiveness and not condemnation. He embodied the dimension of Divine and human sovereignty that cannot be legislated, a level of being where freedom, creativity and the power of forgiveness reigns at all times. The source of this righteousness is the Unconditional love that is forever pouring out of Divinity. Abraham, although living under the old dispensation, had, for an instant, a foretaste of the new way of ordering cosmic and human life.

The Age of the Son

The Age of the Son began to bear fruit with the coming of Jesus Christ. The belief was that it would reach its fulfilment during Joachim's lifetime. The theme of this status is the power of redeeming love through the sacrifice of the Divine Word, the Son made flesh, the self-sacrifice that is demanded of all who would be channels or instruments of this self-emptying love in the realm of human history. It is the path of suffering and many trials and the knowledge that comes from being able to embrace true humility, a transparency that allows love to shine forth and be manifested no matter the consequences.

Under the nurturing and discipline of the Father, children begin to grow up. Under the guidance of the Son they set out on the path of discipleship. Through the gift of a Love freely given, men and women are empowered to become brothers and sisters of their Elder Brother, Jesus Christ. From a child-like way of perceiving life they begin to make their own judgements by learning from their mistakes, how to handle criticisms and the ability to cope with conflict in a positive manner. In the second age individuals begin to grow in Wisdom. From being dependent on Nature and the authority of the Father, individuals learn how to stand on their own feet and to exercise control over the forces of Nature, forces that are no longer 'out there' or 'up there' but are somehow mysteriously 'within me'. From feeling helpless, individuals begin to fashion their own destinies by learning how to co-operate with the Divine.

The early Christian centuries celebrated the dignity and worth of each individual, doing it, paradoxically, through people who left the world in order to discover more about the true meaning of the world. Their rejection of the world helped to reinforce human autonomy and the reality of the freedom necessary if one is to take responsibility for one's life. The legendary St Anthony of Egypt (d.356) broke free of family, social and State ties, in order to be his own government. He was the pioneer for a whole generation of men and women who were more than ready to step beyond the limits or boundaries set by society, in order to attend to their spiritual health and salvation. They were the spiritual explorers and adventurers of their day, who would allow nothing to tie them down. They were 'slaves of freedom', who would not give up on the challenges set before them in the Garden of Eden. Commitment to the Good News taught by Christ made these Christians true subversives, dedicated to the path of self-mastery that was an integral part of their experience of the Divine. They acted in ways that were not expected of them. Like modern-day athletes, spiritual exercises became their guiding principles: the practice of virtue (*virtus* is Latin for strength) or power over oneself, became the means to grow in closer communion with the Divine. Such virtue is a voluntary thing, subject to nothing but the action of Grace, freely sought and freely received. Martyrs among these early spiritual pioneers took individuality to the extreme, by defying imperial power and courageously standing up to worldly tyrants. In a strange sort of way, these martyrs also played their part in stressing the absolute value and worth of each individual person.

These Christian pioneers celebrated the freedom of the human will, the power of choice and the gift of moral responsibility. Many of the early Church Fathers referred to this as our glory and dignity as beings created in the Divine Image. They, too, knew of Sovereignty. Each individual person manifests this royal quality by virtue of the fact that it is governed and ruled autonomously by its own will. In the Sermon on the Mount, Jesus demanded of His followers control of their natures by taking responsibility for their actions e.g. by mastering such responses or drives as anger and sexual yearnings (Matthew 5:21, 27-28). The Good News revealed in the Age of the Son is that human beings have the power to constitute their own being, to choose their own destiny. Adam's disobedience did not affect our individual freedom but highlighted the glorious gift of choice given to us by the Divine One, and the potentiality in every one of us to grow in the knowledge of good and evil. The Edenic disobedience was the beginning of human history and not its end. It is our initiation into the adventure of freedom, an awakening to the human predicament. This includes freeing ourselves from idolatrous views of Divinity, the childish projections which deprive us of our own divine nature and creativity. The temptation is always there to surrender our rational powers, self-awareness and moral responsibility, the temptation to go back to an illusory state of perfection and innocence, the fear of reaching out and grasping Wisdom's fruit, the solid food of the spiritually mature. It is the temptation to refuse to grow up and thus to accept the responsibility of adulthood.

The Age of the Son is the time when disciples, according to the Letter to the Hebrews, learn the 'first principles of the Divine oracles', the elementary teachings about Christ (5:12, 6:1). In other words, the foundation of the Faith. These include the need for repentance from acts that lead to death, trust in the actions of the Divine One, instructions about baptism and the laying on of hands, and teaching about the resurrection and judgement. In the Age of the Spirit one matures and goes on to the second principles, the teaching about righteousness and holiness which lies beyond rules and regulations, especially religious ones. It is the time when individuals leave the milk of the Second Age and go on to the solid food of the spiritually mature, who have been trained to accept full responsibility for their lives and their role in shaping human history.

The Gift of Freedom

In order to enter the world of human responsibility and creativity, each individual must make an act of freedom and heroism. This must be something that everyone discovers in, and for, oneself, and not be something accepted from without. Only in this way will freedom become the creative basis of history. In fact, without freedom there can be no history. It is important, therefore, to understand that there are two kinds of freedom, or that freedom has two aspects, its feminine and masculine poles.

First of all, there is primordial or original freedom, which lies at the root of life, both Divine and human. It is the freedom which precedes being itself and is irrational in its nature. This is the freedom that can never be neatly packaged and explained. It is infinite and ever-increasing in its potency. It is the inmost principle of life, self-determination in the depths of one's being. This freedom is only fully understood by entering into its tragic aspect, which entails acknowledging that it can degenerate into its very opposite, which is slavery. This is the freedom to choose Good or Evil, the inner creative energy to mould the forces of Nature by the principles of heaven, a Nature that can be sanctified by love and illuminated by truth. This freedom was not lost in Eden, but the awesome nature of its responsibility was revealed for all to see: the freedom to choose The Good.

The second type of freedom is freedom in the Truth, the knowledge that empowers us to be the Truth. It is the freedom that uses the faculty of reason and emotion to help one know the truth and consequently to practise and realize it in one's life. In order to obtain the divine freedom which is given in the knowledge of the truth one must recognize and choose the truth in the first place. This is possible only in relation to the original freedom that every person must discover and confront. This second freedom is victory over the power of compulsion and necessity. Without this rational freedom the initial freedom degenerates into self-will and the pride of self-affirmation. Anarchy then follows and freedom is destroyed. However, without the freedom to choose for oneself, the freedom of the spirit is replaced by the need to control and organize the life of the individual, be it in religious or social terms. This is an arbitrary or superficial step where freedom is negated and necessity rules — a characteristic of the First Age. It is for freedom, however, that Christ has set us free (Galatians 5:1), freedom to realize and manifest the Good in our lives. Paul goes on to declare:

> Stand firm, then, and do not let yourselves be burdened again by the yoke of slavery.

Not only the slavery of Nature's deterministic patterns but also the slavery of religious law. Freedom lies at the heart of the human adventure and for that reason has an inescapable tragic aspect. No modern writer has expressed this better than Fyodor Dostoyevsky, an older contemporary of Vladimir Soloviev and one of Russia's greatest spiritual teachers and novelists. In the novel called *The Brothers Karamazov* the tragedy of freedom is profoundly described in these words

> Nothing has ever been more unbearable to man and to human society than freedom! (p. 296)
> Instead of gaining possession of men's freedom, you gave them greater freedom than ever!
> Instead of taking possession of men's freedom you multiplied it and burdened the spiritual
> kingdom of man with its sufferings for ever. You wanted man's free love so that he should
> follow you freely, fascinated and captivated by you. Instead of the strict ancient law, man had
> in future to decide for himself with a free heart what is good and what is evil, having only
> your image before him for guidance. But did it never occur to you that he would at last
> reject and call in question even your image and your truth, if he were weighed down by so
> fearful a burden as freedom of choice? (p. 299)

The New Age of the Divine Spirit

The Age of the Spirit began, writes Abbot Joachim, with St Benedict in the sixth century. Unlike the second age which was governed by clerics, the third age was the era of the Monastic Orders which would last until the End Time. The New Testament would not be superseded, although Joachim suggests that the coming New Age, while not unrelated to the previous age, would nevertheless be superior to what had gone before. Something brand new was emerging. Importance was therefore given to groups that were neither fully lay nor clerical but occupied an intermediate ground between the secular and monastic lifestyles. These groups were open to all genuine seekers of the Truth, all who sought an inner or visionary spirituality. Institutional aspects of the religious life were kept to the minimum. Life was ordered but in an informal way, led but not directed, Christian but non-sectarian. Many such groups were not averse to creating controversy because they did not come under any ecclesiastical control, and stressed personal spirituality over dogma. In both senses the spirituality of these groups was a hidden affair, because to secular and religious eyes their followers looked no different to anyone else, while inwardly they were devoted to a strict discipline aimed at a knowledge acquired directly from the Spirit.

One of Joachim's major preoccupations was with human life as a continuing quest for the most perfect form of monastic or, to be more accurate, contemplative life. He wanted to see the ideal religious life not only manifested in history but actually changing the course of human history, the kind of life that would bring to perfection all human potentialities. Joachim had no difficulty accepting the fact that religious orders like the Cistercians and his own, were nothing more than an interim phase and not the final flowering of the contemplative lifestyle. They were the heralds of the dawning of the perfect spiritual status of the New Age.

Joachim prophesied two stages in the dawning of this Third Age, represented by two new religious Orders. One would be an Order of Preachers in the spirit of Elijah, the other an Order of Hermits in the spirit of

Moses. This prophesy was fulfilled soon after Joachim's death with the appearance of two mendicant orders, the Dominicans and the Franciscans. But even they were not the final word in history's journey towards the perfect earthly state of contemplation. Both were to be at the forefront of the Church's witness against the Anti-Christ. Joachim's spirituality was not divorced from the social and political struggles of the Church in the world. He calculated, in fact, that the Anti-Christ would arise within the Church and hold office — a novel idea for the time!

With the emergence of the New Spiritual Age, an urgent question that arises concerns the future state of existing Church institutions, especially the role and authority of clerics. Joachim was no elitist concerned only for the elect few. While the third status does not produce a new set of institutions, it does bring about a new quality of life which, in every generation, radically overhauls and transforms existing institutions, until they become more perfect vehicles for the contemplative life. This will entail a new examination of the whole question of authority within the Church and hence liberation from false ideas of sovereignty, which in the past has been associated with some form of servitude and submission. Some churches have turned the doctrine of Grace, for example, into a means of exercising power over the laity, both men and women. Grace, and therefore the sacraments, have come to be regarded as the sole prerogative of an organized male hierarchy and have been used as a means of theological and social control. Anyone whose status and prestige is dependent on such a system is bound to be alarmed with talk of a new outpouring of the Spirit. The Spirit is freedom and hence the inevitable weakening of hierarchical authority. The awakening ushered in by the Spirit cannot be controlled and therefore cannot be legislated. It can only be channelled and then only in humility and love. With the Spirit comes a new kind of authority and with it the eventual withering away of all human institutions. Meanwhile, the challenge of the New Age is incumbent upon everyone, because Joachim's 'New Order of the People of God' embraces clerics, monks and lay people alike. All are to be converted to the new spiritual life, where different vocations will cross-fertilize each other, producing, in time, a non-hierarchical and egalitarian community.

The germ of this idea has always been a feature of the Eastern Orthodox and Celtic churches. Neither teaches that the ordained ministry of bishop, priest and deacon or the monastic life, are 'higher' or more 'perfect' than the lay state or the vocation of marriage. Every vocation has its own particular challenges and responsibilities. Furthermore, the New Testament makes it quite clear that all Christians are priests by baptism, all are called to the life of praise and thanksgiving at the altar of the Holy Communion and then at the altar of a neighbour's heart.

The freedom of the Crucified One brings liberation from Sin for Christ's brothers and sisters. Freed from the obsessive need for self-justification they are able to enter into a loving fellowship with each other. In community they begin to grow in understanding and by making mistakes they begin to distinguish Good and Evil; the dizziness of Freedom, the torment of choice. In the Age of the Father one grows in the awareness of the polarity of necessity and freedom. Under the sovereignty of the Son one comes to terms with the tension between Freedom and Right Choice. While in the Spirit one is empowered to put into practice the Good, the True and the Beautiful. It is Christ who makes us free for freedom while the Spirit helps us to realize that Freedom. Similarly, it is through Christ's action that one is justified for greater and greater Glory, one's robing in Sophianic majesty and beauty. In the words St Paul:

> Now the Lord is the Spirit and where the Spirit of the Lord is, there is freedom. And we, who
> with unveiled faces all contemplate the Lord's Glory, are being transformed into his likeness, with
> ever-increasing Glory, which comes from the Lord, who is the Spirit. (2 Corinthians 3:17-18)

The human journey through history is one from slavery to greater and greater freedom and Sophianic Glory, from the state of slaves and childhood dependency to young adulthood and finally to the status of

Divine friends and lovers. All this is made possible by the initial self-emptying of the Father, His Eternal pouring forth for the sake of 'the other', both within divinity and humanity. The original sacrifice of the Father is for the sake of the freedom, and thus the sovereignty, of His children, as they grow into the full maturity of gods and goddesses, sons and daughters of El Elyon. In one of the most poetic passages in his writings, Joachim summons his readers to the Eternal Quest, with these words:

> Clear the eyes of the mind from all dusts of earth; leave the tumults of crowds and the clamour
> of words; follow the angel in spirit into the desert; ascend with the same angel into the great
> and high mountain; there you will behold high truths hidden from the beginning of time
> and from all generations ... For we, called in these latest times to follow the Spirit rather than
> the letter, ought to obey, going from illumination to illumination, from the first heaven to the
> second, and from the second to the third, from the place of darkness into the light of the
> moon, that at last we may come out of the moonlight into the Glory of the full Sun.
>
> *(The Influence of Prophecy in the Later Middle Ages*, p. 292)

The Eternal Gospel

With the coming New Age of the Spirit and its New Contemplative Order comes the Eternal or Third Gospel, written, ultimately, not on paper but on the human heart. It has no written word, or at least no words given or written from on high. It is the wisdom that grows out of the free and loving response of every human being to the Divine. It will celebrate humanity's gift and accomplishment or it will not come into being at all. Since each age is pregnant with the other, the Eternal Gospel had been revealed under the dispensation of the Father, as when Jeremiah foretells the coming of the New Covenant:

> I will put my law in their minds
> and write it on their hearts...
> No longer will a person teach his neighbour...
> because they will all know me, from the least
> of them to the greatest.   (Jeremiah 31:33-34)

The liberty and spiritual understanding of the New Age does not mean that individuals can turn their backs on the authority of both previous Testaments. Nevertheless, they are to be entrusted with the glorious treasures of spiritual understanding. Joachim saw the Older and New Testaments as two cherubims, guarding and guiding members of the Eternal Church into the Wisdom of the Age of Glory, the unveiling of Sophia. In a passage in his first letter to the Corinthians, where he is talking about the hidden Divine Sophia, 'destined for our Glory before time began (v. 7), Paul is already celebrating the dawning of the Third Testament when he writes:

> We have not been given the Spirit of the world but the Spirit which issues from The Divine
> One, in order that we may understand the significance of the free Divine gift given to us.
> This is why we speak in words taught by the spirit and not in the words of human wisdom.
> Spiritual words interpreting spiritual truths to spiritual people.   (1 Corinthians 2:12-13)

The Eternal Gospel is also celebrated in the Johannine tradition, when Jesus declares that 'a time is coming and has now come when the true worshippers will worship the Father in spirit and truth, for they are the kind of worshippers the Father seeks. The Divine is Spirit, and true worshippers must worship in spirit and in truth'.   (John 4:21, 23-24)

In our own century, one of the greatest prophets of the Age of the Spirit, and a worthy successor to Joachim of Fiore, is the Russian contemporary and close friend of Fr Bulgakov, namely Nicolas Berdyaev (1874-1948). His writings abound with references to the New Era that is already dawning, and he wrote about it not from the perspective of an academic but with the passion of one already caught up in the creativity of the Spirit. In *Freedom and the Spirit* (1935), one of his most challenging and informative books, Berdyaev writes what can be regarded as the manifesto of the Third Age:

> We are entering upon a period of new spirituality, which will be the counterpart of the present materialism of our world. There will also be a new form of mysticism corresponding to this new period in Christian history. There is no longer any room in the world for a merely external form of Christianity based on custom. It is precisely the mystical and spiritual life which leads to victory over sin. The world is entering upon a period of catastrophe and crisis when we are being forced to take sides in which a higher and more intense kind of spiritual life will be demanded from Christians..The sort of Christianity...which possesses eternal significance and an inner mystical quality which is growing more intense and stronger.   (p. 268)

The Fourth Age of Glory

Based on the teaching of Genesis that describes the creation of the world in six days, the traditional philosophy of history in Joachim's day spoke of the seven ages of world history, the first six characterized by labour and toil, while the seventh day, on which the Creator rested, became the weekly Sabbath rest, a foretaste of the Eternal Divine Day of Endless Glory. A closer study of Joachim's Ages of the Trinity reveals, in fact, the presence of the Fourth Age of Glory. It was not to Joachim, however, that the full mystery of 'the fourth state' was revealed. That was left to the Russians in a later generation, and the dawning of a new millennium. In this Age will take place the consummation of the Triune One's Reign of Glory: the perfection of the Father's creation, the universal establishment of the Son's gift of freedom and the fulfilment of the energies and gifts of the Spirit. We are privileged to live at a time in transition from the Third to the Fourth Age. This is why the face of the Divine One in our time is predominantly a feminine face. The Divine Spirit, in all Her beauty and power, is preparing humanity for a new indwelling of the Shekhinah — and not only homo sapiens but every aspect of creation is waiting. Vladimir Soloviev in his comical mystical play (first published in 1893), *The White Lily*, describes an individual's search for and final encounter with Sophia, embodied in the White Lily. After much reflection on the 'fourth dimension'(the state where the contemplative vision of Sophia, the Empress of Beauty, is a reality), the hero declares:

> She! She is everywhere! Only about her
> Do all the voices of yearning nature speak.
> Not I alone — but also the river, the forest, the mountains,
> The trees, the beasts, the sun, and the flowers
> Call her and await her.
> If she were to come, the snowy peaks
> Of the cloud-piercing mountain would
> Bow down before her at once; the sumptuous flowers
> Would unfurl their wide carpet before her....
> Yes, that is so! But, my God, when?
> When, when? This insignificant word
> Contains despair and joy, life and death.   (p. 45)

As the new millennium dawns, humanity will experience within history, a foretaste of the blissful fourth dimension. Sophia, the Mother Goddess, resplendent in all Her Beauty. Sophia, Perfect Humanity, the World Transfigured, the Marriage of Heaven and Earth. In the words of the Wisdom of Solomon:

She is more beautiful than the sun
    and excels every constellation of the stars.
Compared with the light she is found
    to be superior.   (7:29)

But it is an awesome responsibility to see Sophia unveiled, to be initiated into Her mysteries. We ignore the words of Ecclesiastes at our peril: 'For with much wisdom comes much sorrow; the more knowledge, the more grief' (1:18). To experience Sophia in Her 'All-in-Oneness' or Unity is to be wounded and torn apart on seeing the divisions and disharmony that dwells in the depths of our human nature and history. It is we who are responsible for Nature's fall and alienation. She lost Her Sovereignty when we we surrendered ours. This is why the Green Man's all knowing stare is tinged with sadness. To help bring about Earth's spiritual transformation we have to follow Christ, Sophia's Son, into the depths of Hades, and ask forgiveness of Sophia's creaturely offspring, the gods and goddesses, the Elohim of old. Our descent will stir up the Underworld, in a way never before experienced, and plunge us into a world of darkness and uncertainty, as old barriers disappear and long forgotten aspects of ourselves reach out for recognition. Here in the depths the task of reintegration must begin. It is here that the union of opposites must first be celebrated. But the ultimate restoration must take place in and through the historical process, when human sovereignty will play its part in realizing, and manifesting, not only the Divine-human unity but also the Divine Unity. The Divine One, revealed hitherto as the Heavenly Father, now bids us honour Mother Earth, the Great Mother, the living cosmos, whose image the devout pagan worshipped under the names of Demeter, Isis and Cybele. She is the world in all is being, from chaos to perfection. She awaits Her transfiguration, Her sanctification through human creativeness. But even now, before Her final transformation, She bears within Herself a spiritual power that can never be quenched for, in the words of the psalmist, the heavens also declare the glory of the Divine One (Psalm 19:1).

History is not the dimension where merely abstract ideas are at work above and outside Nature. It contains and is defined by the fullness of cosmic being. All history is also Nature and all Nature has a history. The Sophianic Age celebrates the interpenetration of history and Nature. In fact, the dynamic quality of history becomes an illusion if there is no dynamism of Nature sustaining it. This is why the message of the 'Word made flesh', the participation of matter in the Divine realm, is the key to the fullness of the Sophianic Age. It brings to fulfilment the longing of Earth for Heaven. It fires the quest for one's ideal image in 'the Other', the passionate longing for Unity and Oneness. It hallows the longing for Sophia in all things, as this prayer by Robert Powell reveals

Our Mother, Thou who art in the darkness of the Underworld,
May the holiness of Thy name shine anew in our remembering.
May the breath of Thy awakening kingdom warm the hearts of all who wander homeless.
May the resurrection of Thy will renew eternal faith even unto the depths of physical substance.
Receive this day the living remembrance of Thee from human hearts,
Who implore Thee to forgive the sin of forgetting Thee,
And who are ready to fight against temptation which has led Thee to existence in darkness.
That through the deed of the Son, the immeasurable pain of the Father be stilled by the
    liberation of all beings from the tragedy of Thy withdrawal.
For Thine is the homeland, the boundless wisdom and the all-merciful grace
For all and everything in the circle of all.

        Amen.   (*The Sophia Teachings, Robert Powell*)

The New Eden: Sophia's Crowning Glory in History
The Good News in the New Testament declares that when we were banished from the Garden of Eden, Christ came with us. The New Adam and Eve was no afterthought on El Elyon's part but is an integral part of the Original Anthropic blueprint. As Christ-Sophia reflects the Divine One, we, in turn, become images ourselves, icons of El Elyon. As we grow in the contemplation of the Divine Beauty and Glory of the Fourth Age, we become reflections of that Glory. Sophia awakens us to the knowledge that every one of us carries the Christic mystery in the depths of our being. It is with Christ that we return to Eden to lay claim to our inheritance, a visit that is also a coronation — our own! — a homecoming to the nobility that has always been ours. We can go boldly into the Divine Presence, without having to grovel. We can take our place in the Divine Assembly, with no veils on our faces and no barriers in our way. Because one true and humble child of Sophia embodies the Ancient Royal cult in Himself — i.e. true priesthood, true sacrifice, true worship and true sovereignty— we can become, if we so choose, divine incarnations ourselves. We can become a Divinehuman 'Yes' for the whole cosmos.

> Our individual priesthoods a universal one
> Our lives a living and loving sacrifice
> Our worship true worship in wisdom and in truth
> Our bodies temples or dwelling places, of The Most High

This dwelling (*beth-El* or House of El) also has a corporate aspect because the Spirit of Sophia makes us members of the Divine or Royal Household. As the new millennium approaches She is still active within human history calling all to follow Her ways, for She walks in the way of righteousness, along the paths of justice:

> Wisdom has built her house,
> she has hewn out its seven pillars.
> She has prepared her meat and mixed her wine;
> she has also set her table.
> She has sent out her maids, and
> she calls from the highest point of the city.
> 'Come, eat my food and drink the wine I have mixed.'   (Proverbs 9:1-3, 5)

> Choose my instruction instead of silver,
> knowledge rather than choice gold,
> For wisdom is more precious than rubies,
> and nothing you desire can compare with her.
> My fruit is better than fine gold,
> what I yield surpasses choice silver.   (Proverbs 8:10-11, 19)

Sophia is the Freedom, the precious gift of Eden, that El Elyon bestows upon us. She is the maturity that we are meant to reach for and embrace. Jesus tells us the story of the father who believed so much in this freedom, that he never thought of standing in the way of one of his sons when he chose to use or experiment with this freedom in a highly risky and irresponsible way. He allowed him to make his own choice and his own mistakes. And when the son finally returned home, the father did not react in a judgemental or authoritarian manner, neither did he patronize his son. He ran and kissed him. It was to protect and safeguard this freedom that another Son died for us.

Sophia is the Knowledge that alone can help us make sense of our lives and discover our place in the Divine Plan. It is Sophia who helps us to become mature, to grow up and thus become responsible stewards of creation and history. It is Sophia who enables us to be 'the Law' ourselves. The writings of the New

Testament celebrate the fact that Sophia has lavished us with the full riches of understanding. Everyone is meant to 'grow up' and become spiritually mature, to move beyond being 'mere infants in Christ' and to begin eating solid foods. We were not created to suckle at the breast for ever, fixated on milk. Sophia's children are meant to become her lovers. But some do not want to grow up. The mature spirituality offered by Sophia is not for them.

This is why the New Testament tells us that some who seek wisdom are going to be subject to guardians and trustees for a while. These include those who refuse to be sovereign, the ones who would rather stay in bondage to the powers of creation, the 'basic principles of the world'. But slavery has no permanent place in the Divine Household. It is alien to the Sophianic way of being.

The New Testament Letter to the Hebrews is particularly concerned about Christians who are spiritually retarded. The ones who ought to be teachers are still in kindergarten being taught the basics, going over and over the same teaching week after week. Others are still in Sunday School stuck on the first collection of Divine principles, the elementary truths of the Gospel. Among these individuals we find those who have turned the Gospel into a new set of laws! The Deuteronomists have their followers in every age. These people are convinced that theirs is the only way back into Eden. They have the spiritual life nicely mapped out. The Spirit is theirs to control and they have a caricature of Christ as their mascot or lucky charm. Whenever Enlightenment is mentioned to followers of this type of spirituality, they deride it by insisting that it is beyond humans to achieve.

But Enlightenment is what homo sapiens was created for. It is what the Edenic Quest in history is all about. It is part of our initiation into the Spirit of Sophia to go on to the second principles of Divine knowledge, the true heavenly food. We are meant to have esoteric knowledge of the Truth and to share in the glorious riches of our inheritance as sons and daughters of El Elyon, riches that, according to the New Testament, are already being lavished upon us. It is our privilege to feast ourselves on the Goodness of the Sophianic Banquet, tasting the Heavenly Gift, the Divine Sophia, having a share of Her and experiencing with our whole being the powers of the New Age that is already dawning in our midst.

NOTES FOR CHAPTER FIVE

Fyodor Dostoevsky, *The Brothers Karamazov*, translated and introduced by David Magarshack, Penguin Books, 1982

Marjorie Reeves, *The Influence of Prophecy in the Later Middle Ages: A Study in Joachimism*, University of Notre Dame Press, Notre Dame (USA) 1993

Nicolas Berdyaev, *Freedom and the Spirit*, Geoffrey Bles, London 1944

Vladimir Soloviev, *The White Lily*, translated and edited by Boris Jakim, The Variable Press, New Haven, Conn. 1995

Robert A Powell, *The Sophia Teachings*, Sounds True: Boulder, CO 1997. See also Robert A Powell, *The Most Holy Trinosophia*, Anthroposophic Press: Hudson, NY 1998

6. Sophia and the Zodiac

Now it may be asked, What are the stars (or planets)? Or out of what are they come to be? They are the power of the seven spirits of God. (p. 641)…There are in him chiefly seven qualities, whereby the whole divine being is driven on, and sheweth itself infinitely in these seven qualities…' (p. 274) (*The Aurora*, Jakob Boehme)

Gentle Son, I counsel thee not to learn this Art, for it is of great difficulty and one may err in it; it is dangerous, for men who understand it best use it for ill, for the sake of the power of the celestial bodies, ignoring and despising the power and goodness of God.

(*Doctrina Pueril*, Ramon Lull)

I have in my possession a copy of a ninth-century painting of Christ, in the form of the sun, surrounded by the twelve signs of the Zodiac. When I first saw this print, I became aware of the fact that something very profound was taking place in my spiritual life. This ancient Zodiac was, like a magnet, drawing me to itself, inviting me to enter a reality that was beyond anything I could begin to imagine. It was a new reality to me and yet I knew that I had always belonged there. The more I meditated on the symbols, the more I began to realize that they were only complete together. To reach the wholeness that it reflected, in my own life, I knew that I would have to enter into a new relationship with The One that lies behind all multiplicity. Although I could not explain what was happening, in any rational way, I knew that to turn away from the harmony of the Zodiac, would be to deny not only an important stage in my spiritual growth but also the richness and wonder of the Divine creation.

Meditation on the Zodiac also helped me to re-connect with biblical knowledge in a new way, by revealing the importance and depth of the Older Testament model of the Divine Assembly. It spoke to me of the balance of male and female, Father and Mother, inner and outer, heaven and earth, personal and cosmic. It also bears witness to the important distinction between the uncreated and the created. In other words, that which issues from The One, and that which is created by The One. The Christian Creed speaks of the 'begotten' and that which is 'made'. The former eternally is, while the latter was called into being as a creative act on the part of the Divine One. This ancient biblical model bears witness to the fact that all the different levels of creation manifest, in different ways, the Glory or Light of The Most High or Transcendent One. Everything revolves around El Elyon, the Divine Source of all things. At first I found it confusing, since there appeared to be many sons or 'offspring' of El Elyon, as they are called. But the more I became attuned to the reality of the Divine Assembly, the more I realized how sophisticated this ancient biblical wisdom was, and indeed 'is', for it is timeless. The Glory of El, for example, refers to a different hierarchy of being to the Glory of Yhwh. Similarly, there are sons of El Elyon who are angels or agents of El Elyon, the sons of Light, who shine from the One, like the rays that pour from the Sun. There are also sons of El Elyon who are the Elohim, the gods and goddesses. The Greek version of Deuteronomy 32:43 bears this out:

Rejoice with him, O heavens,

Bow down to him sons of God   [i.e. The Elohim, sons of El],

Rejoice with his people, nations,

Confirm him, all you angels of God.   [i.e. divine messengers of El] *(The Great Angel*, p. 43)

No aspect of creation is left out of the Divine Assembly, a characteristic that we find in all of the Middle Eastern models of the universe. One of the oldest of these cosmic blueprints goes back to Sumer, the birthplace of astrology. The Sumerians, who lived in what is today Southern Iraq, had a profound awareness of the overall oneness of life, the interdependence of all things and the harmony that issued from such a wonderful sense of balance. The universe was for them a unified organism (the macrocosm) which is reflected in each individual person, who is consequently a microcosm or mini-universe in itself. Using a system that united the seven known planets of the day with the characteristics of the zodiacal signs, the Sumerians worked out the general patterns involved in each individual life. This in no way detracted from the freedom that is the birthright of each human being and the fact that each person is ultimately responsible for his or her own destiny. To this day the motto of genuine astrology remains the same, namely 'The stars dispose but they do not determine.' By the third century BC the final form of the Zodiac as we know it today had taken shape. The seven days of the week still pay homage to the planetary deities:

Day of the Moon or Monday (*dies lunae*) in Welsh, *Dydd Llun*

Day of Mars (*dies Martis*) becomes *Dydd Mawrth*

Day of Mercury (*dies Mercurii*) becomes *Dydd Mercher*

Day of Jupiter (*dies Jovist*) becomes *Dydd Iau*

Day of Venus (*dies Veneris*) becomes *Dydd Gwener*

Day of Saturn (*dies Saturni*) becomes *Dydd Sadwrn*

Day of the Sun (*dies Solis*) becomes *Dydd Sul*

I found the Christ Zodiac in the early eighties. Since then my collection of zodiacs has grown, along with complementary models of the universe. These models are an important part of the human way of understanding and making sense of life, the way that the cosmos works and homo sapiens' place within it. The model that I have developed in my own work consists of revolving circles of different sizes, 'wheels within wheels', each one representing a different dimension of creation. Each circle, in turn, is divided into different segments, three, for example, representing the Divine Trinity, and seven the planets or the Archangels. The twelve signs of the Zodiac are fixed and form the basis of my universe. This model evolved over many years as I endeavoured to bring together, in my own life, the energies and principles of heaven and earth, from the most basic to the most refined. In a stylized way, I am thus able to celebrate the expansion or birthing of the Divine One into the all or many of creation, and the return or redemption of the all back into the One. As I ascend or descend the ladder of being I am thus able to contemplate the Divine-cosmic mystery in all its beauty and power.

The Gods and Goddesses

The gods and goddesses are an integral part of an ancient wisdom that is as relevant to our self-understanding and growth today as it ever was. They form an important part of the Universe, both personal and cosmic, and have their own part to play in the human journey towards greater health and wholeness. The cosmic and mystical model that I built was only complete when the gods and goddesses had taken their place. Rooted in my own native spirituality is an unbroken affinity and relationship with the ancient ones. There has never been a time when they have not been honoured. Through the mediation of the Ancient One in the sanctuary at Pennal Church, I was introduced to their company in an exciting and intimate way.

The gods and goddesses are symbolic representations of created powers and energies, the raw material of cosmic life in all its diverse aspects. They represent specific drives or impulses which need to be expressed and satisfied, each deity set apart for a purpose, each denoting an aspect of created Wisdom. Jakob Boehme refers to them as seven principal qualities or properties of divine power within creation. The signs, in turn, represent qualities that everyone needs to acknowledge and develop during their lifetime, each individual thus expressing planetary energies in a unique and personal way. Nowhere does the Bible deny the existence of the elohim, the gods and goddesses. Even in the New Testament it was acknowledged that they were plentiful namely 'many gods and many lords' (1 Corinthians 8:5). The Older Testament, in fact, bears witness to crucial stages in the development of our Western understanding of the deities. Along with their neighbours, the Hebrews accepted the presence of a rich array of deities, but they viewed them in a different way. Long before the coming of Christianity, for example, pagans had humanized their gods and goddesses. From being supernatural beings 'up there', they became natural principles 'down here'. In the process the deities were de-mystified and eventually became metaphors for dynamics at work within the human psyche. In Hebrew consciousness the gods and goddesses underwent a totally different transformation altogether.

With the existence of so many gods and goddesses, there was great rivalry, competition and conflict. This can be seen, for example, in the rivalry between Yhwh, the god of Israel, and Baal, the Canaanite god of fertility. In time, different communities produced a god or goddess that was regarded as being more important than the others, and consequently we see the exclusive worship of one god among many, for example:

> You shall have no gods before me.   (Exodus 20:3)
> Ascribe to the Lord [i.e. Yhwh], O mighty ones, ascribe to the Lord glory and strength.
> (Psalm 29:1)

The Hebrew began to confront the elemental powers of the Universe, refusing to bow down to them or to bind itself to any one of them. The writings of Isaiah of the Exile declare that the gods and goddesses, or the lesser deities, had been defeated and judged. In a very real sense, for the Hebrew they had ceased to exist: 'But you are less than no thing and your works are utterly worthless' (41:24). This process reached its climax in the realization that all the gods and goddesses were different aspects of one divine being. Deuteronomy proclaims that Yhwh our Elohim, Yhwh is One(6.4). Yhwh came to sum up all the Elohim. The totality of created power was focused and harnessed into one divine being, Yhwh of Hosts. All pluralistic concepts of divinity were therefore unreal. Yhwh became the Mighty One, a divine being so powerful that not only is 'He' the All of Nature (a role occupied by Pan in pagan mythology), but also the supreme power at work in human history. Yhwh's very name bears witness to this, namely 'the one who causes everything to happen'. No aspect of creation was outside His domain. Although to this day Yhwh is referred to in masculine terms, He embodies both polarities of being, the male and female powers. In Isaiah 42, for example, in one verse Yhwh is described as a woman in labour, whereas in a previous verse He was a mighty warrior triumphing over His enemies. Yhwh had grown into a being or level of creation that absorbed all the different qualities of individual deities, which included the fundamental cyclical pattern of death and rebirth, growth and decay. In one of the most startling revelations in the Older Testament, Yhwh is heard to declare that

> I form the light and create darkness.
> I bring prosperity and create disaster.   (Isaiah 45:2)

Being many gods and goddesses, Yhwh cannot have one name, for 'He' had many. He cannot be summed up by any one of His aspects. His became the Name that contained all names: 'I am who I am.' Yhwh was creation as one. Various models developed to describe this totality of created being, e.g. the prophet Zechariah speaks of the seven eyes of Yhwh which cover the whole earth (Zechariah 4:10), represented in Temple furniture by a solid gold lampstand with a bowl at the top and seven lights on it, with seven channels to the lights. The priest Ezekiel saw a fourfold vision of Yhwh, an early astrological model, this time in the form of four living creatures, representing the four fixed signs of Taurus, Aquarius, Leo and Scorpio. Both models re-appear in the last book of the Bible, the Apocalypse of St John, namely. the seven spirits of El Elyon (Revelation of St John 4:5) with the four living creatures surrounding the Throne of the Lamb [i.e. the Risen Christ], who itself had seven horns and seven eyes.

In his Letter to the Romans (8:38-39), St Paul, while addressing a generation who lived in fear of the cosmic powers, alludes to an astrological model in order to celebrate the Good News of what Christ's redemption had accomplished. All the polarities of being, he says, cannot separate the redeemed individual from the Divine Love manifested in Christ, namely Death and Life, Angels and Demons, Present and Future, Height and Depth. This last pair refers firstly to the Ascendant or the Path of the Sun, which the Greeks called the 'horoscope', the determining hour of one's birth. This term is now used to refer to the whole of one's celestial chart at the time of birth. This 'rising sign', as it is also called, is balanced by the Descendant, which coincides with an opposite sign from the Ascendant and embodies the reality of conflict among different forms of energy. Such dynamics are simultaneously contradictory and complementary.

Yhwh, in addition to being the sum total of the gods and goddesses, also became the rule or principle of Divine Order and Harmony, similar to the role of the Logos in pagan religion and philosophy. Yhwh was the bond which kept all the gods and goddesses together as a unified whole. It was Yhwh who mediated between the opposites, keeping every part in its appointed place. It was Yhwh which represented the way in which the divine order of things is meant to operate. Since Yhwh embodied the standard set 'He' also mirrored or judged, of necessity, any part which acted contrary to the ordered pattern. While in Greek mythology Zeus was also the principle of order and measure, he was still, nevertheless, one of the many. Yhwh, however, had come to represent something very different. For the people of Israel Yhwh was 'the many'. He was one divine being that comprised all of the deities. Yhwh was the absolute power of nature. While some in Israel saw Yhwh as the manifested power of El Elyon in creation (a kind of second Divine being), others came to equate Yhwh with El Elyon, a radically different proposition! Two different theologies developed that were eventually to split the ancient religion of the Hebrews in two. We return to this theme in chapter seven.

The planets

The gods and goddesses exist, as do the signs of the Zodiac, in a complementary relationship with one another. They provide each individual with a map or model of the dynamics that he or she will encounter in life. The Sun and Moon represent the male–female polarity that governs every aspect of life, from consciousness to unconsciousness, light and darkness, rational and irrational, etc. Some astrologers and psychologists refer to this as the Apollo-Dionysian polarity, the former representing masculinity, light and dynamic movement, balanced by the latter's femininity, darkness and passivity (a quality, however, that should not be confused with inactivity). Others speak of the primitive Dionysian phase of consciousness (unashamedly pagan), more in tune with the veiled secrets of Mother Nature, balanced by the more aggressive energy of the above-ground Olympian pantheon, the religion of conquerors and the human will-to-power. This aspect is, for example, reflected in the struggle of any nation or people to establish and assert itself, and Israel was no exception, as the Older Testament bears witness.

The interplay of Apollo and Dionysius also highlights the need for things to take form by the energy or vitality that is continually waiting to be shaped into some pattern or other. The inherent tension between these polar opposites, between order and free movement, is regarded as being basically negative, with the opposites in constant conflict or as being positive and therefore perpetually engaged in a creative and complementary relationship with each other. In fact, it is important to realize that not only is a god or goddess in polar relationship to another, but each deity is made up of alternating qualities of male and female, or, as the Chinese say, of yang and yin, positive and negative. One needs to be careful in labelling a particular deity as being feminine, for example, since that femininity is a complex reality, dependent on the right balance or rhythm of her own positive and negative poles.

The fundamental male-female polarity accompanies us throughout our lives, the constant interplay of the need for independence and separateness balanced by the need for interdependence and community.

A significant part of our lives is governed by our ability to handle the freedom needed for growth and individuality, for change and spontaneity which is forever countered and resisted by the predictable and unchanging. We cannot escape the play of opposites, and the art of being human is the ability to honour both sides, thus not taking either to extremes. Like the ebb and flow of the tides, we need to weave the polarities of life into a creative pattern and rhythm.

Mercury is the god who cannot easily be tied down and and labelled. Hermes, as he is also known, is the quicksilver of our own dynamic self. He is the ability to communicate and pass on the knowledge of each one of the gods and goddesses, as the need and opportunity arises. Mercury is the youthful, enquiring energy of human curiosity, that stimulates the power of reflection and empowers each person to travel courageously towards the future. As each individual begins to draw from the wisdom of the parental and nurturing energies and principles of Sun and Moon, it next encounters the polarity of Venus and Mars, the dynamics of human sexuality and power. It is the mysterious power of attraction that lies at the heart of all relationships, coupled with the energy needed to establish and assert oneself in the world. Venus, or Aphrodite, is the goddess of love and beauty, that yearns for union on many levels, both earthly and heavenly. Mars is the warrior that helps us to master situations as well as to be combative when required. This polarity celebrates the reality of human pleasure and satisfaction as well as the privilege of being responsible for creatively handling power in all its rich and varied guises.

The next polarity that the maturing individual encounters is of a more transpersonal nature. Here we have to face and cope with principles traditionally related to philosophy and religion, the questions or issues that lead us deeper into the meaning of life. This is the territory where Jupiter and Saturn hold sway and where many religious people struggle to make sense of life. Jupiter, or Zeus, is the epitome of sheer optimism towards the human condition. He is the bringer of good fortune and joy and represents the divinely ordained all-providing energy of life. Saturn, however, is the principle of darkness, limitation and suffering. He is the shadow side of human life, closely related to the senses and earthly pleasures, hence his association in traditional Christian consciousness with the underworld and evil. Saturn is the Wise Old man or Hag who insists that we learn the value of pain and suffering. It is our saturnine nature that helps us to come to terms with the anxiety and frustration that is an inexorable part of being human. It teaches self-discipline and patience. Failure to acknowledge this aspect of life turns Saturn, from the human perspective, into a cruel and ultimately sadistic presence. When this happens we become slaves to our worst fears, we find ourselves in bondage to the paralysing forces of inertia. Unable to face the unknown, we end up clinging on to anything that can provide us with temporary comfort. Our world becomes a small and ultimately suffocating world. The traditional word for such a state of affairs is hell! Instead of being an aid to greater freedom and spaciousness, life's many challenges become an excuse for remaining trapped within our own self-made little world. The self-discipline, which Saturn encourages, eventually becomes destructive and demonic, causing us to turn in completely on ourselves. Retreating into our shells, we becomes more and more isolated from the Whole. These dynamics apply to all aspects of life, the personal and collective, the social and national. Jakob Boehme describes the outward Saturn as wrathful, a quality that encloses and makes hard, while Jupiter, in contrast, is an unsettled zest for life that opens the darkness.

In religious terms what many in the West struggle with in every generation is a combination of the Jupiter-Saturn polarity in its most negative aspect. The former in this guise becomes The Great Father, on whom many of us project our often unrealistic expectations. He is in perpetual conflict with Saturn, the deity whom many have transformed into Satan, the eternal scapegoat for all human failings and sin. Religious people are particularly good at setting human joy against the reality of pain and suffering. Failure to integrate this polarity positively in our lives leads to the immature attitude of siding with one principle against the other. The ongoing human journey to wholeness includes re-cognizing [i.e. re-knowing] and honouring the creative powers of all the gods and goddesses. If we continue to fight against Saturn, or any of the deities, we are ultimately fighting against ourselves. Jesus gave a clear warning of what happens when an individual falls into this trap, namely 'Every kingdom divided against itself will be ruined' (Matthew 12:25). It is only when we have firmly and creatively established our sovereignty within the realm of Venus-Mars and then Jupiter-Saturn, that we can move on safely to meet the outermost deities of growth and change, the masculine planet Uranus and the feminine and fluidic Pluto and Neptune. All three planets are continually testing and pushing at the boundaries of tradition and convention.

Uranus is the principle that urges us to get rid of old and outworn ideas, habits and behaviour. While Saturn plods along resisting all talk of change, Uranus with his nonconformity and individuality is already smashing or breaking down anything that gets in his way in order to make way for something new. The challenge, as with all polarities, is to discover a wise mean between the opposites. The middle way when Uranus confronts Saturn, for example, is best summed up in the words of Jesus — 'Every teacher of the law who has been instructed about the Kingdom of Heaven is like the owner of a house who brings out of his storeroom new treasures as well as old' (Matthew 13:52). When Uranus approaches barriers tumble and veils are lifted, and a more spacious picture of ourselves and our universe is revealed.

Whereas Uranus is the Magician who can work wonders in what is often a cold and sterile world, Neptune is the Mystic who draws us into greater and greater union with that which lies beyond all differentiation. When our neptunian qualities are activated we become part of a more embracing unity and oneness, and experience the bliss of contemplation and divine ecstasy. Elements of our character that have been kept underground are also drawn into this cosmic spaciousness. Pluto, a feminine planet, like the masculine Mercury, is also not easily tied down and labelled. It also works, mysteriously, through the whole constellation, the irreversible principle of decay and death, both literal and physical, and the change and renewal that always follows in its wake. Pluto is the principle that draws from energies deep down in the Underworld, inviting us to face the ultimate darkness that is also an integral part of wholeness. Here lies our personal and collective monsters, the horror of human pain and suffering, anger and hurt. In other words, all those things in the human condition that can so easily be rejected and damned. Pluto is the power that transforms all that we regard as being black and dirty into pure gold, in order that our sovereignty may be complete.

The Power of Detachment

One of the major challenges that faces us as human beings is the need to realize that while we are a part of Nature we can only become fully human by standing apart from her. It was a great breakthrough in the development of human awareness to realize that 'I' had a consciousness that could be aware of itself! In the sixth century BC, for example, the Deuteronomists, and later on their followers, as they turned away from the power of myriad gods and goddesses, came to rely more and more on the power of their purely inner or mental relationship with the Divine. Mainstream Judaism went on to reject all types of magic, the use of sacred objects, religious ritual and astrological calculations, as part of its spirituality. It found prayer, study and good behaviour efficacious enough to channel Divine help, although it can be argued that for some Jews the Holy Scriptures became a sacred cult object and that ritual was replaced by an almost obsessive code of human behaviour. The absence of few or no external aids left each individual to rely increasingly on the power of the human mind. A consciousness developed highly conducive to studying and analysing the minutiae of the Law, which served to increase the importance of making choices based on purely rational arguments. It is not surprising that the formal and public face of Judaism is dominated by men and their intellectual processes. But Judaism, in contrast to Christianity, grew up as a world-affirming spirituality, with stress on family life, the sanctity of human sexuality and the importance of worldly occupations. It is ironic that Christianity, whose central doctrine is built on the mystery of the Divine Word or Logos becoming flesh, developed in the totally opposite way. To this day many Christians view the physical part of being human as an embarrassment. This is primarily because of the flesh's association, in the prevailing pagan philosophy of the day, with femininity, bondage and evil. The pleasure and enjoyment of the human senses were acknowledged as a curse.

The initial step taken by the early Christians had been a brave and creative one. The birth of Christianity coincided with the collapse of the ancient and classical world and the breakup of the Old Order. A new journey was undertaken by the first Christian ascetics and monks, of both sexes (a quest started by groups and communities such as the Jewish Essenes), into the mystery of understanding the dynamics of one's inner self. A new focusing of human energy and spirituality took place, as individuals struggled to rediscover where the sovereignty of homo sapiens lay. A transition took place from a world dominated by the power of natural-magical forces to one where Otherworldly and mystical forces held sway. In the former the ego is central and is strengthened in order to master the natural forces it seeks to control. In the latter, the ego, after consolidating itself, is transcended, as the individual goes on to achieve union with the Divinity which lies behind all phenomena. On the positive side, these individuals faced the gods and goddesses, the forces of Nature 'head on', and, in one sense, achieved liberation from her. With great discipline that was strengthened the more temptations one faced and triumphed over, these individuals were able to rise above their natural impulses and thus celebrate the core of their humanity, the gift of freedom and the power of discrimination. In rising above Nature they affirmed the presence and reality of the Transcendent One and the positive qualities that issued from union with it. In what had become a hard and cruel world, this was Good News indeed, namely the salvific power of kindness, compassion, nobility, patience, gentleness and joy.

Living in a transitional period, however, Christians displayed great ambivalence towards the forces that surrounded them, 'the rulers and authorities in the heavenly realms', to quote the Letter to the Ephesians (3.10). In chapter six of this letter these forces are so evil that the Christian must engage with them only when protected by full divine armour. Spiritual weapons were needed to fight spiritual evil. In St Paul's first Letter to the Corinthians, these powers are even called the enemies of Christ (15:26). In the Letter to the Colossians, however(written in all probability by a follower of St Paul), we are told that these powers were created by Christ! So overwhelmed were some individuals in facing the stark reality of a cosmos filled with a hierarchy of gods and goddesses, many of dubious origin, that they did not think of them as principles to be assimilated and integrated (and redeemed if necessary) into their personal universes. Rather, they were powers to be banished to the nethermost depths of the human psyche, because it was their influence that resulted in such sins as sexual immorality, witchcraft and drunkenness. Furthermore, all were sins of the flesh. Generally speaking, there was little or no positive appreciation of the gifts of the senses. Nature was gradually de-animated and everything natural came to be regarded as being lower or base, and ultimately evil, when compared to mental or spiritual influences. A dualism developed that set one's inner life or mental dynamics against the power of the flesh. To this day we in the West, for example, still refer to 'physical education', thus perpetuating the belief that the body is 'just an instrument' or a machine to serve the mind.

The 'idea' of Spirit came to be synonymous with everything that was non-physical, as individuals struggled to grasp the heavenly gifts that had sealed their salvation — a salvation from the world not salvation of the world. If there was little or no hope for this world of creation one could at least be assured of a place in the new creation to come. There are plenty of verses in the New Testament that can be taken out of context to reinforce an Otherworldly spirituality, e.g:

> Since with Christ you have been raised, set your
> hearts on heavenly things, where Christ is seated at El's
> right hand. Set your minds on things above and not on earthly things.   (Colossians 3:1-2)

Such passages, however, are not decrying earthly realities *per se*, but their abuse. But the time, nevertheless, was still one of uncertainty *vis-à-vis* the gods and goddesses. They were not to be trusted. Consequently the key words that we encounter in the writings of most Christian theologians in relation to Nature and the flesh are 'conquer', 'renounce' and 'overcome'! Traditional Christianity's treatment of the god Pan illustrates very well the failure of the Church to deal creatively with one of the great deities of Mother Earth. It set up a false dualism between Christ and Nature's All-encompassing One. Originally the god of graze or pasture that brought nourishment to sheep and goats, Pan's phallic representation came to be considered perverse. Instead of honouring the life-giving fertility of All-Nature, the Church set out to convert Pan into a version of the Western devil — horns and all. In severing its links with Pan, the Church became part of a culture that has for centuries raped and exploited Mother Nature. Ironically, homo sapiens was given the privilege, according to Genesis, to cultivate Nature, to 'work [i.e. till] the ground' (3:23). The Hebrew phrase means 'to serve the earth', in the sense that humans are to bring it greater strength and fullness, a Nature renewed and rejuvenated through the creative actions of human beings.

Emotion and Reason

As the new millennium dawns, more and more individuals and groups are being initiated into the wisdom of the Underworld. It is time for us in the West to grow up! Spiritual maturity empowers individuals to undertake the journey back to embrace the wisdom of Nature. This wisdom never died out, even when Sophia was banished in sixth-century BC Israel or the Goddess in the Christian Middle Ages. It has always been an integral part of any path that would celebrate the Wholeness that the Zodiac bears witness to. As the Divine Feminine re-awakens in our lives, She does so, not to pit the feminine against the masculine but to balance the two and thus bring about a new harmony between the forces of heaven and earth. Sophia's all-embracing power is mirrored in Nature in the character of Hecate, the Underworld goddess. Guided by the Green Man I was privileged to enter her realm and, by drawing closer to her, learn of the true order of things. As a Thanksgiving, I dedicated my rose garden in her honour. A rose known as Blue Moon is one of my favourites. Hecate fulfils a mediative role between opposites and thus is a challenge to the masculine, dualistic view of the world. This is possible because, although her realm is in the Underworld, she also has power in earth, sea and sky. My time in her presence brought much enlightenment and vitality, as these words from my Journal record:

> I sat cross-legged beneath the graceful willow tree, my spine against its living trunk, my horns growing and mingling with its branches, until they were intertwined and I was held fast. Suddenly, I was not alone. From deep below the willow's roots, a figure took shape. She too was inseparable from the tree, her body pressed close to its cool grey bark, her hair falling as she bent to embrace me. I emerged from the Underworld with my hair and beard saturated in the willow's sap. My body coated in rich brown earth and an array of fresh roots that looked like small fragile arteries, each one eager to touch me, so that they, too, could fulfil their part of the Blessing. The smell and taste of that good earth will remain with me for ever.   (5 June 1992)

The traditional Christian, and in particular Gnostic, dualism of body and mind or flesh and spirit, continues to exercise its influence on Western religious culture. The 'idea' of the rational (a masculine trait), is still generally 'thought of' as being superior to the sensual, emotional, and hence feminine life, which is regarded as a hindrance to, and in some cases, the enemy of, an ordered, calm and rational life. But the belief system that for centuries has subordinated everything associated with the feminine is now itself being challenged. We are witnessing a total reversal of patriarchal values. As the new millennium dawns, we can celebrate the fact that the emotional dimension has always been the core or essence of our lives. It is the raw material that goes to make up the gods and goddesses, the very basis of our human nature. The emotional life is primary and not secondary or subordinate. Neither is it unruly, bad or evil. Consequently, the intellect is derivative. It emerges out of the sensual and emotional life, is nourished by it and receives its direction from it. A wholesome emotional life means a healthy intellect to serve it. The intellect is instrumental. It is concerned with its object and not itself. Its desire is to know about things, which it does in a piecemeal fashion, analysing aspects of being, dividing up reality, abstracting from it and substituting parts for the Whole and concepts for reality itself.

But life is more than thought, and reason is more than intellectual ability and power. There is reason in the emotional depths. The danger of an intellect divorced from the emotions is that its cold, calculating and clinical observations can so easily lead to a distorted view of life. Many of the 'heresies' of our modern society are the product of such 'thinking'. This is the temptation to make one known concept, or aspect of life, the principal meaning of the Whole. Psychiatrists, social reformers and theologians, for example, fall into this trap when they attempt to explain all human behaviour in terms of either childhood sexuality or biology, socio-economic factors or 'Original Sin'. Some philosophers have even made the intellect itself the ultimate principle of life!

The Challenge of the Gods and Goddesses

The human personality is a rich mosaic of powers, hence the need to face and embrace the gods and goddesses. This demands great courage and commitment, because in order to educate ourselves we cannot but become fascinated by each god and goddess, some more than others. They have the potential to exercise a seductive power and hold over us. Hence the need to be aware of those who can offer immediate satisfaction, or at least the promise of satisfaction. Genuine human needs are never easily met. It is imperative, therefore, to step back from pleasures that appear immediately at hand. Similarly, over-identification with a god or goddess can lead to possession by them. Anyone desiring emotional, and hence spiritual, maturity has to be prepared to take this risk. Possession becomes obsessive when a deity, masquerading as the whole, becomes the sole principle of an individual's life. In religious terminology this is called idolatry, the worship of one aspect of life. Idolatry becomes demonic or pathological when an individual is so taken over or swallowed by a god, or combination of gods, that he or she draws in completely upon oneself to the exclusion of all else.

By learning to step back, we slowly become aware of the gap between 'Who' or 'What' I think I am (neither 'this' nor 'that') and 'that which I can actually become'. It is a painful condition, but it is only in this state of positive anxiety, and even despair, that we can discover our real selves. In facing the company of gods and goddesses, not only does my true self emerge but also the knowledge of The One that lies behind and beyond all multiplicity. This free exercise of my emotional resources and wisdom involves a continuous effort to discover the real values of life for myself. It is in this way that my sensuality, for example, becomes more and more refined. In the process I also learn how to exercise authority over the gods and goddesses and the responsibility that goes with it. I thus become a more mature and disciplined person, a discipline born out of the depths of my emotional life and served by a discerning intellect, and not a discipline that belongs to another. In fact, discipline imposed by another destroys our ability to experience and think for ourselves. It prevents the spontaneous exercise of an individual's emotional and sensual life.

Knowledge of the gods and goddesses is consequently only part of our emotional education. In order to weave them into a creative and integrated whole, the gods and goddesses must be loved. They must be acknowledged, accepted and embraced as integral parts of the human personality. The old practice of coercion, repression and punishment, when the need arose, will no longer do. It is this negative tradition that has resulted in the seamless robe that is the human soul being torn asunder by principles that are wrongly believed to be in conflict, principles that are regarded as being 'nothing but', and even worst, mere 'its'. Every god and goddess is to be embraced as a 'loving thou'. And the test or fruit of such loving harmony and integration is the growth of a freedom that itself grows out of genuine spontaneity and love, which is impossible if we are driven by the gods and goddesses. There can be no lasting satisfaction and genuine sensual pleasure when the gods and goddesses are unloved, undisciplined and immature.

The emotions have their own wisdom. Human drives and yearnings are not ignorant and unruly. They cannot be reduced to 'mere impulses' without serious repercussions for our well-being. They are component parts of a complex process, possessing their own significance and inherent unity. These natural principles are not free in the sense that an individual human being is free. But every principle can, nevertheless, develop imperial tendencies of its own. Herein lies the paradox of our relationship with the gods and goddesses. Without humility and compassion they can become caught in the vicious circle of our individual and collective quest for self-justification and self-aggrandizement. They become part of human pride and arrogance, and gradually find themselves estranged and alienated from their true source or centre. These created principles are not 'neutral', because in being part of an individual's freedom they acquire a degree of power over that individual. In a personality devoid of the experience of sovereignty they come to be regarded as autonomous rulers within the human psyche. Divorced from their true centre, they become tyrannical, limiting agencies, usurpers, whose sole aim it is to enhance their own self-importance and glory. In this alienated state, the gods and goddesses do influence human behaviour in a negative, disruptive and ultimately sinful way. It is our privilege and responsibility as individuals to mould and give shape to these created principles. As human beings we can choose to be ignorant of, and thus driven by, the gods and goddesses, or we can exercise our sovereignty by facing and fashioning them with a positive and creative meaning that embraces them all.

El Elyonic Spirituality

There is a Christian, biblically-based astrology, that draws on the major theological and cosmological insights of the Judeo-Christian tradition. Its roots go back to Israel's ancient faith, the Ageless Wisdom that King Solomon patronized nearly three thousand years ago. It is a system that honours the Divine and the human, the relationship between the powers of heaven as well as the forces of the earth. In the words of Jakob Boehme:

> The Divine must become human, the human must become Divine; heaven must become one thing with earth, the earth must be turned to heaven. If you will make heaven out of the earth, then give the earth the heaven's food, that the earth may obtain the will of heaven.
>
> (*The Signature of All Things*, p. 121)

This is the harmony ordained by El Elyon, from whom everything in heaven and earth originates. As the New Testament era dawned, the praise of the Most High One was still being sung. Ben Sirach 42:15–43:37 is a lengthy hymn celebrating the wonders of a Universe which reflects the unfathomable Glory of El Elyon. Had El Elyon been nothing but a primitive deity — and a pagan one at that! — it would surely have been swallowed up by the more nationalistic Yhwism and the purging of the sixth-century BC reformers and their followers who survived the Exile. But El Elyonic spirituality not only survived and grew, it also became the focal point of Hellenistic Judaism and Christianity. Philo (20 BC–AD 50), a famous Alexandrian Jewish philosopher, followed a tradition that was very different to the Orthodox Jewish one that is normally associated with first-century Judaism. But it was Jewish, nevertheless, and, like the Jewish sectarians who later became 'Christians', it drew upon an alternative, but equally ancient, faith. Philo also spoke of the Supreme or Ultimate Reality as El Elyon, the Transcendent Source of all things, the same Divinity that Jesus honoured with the words, 'I praise you Father, Lord of heaven and earth' (Matthew 11:25), and that Melchizedek knew as 'Procreator of heaven and earth' (Genesis 12:9).

The sons or offspring of El Elyon were still active in New Testament days, the Archangels or Chief Messengers, forever radiating from the Uncreated Divine Source. They are not separate entities but aspects of El Elyon. Their names bear witness to the fact that they partake of, and manifest, the core of the Divine nature, in a unique way. For example, Rapha-El (Healing of El), Gabri-El (Strength), Zadki-El (Righteousness), Tami-El (Perfection). In Luke's Gospel it was Gabriel who greeted Mary with the news that she was to give birth to the Son of El Elyon (1:32), the Firstborn, and clearly of a sonship different to that of the Archangels. The power of El Elyon would overshadow Mary, i.e. the presence of Shekhinah El or Sophia. The aged Zechariah, the father of John the Baptist, called Jesus a prophet of El Elyon, while angels praised El Elyon saying, 'Glory to El in the highest and on earth peace to men on whom his favour rests'(2:14). The Gospel account goes on to say that the child Jesus grew and became strong: he was filled with the spirit of Sophia and the grace of El Elyon was upon him. And Jesus grew in wisdom and stature and in favour with El and humanity. In Matthew's Gospel it was an unnamed messenger who appeared to Joseph in a dream, thus fulfilling the prophecy of Isaiah of Jerusalem.

The Virgin will be with child and will give birth

to a son and will call him Immanuel. [i.e. Immanu-El, El Elyon with us]   (5:2)

We note, once again, that Jesus is the Son of El Elyon and not the Son of Yhwh. He is a new and unique manifestation of The Most High, whose coming was acknowledged and celebrated by El Elyonic Arch-Messengers. These ancient sons of El Elyon did not disappear with the coming of Christ but they took on a new guise. People's perception of them changed and by the sixth century AD — especially in the writings of Dionysius the Areopagite — they had been integrated into a theology that knew them as the Divine Names. These included, among many others, Righteousness, Perfection and Goodness, for the Divine One sends forth upon all things the rays of Its undivided power. All goodness in creation is therefore good because it participates in this original Goodness. The key link in transmitting this ancient El Elyonic wisdom to the West (preserved in the teachings of Dionysius and the Greek Fathers) was the ninth-century Irish Celtic holy man known as Eriugena. In his cosmology the Divine Names, which issue forth from the One, are acknowledged, although he refers to them as 'Divine Principles'. These are the primordial or original causes of everything in creation. The Greeks called them 'Ideas', and they form the proper or true qualities of everything that exists. There is no astrology, however, in Eriugena's system. The same cannot be said for the Great Art of Ramon Lull, where the wisdom and principles of heaven and earth come together in a holistic discipline that is as relevant today as it was in the Middle Ages.

The Lullian Art: A Christian Astrology

Ramon Lull (1232-1316) was a native of Palma in Majorca, and to this day is honoured as one of the greatest Catalan writers and thinkers. From an early age he was in contact with a rich variety of religious and spiritual traditions, especially Muslim and Jewish. He lived during a time of great piety, cultural energy and spiritual growth. Steeped in Dominican scholarship, Lull believed passionately in the power of the enquiring mind to acquire all truth. He used his talents to produce a synthesis of Christian and Muslim theological thought. A member of the Third Order of Franciscans, Lull also became a 'Fool of Love', a holy troubador singing the praises of Divine Love, especially as revealed in the person of the Crucified Christ. In his thirties, he was granted a vision of the Crucifixion, which was repeated five times. At the core of his work as a scholar and mystic was the Divine or Great Art, that was revealed to him in a heavenly vision on Mount Randa in 1274. He believed that he had been given this special revelation in order to demonstrate, in as scientific a way as possible, the essential truth of all things, including the act of creation and the mystery of redemption. Lull devoted the rest of his long life to elaborate and promote this mystical system, which brought together heavenly and earthly dynamics into an all-embracing and integral discipline.

Like Eriugena, he too believed that each divine principle or attribute was manifested on every level of creation, culminating in the life of every human being. It is by living in harmony with these principles that all created perfection is brought about.

Contemporary with Lull, in thirteenth-century Provence (in its Western part called Languedoc), there also appeared a mystical form of Judaism called Cabbalism. From here it was transported to Aragon and Castile, in Spain, where its classical shape developed. This Jewish system also highlighted ten cosmic (or Elyonic) powers or potencies, which manifested the living and dynamic unity of the Divine One. These powers were known as *sefiroth* (from sapphire), each one being a reflection of Sophia, the Divine Beauty. In some sources they are also called 'paths of Sophia' and are not individual entities but share and reflect the One Divine Glory. The classical text of Cabbalistic lore, *The Zohar*, appeared in Gerona in Northern Catalonia in 1275, the year after Lull received his vision. Both Christian and Jewish mystical schools were rooted in a spiritual tradition that celebrated The One and the Many, a tradition that taught that The One could be known and experienced by contemplating its manifestations in the world.

Ramon Lull's Art was based on what he called the New Astrology, which viewed the old astrological principles, the heavens and the planets, in a way different to what had been taught in the past. The warning given by Lull at the start of this chapter, is a warning against the errors of the old astrology, which was based on natural principles, which were believed of necessity to rule over the world, including homo sapiens. The Freedom which we see celebrated in the New Testament could not, however, submit to fate or necessity of any kind. The New Astrology was based on the Divine Principles, or Dignitates as Lull called them, which exercised a higher influence on the planets and signs, since they originated from beyond even the highest of the created heavens. These are Goodness, Greatness, Eternity, Power, Wisdom, Will, Virtue, Truth and Glory. In Cabbalism they are Crown, Wisdom, Understanding, Mercy, Judgement, Beauty, Power, Glory, Foundation and Kingdom. These principles enable individuals to draw nourishment and wisdom from Divinity itself, and for Christians, from the Trinity. For Lull the doctrine of the Trinity was not merely a profound theological truth, it was a fundamental fact in the existence of the universe. The Son or Word mediates the Father's Will through the use of the Names or Principles, while the Spirit presides over their subsequent effects in the world.

Lull's higher astrology does not draw a wedge between Divinity and creation, the One and the many. On the contrary, he helps bring the gods and goddesses into a closer and more intimate union with the Divine principles, which inform their movements. They thus become vehicles for the exercise of a different kind of power. The deities have also been set apart to fulfil a Divine purpose. Each one denotes the Wisdom of the Creator within creation. In truth it can be said that the stars and the elements nourish us. The very matter of our bodies pulsates with them and it is by their impulses that we are grounded in our Nature. Every planet has its 'proper qualities', i.e. the divine principles which enable the planets and signs to be in harmony together. They also have their 'appropriated' qualities or aspects, namely

Sun: principle of integration	Jupiter: optimism & expansion
Moon: reflection	Saturn: restraint & rigidity
Mercury: communication	Uranus: individuality
Venus: beauty & harmony	Neptune: dissolution
Mars: aggression	Pluto: transformation

These created principles, in different combinations and in relation to the fixed signs (Aries, Taurus, Gemini, Cancer, Leo, Virgo, Libra, Scorpio, Sagittarius, Capricorn, Aquarius and Pisces), make up the raw material of each individual person.

Holistic Healing

With a deep love of myth, a grounding in the insights of Jungian psychology, and an ever-increasing 'feeling for the mystical', I was myself slowly drawn into the profound wisdom of Cabbalism, both in its Jewish and Christian guises. I adopted it as the unifying discipline and model for my spiritual growth and development: the foundation of my 'wheels within wheels'. No longer did I have to keep psychology, mysticism and theology in separate compartments. The Divine Spirit embraced them all and provided me with a practical, 'tried and tested' discipline to help me integrate the different dynamics at work in my life, from the most basic to the sublime. My interest in another ancient tool of higher consciousness, the Tarot, emerged out of many years of growing up with the Cabbalistic 'Tree of Life', as its central motif is called. The Tarot is now a valuable complementary aid to my healing work. My favourite deck is the Russian tarot of St Petersburg by the late Yury Shakov (1937-1989). I hope one day to complete my own Biblical Deck of Tarot cards.

Central to the wisdom of these spiritual exercises is the importance of the symbolic way of perceiving ourselves and our world. On a family pilgrimage to Brittany in 1990, it was a delight to come across the small village of Trehorenteuc in the Forest of Broceliande. Its 'Grail Church' made sacred my love of symbolism. Similar in size to Pennal Church, it is dedicated to Tristan's sister-in-law, St Onenne, and is full of paintings and windows commemorating scenes from the tale of King Arthur and the Quest of the Holy Grail. The East window depicts Christ and Joseph of Arimathea, while a beautiful white stag, surrounded by four red lions (representing the four evangelists), adorns the west wall. The church was restored to its present glory by Fr Henri Gillard, Rector of Trehorenteuc between 1942-1962. All his work is impregnated with symbolism, as the church and a host of brochures on subjects as varied as the Zodiac and Medieval books of hours attest.

No genuine spirituality exists in isolation from the life and achievements of the past. Living spiritual traditions take us out of ourselves and thus prevent us from becoming prisoners of our own subjective feelings and beliefs. They provide us with the opportunity of sharing in the creative ongoing life of the Divine Spirit. They help ground us as whole persons in the Eternal. They empower us in the present to shape our inheritance with confidence for the sake of the future. My visit to Broceliande was a kind of homecoming.

The human soul lives and breathes and grows in images. Symbols are its language. The mystery of what it means to be human can never be adequately explained by the use of reason and logical concepts. This is only possible by means of symbols, which operate at a deeper, and more creative level, of human consciousness. Paradoxically, even when illuminating aspects of our human individuality, symbols also safeguard the mystery in the process. They provide a safe and creative way of participating with cosmic forces, a process that involves the whole person, thought and imagination, the will and emotions. Sacred symbols awaken and challenge, stimulate and nourish each one of us in ways that honour the uniqueness of each human being. They invite us into the intimacy of meditation and contemplation. Through symbols we discover our own spiritual alphabet, and grow up in ways that honour irrational dynamics as well as rational ones. Every aspect of the human personality is thereby brought into harmony with the Divine Will and purpose.

The Divine-human 'I Am'

There is always a danger, when discussing our place in the cosmic scheme of things, of losing sight of our sovereignty as human beings. We can so easily be swamped by talk of angels and hierarchies, gods and goddesses, elemental beings and the like. In his writings, Nicolas Berdyaev never tires of reminding us of our sovereignty within the cosmos. The Good News is that homo sapiens is not a temporary being but a unique Divine-human creation.

Man is not a transitory fragment of the cosmos, a mere step in its evolution; he is superior to the cosmos, independent of its infinity and in principle embraces it completely.

(*Freedom and Spirit*, p. 276)

Drawing from the eighth chapter in Berdyaev's Freedom and Spirit, I bring this chapter to a close by listing seven principles to guide the ethos of the developing global spirituality of the new millennium. May we affirm, both individually and collectively, that

I am the highest order of being and am superior even to the angelic hierarchy

I am created in the Divine image and likeness and am not the product of cosmic evolution nor subordinate to it

I am Divine-human and cannot be eclipsed by a new race, whether of super-human or angelic origin;

I am rooted in the very heart of Divine Life in and through the Humility of Christ

I am the Child of the Divine and nothing in the whole of creation can separate me from that Divinity

I am the recipient of the Divine gift of Freedom and am thus free to mould creatively the forces of nature to the service of humanity and to the glory of The Divine Life

I am an integral part of the Divine plan on earth. A design that cannot be modified or transcended by any process but only realized or destroyed by me.

NOTES FOR CHAPTER SIX

Jakob Boehme, *The Aurora*, John M. Watkins, London 1914

Frances Yates, '*The Art of Ramon Lull*', Journal of the Warburg and Courtauld Institutes XVII, pp 115 -173 1954

Margaret Barker, *The Great Angel*, SPCK, London 1992

Jakob Boehme, *The Signature of All Things*, James Clarke & Co Ltd, London 1969

Nicolas Berdyaev, *Freedom and the Spirit*, Geoffrey Bles, London 1944

The Challenge of the Christic Way of the Cross

A Meditation
It is by coming to terms with the Challenge of the Gods and Goddesses
that we begin to make sense of the Challenge of the Cross.
Similarly, it is only through the Cross
that we can approach the gods and goddesses,
and play our part in their, and our, redemption.

It is by dealing creatively with the reality of human power,
as symbolized by the gods and goddesses,
that we can grasp the meaning of the Pauline myth,
where The Divine One sets a trap
for the fallen powers of the world.
That trap was Christ!

Because of our failure to surrender our powers
to the reality of Agapic or Unconditional Love,
the gods and goddesses become totally self-absorbed.
They become so self-centred
that they fail to recognize the gift of liberation.
They become imprisoned in their own little worlds.

And so Paul, through the profound language of myth,
tells us that a trap was set for the gods and goddesses.
That trap was Love.

But surely Christ could have persuaded the powers
by argument or by some other wise gesture,
less painful, maybe, than the Cross?
But this is the whole point.
Christ would then have to prove who he was
and what he stood for, and he would have to do so
by the use of human power, however subtle and refined
that power may have been.

Christ confronted the powers as manifested in the
religious, political and military,
authorities of his day.
This act of Crucified Love was a radical breaking through
of all the religious and conventional taboos,
the most desegregated event imaginable.
All worldly labels and roles were rendered totally irrelevant.

All expectations were rendered null and void.
Christ is not what we would have created for ourselves!
He is truly the sign of peace and healing
because he is the sign of contradiction.

What Christ represented could only be known to be genuine
in an act that was so absurd and ridiculous
that it would prove nothing
and yet reveal everything
about Divine love.

Christ was no threat to the gods and goddesses.

Christ had nothing to prove because he had no power to
demonstrate and nothing to justify
or to seek approval for.
Confronted by such powerlessness,
the gods and goddesses were liberated from the
human need for constant self-justification and self-glorification.
It is in and through the foolishness of The Cross
that we are liberated from the powers,
and therefore from ourselves.
No longer need we fear the gods and goddesses.
No longer need we fear ourselves.

Liberated from our pride,
the gods and goddesses can also fulfil themselves.
Redeemed through Agapic love and humility,
the whole of creation, along with us,
can become part of the Divine Fullness.

In the Letter to the Philippians
we see the pattern of the lifestyle
that deepens Divine Love is us:
Do nothing in an egocentric or vain manner:
Be humble and think of others as better than yourselves.
Christ did not use his divinity to prove anything:
he never grasped at anything in the whole of creation,
he made Himself as nothing,
he took the form of the servant,
he totally embraced his and our humanity,
he surrendered to humiliation and even death,
in order to bring a genuine and wholesome life to all.

The secret has been revealed.
The mystery of mysteries has been laid bare.
It is the Divine Word and Action in all its fullness,
and that dynamic word is Agape, Christic power,
Divine Love incarnated in our midst.

By the Cross, homo sapiens is challenged to live
the life of humble and unconditional love.
It means embodying the Philippian lifestyle in our lives —
to give up grasping at anything,
to become nothing,
to serve,
to become fully human,
to accept humiliation when it comes,
as well as the different deaths
that are an integral part of living,
including the final death,
with trust and love.

In the words of the Tao Te Ching:
a Christ-like, kenotic or self-emptying consciousness,
results in this kind of behaviour —

> The perfect person employs his or her mind as a mirror.
> It grasps nothing,
> It refuses nothing,
> It receives everything,
> but does not keep.   (Chuang Tzu)

The ultimate Sophianic challenge is to involve
all of the gods and goddesses
in serving an all-embracing meaning.
That meaning is Unconditional Love,
which is continually being poured forth into creation.
The challenge is to love the gods and goddesses:
to invite them to share the wheel of life with us,
to share table fellowship,
at which they can all sit as equals.

The mystery of Love has great power.
It is the potency of no-power.
United in and through love,
the gods and goddesses become more attuned to each other.
Because the powers are in tune
order and balance reigns.
Because of such harmony,
human creativity receives expression in manifold ways.
Love flows, drawing out the hidden meaning of our lives.
It reveals the truth,
and sets us free to be ourselves.
The realization of our destiny
brings a feeling of well-being,
which in turn brings forth more love,
more 'loving power'.

The gods and goddesses challenge us.
Agapic love challenges the gods.
Because of the power of All-embracing love,
not one of the gods and goddesses
is lost, discarded or ignored.
Each one can return to its rightful place
in the order of things,
and become part of a rhythm
that in and through freedom
not only transcends Nature but also transforms her.

With the humble and loving Christ
in the centre of life
as no threat to anyone,
the gods and goddesses no longer have to justify themselves.
They can be themselves.
This is possible because Christic love
is the focal point that alone can
command the loyalty of such heroes.
Agapic love is about transformation and not manipulation.
The gods and goddesses are accepted and loved
in a relationship that enables us to
acknowledge, assimilate and affirm
their values and qualities during our lives.

The Christic Zodiac is an ancient invitation for us
to be at one with everything in creation.
It is all about Sophianic togetherness.

The Zodiac reminds every one of us of our holiness
ie. that we are 'set apart' to fulfil a divine purpose,
weaving together the powers of heaven and earth
into something beautiful and unique.

The Zodiac, however, is not a rational and closed system.
On the contrary, it is a system
that also honours the wisdom of the irrational.
It is the celebration of that Wisdom
that no human faculty or aspect of creation
can ever fully understand,
and least of all control.

The stars dispose but they do not determine.
The Zodiac celebrates freedom and growth —
'powers' that cannot be ordered or manipulated.
In fact, the Zodiac enables us to live the mystery of life
and to cope with the fact that real life is ambiguous,
and that disorder is as much a part of life as order.

The Zodiac helps us to begin to come to terms with the fact
that we must learn to live with contradictions.
In fact, that we are a contradiction!

There is a pattern after all.
There is a way from chaos to cosmos,
from fragmentation to wholeness,
from isolation to community.
My wholeness as a human being lies in my fragmentation:
for community to grow isolation is needed,
just as order makes no sense without disorder

Here, on the Zodiac,
we meet the gods and goddesses
as divine qualities,
each manifesting a particular spiritual potency.
At the beginning of creation
these powers were at the Creator's side.
When homo sapiens was created
their nakedness was clothed with them.

Christ is the centre that holds the Zodiac together,
forever radiating out Agapic Love.
In true humility we see that Christ does not lord it over creation,
like a temporal king or ruler,
but rejoices that he is as much part of creation
as the gods and goddesses are of Him.
And as Christ surveys the fullness that surrounds Him,
the richness of his Father's creation,
we hear Him echo the sentiments of Isaiah of Jerusalem, namely
'Here I am and the Children the lord has given me;
We are signs and symbols from the lord.'

Rooted in the gift of Agapic love,
we are enabled to mould creatively the forces of
heaven and earth.
This is real magick:
the conscious, imaginative and loving working
of the gods and goddesses.

Our destiny as human beings is to be wise custodians
of all that The Divine One has created.
In Wisdom, Divinity invited us to become wise stewards
of all the beasts that had been created.
It was also homo sapiens' privilege to name
the beasts according to the particular quality or essence
divinely appointed them.
We are meant to enter into intimate communion with them,

in order to become more aware of the workings of nature,
and thereby grow in knowledge of the human soul.

It is interesting to note that some of the earliest
paintings of Christ show Him as a beautiful figure,
surrounded by the beasts of the field
and not hanging on the Cross.

Christ at the centre of the Zodiac is the Cosmic Lord,
the new Adam and Eve,
and it is our destiny as human beings
to clothe ourselves
once again,
in our Edenic identity.

The key to that clothing is Christic humility and love.

The word 'zodiac' is actually made up of two Greek words, viz.
zoe-diakos, meaning the Wheel of Life.
But zoe is also linked to the word zoon,
from which we get zoology and zoo, which means animal.
For centuries the Zodiac has also been known as
the Path of the Animal.
The original zodiac consisted of twelve animals;
eight of the current signs are animals.
Virgo, the Lady holding a piece of wheat
is also represented by the hare.

Two-thirds of the signs are therefore animals,
Not a bad way of making sure that we
honour our earthiness
as human beings!

The Challenge is to enter the world of the Zodiac
and to walk its many paths.
To embrace the depths and heights of the Universe,
the mysteries of the One and the Many.
The challenge is to know ourselves to be microcosms,
containing all the richness of creation,
and brimming over with the fullness of Christic love.

By meditating upon the Zodiac
a pattern slowly emerges.
The rudiments of a Cosmic Dance is unveiled,
and we are invited to move in rhythm with it.
Here, in embryo, is the adventure of a lifetime.
The sacred dance which takes us deeper into the mystery
of the One and the many.

For some the dance is a simple one,
and they slip into it effortlessly.
But for most of us it is a complex one,
where we have to struggle even to master the basic steps.

The dance is all about letting go,
being open to, and knowing,
the powers of creation,
without being overwhelmed by them.

It is the Dance of Love.

It is movement towards the single point,★
towards The ONE,
where, en route, we encounter the Many,
and thus learn to see the many in The One
and the One in the many.

It is the Dance of Harmony,
that celebrates the Fullness of creation.

It is the Dance of Sophia
when Divinity becomes All in all.

The rhythm is never easy to get into.
The Dance is full of risks,
for the paths to Wholeness are many,
and mistakes have to be embraced and honoured
as integral parts of our salvation.
We run the risks involved in the story of King Solomon,
who, in his quest for Wisdom,
became infatuated with many gods and goddesses,
and was seduced by some of them.
In the eyes of some he may have failed,
but unlike the majority,
he did not shy away from
the Challenge of the Gods and Goddesses.

★ The Greek word *hamartia* means missing the mark or the point, as with an archer missing the bull's eye. The New Testament uses this word for sin, not in a moral sense but in the sense of failing to be focused on The One. It means missing the vital centre and focusing, instead, on a part of the Whole, which can so easily lead to division and fragmentation. When this happens we become alienated from the Source.

7. Sophia: The Quest for Unity

I shall not argue with the contemporary opponents of religion, because they are right... the contemporary state of religion calls for rejection, because our religion is not what it ought to be.

Speaking generally and abstractly, religion is the connection of humanity and the world with the absolute principle and focus of all that exists. Clearly, if we admit the reality of such an absolute principle, it must determine all the interests and the whole content of human life and consciousness....Only then can unity, wholeness and harmony appear in human life... If the religious principle is admitted at all, it must certainly possess such all-embracing, central significance.   (*Lectures on Divine Humanity*, Vladimir Soloviev, p. 1)

The Sophianic Ideal

Sophia, the most exalted Divine Mother Wisdom, the All-Encompassing Form, One with Divinity from all Eternity and One with creation for all time. She is the living soul of nature and cosmos, the absolute unity of all that is. Like the ray of light proceeding from a single point, Sophia extends to every dimension of life. Having oneness with the Source of life, Sophia unites to it all that is. Her motto is profound in its simplicity, viz. 'I join all things'. Sophia, the love of The One for the many, the love of The All for the all. She is the Primordial Unity of the Cosmos, the Harmony which is the innate quality of Femininity. Only in Her spaciousness can balance be achieved between opposites, and hence the reconciliation which is the goal of creation. Sophia, the Divine and cosmic yearning for union and ecstasy. It is Her kiss that awakens in us the true desire for wholeness and holiness. It is Her beauty that calls us to become that which we contemplate. It is her splendour that draws us into deeper union with the Divine.

A superficial glance at the above words from our Divine liturgy can easily give the impression that Sophia is all that matters in our spirituality. In fact, one of the criticisms most often levelled against Sophia, and by association against Sophiology, is that She swamps everything with Her presence. Even the Divine Trinity, it is argued, pales into insignificance, when compared to Her. I can only imagine that those who promulgate this belief do so out of ignorance of Sophianic reality. Sophia does not seek Her own glory. She is pure transparency on every level of creation. As the Seat of the Divine Trinity, for example, Sophia mirrors to us the mystery of intra-divine life. She is the Understanding that is our initiation into Divine knowledge. This knowledge is ultimately not only about belief but is also about our participation in the drama of divine love.

Sophia is the Divine Ideal that, one day, creation, in all her aspects, will radiate with divine light, its Sophianic glory. The Eastern Church calls this *theosis*, the process whereby every part of creation (with homo sapiens as its pinnacle) grows into the Divine, the movement where contemplation becomes participation, the mystery of humanity's elevation into the Divine life. It is the sacred union of the Divine and human, our Sophianic nature perfected. It is the marriage celebrated in the person of Christ, the perfect 'Divine-human', the union that we, in turn, are called upon to realize in human history.

Because of our Sophianic nature, the Divine and human can never again be treated in isolation. They belong together. What the Divine has joined together, no one may separate — not even the theologian! This bond between the Creator and creation is not limited to a disembodied realm but embraces the holiness of 'the flesh'. Because of Wisdom incarnate, Sophia-Christ, matter becomes the vehicle of the Creator's will and purpose. Nature is divine, humanity a Divine temple. A genuinely incarnational spirituality empowers individuals to acts that help transform the world, the realization of Sophia as Perfect Humanity, the Divine-human ideal. No longer can we distance ourselves from the world, taking refuge in an illusory 'inner-life' or in a utopian dream. Genuine mystical experiences of Divine joy and Bliss plunge us deeper into the world, and we become urgently aware of all that makes for alienation and separation, the evil that is the culminative effect of sinful humanity, its prejudices and weaknesses, its anger and hatred, its spiteful projections and vain, often perverse, illusions. In a sentence, the fruits of pride and arrogance, of human egotism.

The will-to-power

There is nothing romantic in following a Sophianic spirituality. Initiation into the Way of Sophia-Christ demands absolute commitment. It entails learning to live with the pain of rejection as much as the pleasure of union. It means living in the real world of struggle and imperfection and embracing its secularity to the full. There is no room for those who want to hide behind a religious veneer. Sophia's call to justice is to be heard in the midst of the hustle and bustle of every-day life. Not in churches and temples, chapels and mosques, synagogues and meditation halls but 'on the heights along the way, where the paths meet, beside the gates leading into the city' (Proverbs 8:2-3). Serving Sophia-Christ means confronting the reality of power in all its guises. It means facing up to and being able to withstand the full effects of the abuse of power. Exposing the false centres of meaning (or idols) that human beings create in order to give a sense of purpose to often empty and meaningless lives. By doing this we usurp the sovereignty of El Elyon, the Transcendent One. The religious instinct is problematic. It can be used or channelled to serve the Truth as well as to hinder its realization. The following example from the Judeo-Christian Scriptures bears witness to dynamics that are at work in this and every age. It is a salutary warning.

A religion developed in ancient Israel which transferred the honour due to El Elyon to Yhwh's 'chosen people', who were originally one divine 'son' or 'offspring' among many. 'If you obey Yhwh our Elohim, he will set you high above all the nations of the earth' (Deuteronomy 28:1), thus giving them praise, honour and fame, qualities which belong to El Elyon alone. Absolute power was consequently appropriated by a section of society for its own use. What's more, the kings of the earth are warned that they must serve this kind of deity with fear, for his 'wrath' can flare up at any moment. It should come as no surprise to learn that some of the heavenly Elohim opposed the plans that this deity had for Israel's future!

We live in a world of power brokers of one kind or another. Monotheistic religions have proved an ideal and popular breeding ground for 'power deities' over the centuries. Psalm 110 is a classical example of the will-to-power at its most perverse. It describes the actions of a power-mad and angry nationalistic deity, who even punishes his own people if they offend him. It sings the praises of a god who makes his enemies his footstool, showing them no mercy, and thereby extending his mighty sceptre from Zion. He thus crushes kings and rulers on the day of his wrath. He eventually judges the nations, finally heaping up their dead. A system of worldly power always benefits from a system of religious justification. It is good to know that 'God is on our side'. The author of this psalm (or a later editor) even mentions the person of Melchizedek (who does not belong to this narrow and aggressive theological tradition) in his efforts to legitimize, and gain prestige for, the actions of his deity.

Lest anyone think that an angry, jealous and vindictive deity is only to be found in the Older Testament, where 'his' cruelty abounds, 'he' is very much part of the Christian and Muslim world as well. In the Book of Revelation, for example, the message to the Church in Thyatira (in present-day Turkey) is delivered by a being whose 'eyes are like blazing fire and whose feet are like burnished bronze' (2:18). It was this angry deity who struck dead the children of the harlot Jezebel, and, after dashing its enemies to pieces like pottery, granted his followers 'authority over them, ruling them with an iron sceptre' (2:22). A deity like this is never short of followers. It is a perverted kind of deity, however, that requires a violent act of power of this kind to fulfil its purposes. No matter how evil or cruel kings or rulers can be (and the twentieth century has witnessed some of the most horrific atrocities in human history), if that which professes to be the ultimate in life can find no better response to evil than fighting evil with evil, is it any wonder that many choose not to give their allegiance to such a monstrous creation. What is disturbing is the fact that countless religious people, of all persuasions, continue to follow such a deity — and devoutly so!

This is not the action of 'the God and Father of Jesus Christ. The Christ of Calvary chose not to act in this power-mad and angry manner during his life and crucifixion. Strange that He should revert to sub-human behaviour after his glorious ascension! The message of The Cross remains alien to many Christians and non-Christians alike. Ironically, to spread the message of the 'Prince of Peace', early European missionaries and evangelists turned Christ into a new version of a 'power god'. In fact, many pagans became Christians because Christ was seen as being more powerful than their own gods, especially in battle. If 'the Christian god, or at least His followers, were seen to be powerless in battle, pagan warriors would not have been impressed with his credentials. Brave and successful Christian kings, however, meant that Christ was the bearer of good fortune and protection. It was Christ who was now in control. He became the supreme cosmic ruler who not only defeats and destroys His enemies in heaven but also on earth. It is little wonder that a pseudo-Christ became the focal point of a new power base, the power of those who claimed that He was the new 'top god', the all-powerful Son who has an even more powerful Father, an All-Mighty Heavenly Monarch.

The will-to-love

Many who have exercised authority and power within Christian institutions down the centuries have found it difficult (and often impossible) to embrace the fact that Christ is the embodiment of Divine, and not worldly, power and wisdom. Many find it difficult to surrender to the fact that 'righteousness', according to Christ, is based on humility and not power. It has never been easy to serve Divinity defined as love (1 John 4:16). It is a vulnerable and risky business, but it is still the only hope for our world in the twenty-first century. This is why immature and sub-human concepts of divinity must be exposed as lies. In Wisdom we have been given an insight into the heart of the Divine nature. That heart is love, a serving, sacrificial and tragic love. The trinitarian dynamics that speak of a divinity made up of a passionate yearning for the well-being of 'the other', rules out the idea of a religion based on the relationship between the Divine and human as one of slavery and dependence, and justifies instead the freedom and dignity of the human being. This is why the Divine Glory entered into Christ incognito and in humility, in order to preserve both Divine and human sovereignty. True divinity knows of no other way of being-in-the-world, least of all of ways that would draw attention to itself, i.e. a show of one kind of power or another.

Wisdom crucified and sacrificed calls every human expression and manifestation of power into question. Every human act and institution is laid bare by the 'non-power' of love. Every definition of what is meant by being rich, wealthy, successful, strong and wise is held up to the closest scrutiny. This is no neurotic worship of everything that is weak and ineffectual. On the contrary, Wisdom judges everything that humans can use (poverty being no exception) as means of manipulating each other. The Way of Crucifixion challenges the authenticity of everyone who claims to speak with reason and understanding [i.e. knowledge of all kind] and all efforts at handling power, in particular in the name of truth or progress or the Kingdom of Heaven. Every aspect of human life and culture is measured in relation to the humility of the Crucified One, El Elyon unveiled. Every claim to ultimacy is tested by the Sign of Contradiction, wherein lies the only assurance that Wisdom will never again be misused or abused. These are fourfold in nature, and include:

> Our human origins and past history and thus the power of human traditions to shape our lives. The memories, both mythical and historical, that seek to give meaning to us but only in relation to the past.

> Our future orientation and the often conflicting solutions that purport to fashion the future for us, e.g. utopian schemes, Messianism, socialism etc.

> Our ability to transcend history and reach for the skies; the yearning for mystical experiences, apocalyptic visions or immersion in an abstract or timeless state of being, be it 'outer' or 'inner'.

> Our reaching out into the whole cosmos, in order to observe its order and harmony, or to contemplate its beauty and wisdom, as well as to analyse its different levels or dimensions of being.

It is of the essence of the way of crucified or 'non-power' kind of love, that it dismantles and renders harmless all human efforts to grasp Wisdom in order to use it to serve selfish human ends, the grasping which lies at the heart of the human weakness for self-justification and self-aggrandizement, the need to use aspects of creation in order to prove that 'I am somebody', that 'I have power', that 'I have understanding'. In and through the wisdom of crucifixion (which is the way of humble and healing love), power and knowledge are forever changed and transformed. In traditional religious language they are redeemed. This is henceforth the true reflection of Divinity, namely Christ, the power and wisdom of El Elyon (1 Corinthians 1:24).

The Way of Humility and Self-Sacrifice. Christ made use of neither power nor knowledge in order that both can become instruments of non-power, servants of a self-emptying, sacrificial and forgiving love. All genuine spirituality must consequently manifest a lifestyle built on the way of a wisdom that seeks the empowerment of individuals and not their submission to a false idea of divinity and the institutions that serve such a divinity.

A Universal Creed?

Abraham has always been a hero of mine, ever since I first heard stories about him and the other patriarchs and matriarchs in the Bible. Abraham, the paradoxical one, the stranger who emerges from among 'the peoples' (i.e. Gentiles or non-Jews), to be the Father of Israel and also a Mediator of blessing for all the peoples of the earth. The Divine Blessing given to Abraham extends to all humanity. Abraham, Hagar and Sara, his wives, are to be the new beginning of a history of hope, and not curses, for a transformed humanity. We see no triumphalism and elitism here. No isolation but faith in an all-embracing future, an ongoing and an open-ended spaciousness.

Abraham was accepted by El Elyon, irrespective of the fact that he was not a Jew. He was allowed to stand in the presence of The Divine One regardless of his particular devotional practices or previous moral standards. Abraham was liberated for all time from the anxiety involved in all human attempts to keep the religious law. Even his shortcomings did not bar him from being showered with Divine Love, for such love can never be ordered or regulated by any human being or institution — however devout! Furthermore, 'the Promised Land was also a Divine gift which cannot be acquired by human effort. Finally, Israel was given a task that it did not ask for. To it was entrusted the privilege, and at times the curse, of spreading among the nations the message of the Universal Fatherhood of El Elyon, a vocation that brought it much pain and anguish. While in a foreign land,

Isaiah of the Exile, after much reflection on the suffering of his people, came to see their humiliation as an integral part of their vocation, as a 'light to lighten the Gentiles' (Isaiah 49.6), to bring the news of salvation to all the earth. Ezra, however, on his return to Jerusalem from exile, promoted an elitist policy, summed up in the words 'Separate yourself from the peoples around you' (Ezra 10:11), the very opposite of the Sophianic ideal of harmony and unity.

The history of all religions (and biblical witness is no exception) displays the tension between a narrow and often aggressively chauvinistic faith and a more universal and inclusive kind of religion. The ancient biblical prophets represent a transitional period between two kinds of spirituality. With them an exclusive national consciousness and identity became more spacious, more open to the universally human. Proudly patriotic, the prophets were, nevertheless, visionaries, who took their message to all, irrespective of race or religion. But not everyone saw their spirituality in such a universal way, as was the case with Ezra. His was a religious ideology closely related to a group or a people's quest for an identity and the power inherent in the search for, and the efforts to protect, this identity. It is a stage in the human search for meaning, especially when that search becomes part of one's struggle for survival. In this context Israel's history is no different from the history of a great deal of early, and indeed current, Christian missionary activity. Both are sustained by a theology that believed their earthly survival and future to be divinely appointed.

When an individual or collective becomes totally preoccupied with its own survival and future [e.g. a nation or a church], it tends to lose sight of 'the other' in any positive way, especially when 'the other' is perceived as being a threat to 'my life', 'my religion' and 'my country'. When this happens, a person has to choose between fighting to survive and possibly having to conquer or 'save' the other (most forms of Christian evangelism are a power trip whose goal is domination), or to retreat from 'the other' altogether and abandon the concerns and challenges of the world. Such individuals end up obsessed with themselves or with other-worldly goals, or both! Divorced from genuine dialogue, a person's attitudes and responses can so easily breed an elitist and exclusivist type of mentality, reflected within one's nationality, political leanings or religious persuasions.

The tension between universalism and particularism will always be a characteristic of human culture. Isaiah of the Outcasts went as far as to declare that the Divine One 'will gather still other peoples beside those already gathered' (56:8). Judaism became for some a universal faith and not an obscure religion of an inward looking people. The Wisdom of Jesus ben Sirach is, in fact, a celebration, by a cosmopolitan Jew, of a religion that he believed was on the same lofty heights as other religions and philosophical movements. At the heart of this religio-philosophical system was the Divine Wisdom.

Abraham's role in Israel's history was used by some, right up to New Testament days, in a narrow and exclusive way. Isaiah of the Outcasts had to confront those who would turn Abraham (as some would do later with Christ), into the figurehead of a narrow religious cult, the leader of an exclusive faith. Isaiah insisted, however, that 'the truly blessed will not bless themselves by Abraham but by the God of Truth' (65:16). In saying this he is not demeaning Abraham but only those who misuse Abrahamic spirituality to serve their own ends. It was to counter this mentality that St John the Baptist, in the tradition of Isaiah of the Outcasts, preached that 'out of these stones El can raise up children for Abraham' (Luke 3:7), when his opponents, in pride and arrogance, maintained that 'we have Abraham as our Father'. This is why the Fourth Gospel speaks as though the Fatherhood of El Elyon was not known in ancient days, e.g. 'No one knows the father except the Son' (Matthew 11:25-30). This is not a new elitism but a counter to the claims of the traditionalists that only they were the true children of Abraham, and hence only they had access to the Divine. Jesus was unequivocal — 'They do not know the One who sent me' (Fourth Gospel 15:21). The Divine loving Father had become a stranger to many. A new revelation was taking place (or the original revelation was shining through once again), which gave hope to a multitude of people who had become so disillusioned in their spirituality that for generations they even doubted whether knowledge of El Elyon was at all possible.

The Son knew the Father in a unique way. It was a message of good news, and the knowledge was available to all, irrespective of their background, knowledge which made them, also, sons and daughters of El Elyon.

Good News

The tradition represented by the likes of Isaiah of the Outcasts came to a climax in the life and teaching of Christ and in the message of St Paul. The universal message of El Elyonic spirituality rang out, again, rooted in the ancient belief that there is 'One Divine being and Father of all, who is over all and through all and in all' (Ephesians 4:6). The parental or caring quality of Divinity was not only the prerogative of the Divine Mother, but motherhood was also a characteristic of The Most High. The love of this Divinity was absolute, unconditional and no respecter of persons. Influenced by the Wisdom tradition, St Paul had become aware of the centrality of Sophia in this all-embracing spirituality. In the past, She had manifested The Divine One in a variety of ways, both through heavenly beings as well as through a variety of wise men and women. This time through Sophia's mediation the Divine was revealed as an incarnated and perfect 'Divine-human' being. Herein lies the secret knowledge of those early Palestinian Christians who were custodians of the ancient El Elyonic tradition. Christ is our Sophia from El (1 Corinthians 1:30), in whom all the treasures of Sophia are manifested, writes St Paul, the One in whom all the fullness of Divinity dwells in bodily form. Christ is the human form of El Elyon, Divine Glory and Beauty incarnated. It is Christ who is the 'Lord' of this tradition, thus usurping the position of Yhwh. It is through His condescension and humility that Christ reasserted the sovereignty of El Elyon as well as the sovereignty of each individual human being. We are all offspring of El Elyon (Galatians 3:26). Paul preached the radical implications of this Divine secret in a world where rival theologies and philosophies, cults and religions, bred division and not unity.

Since there is One Father, 'from whom all things come and for whom we live' (1 Corinthians 8:6), there is one family and therefore the Gentiles are heirs with Israel. They too are given the full riches of complete understanding. They, too, can administer and serve the Righteousness or Justice of El Elyon. Other spiritual traditions excluded the Gentiles from Divine citizenship, giving them no hope. In and through Christic humility, there is through the Spirit one access to Divinity open to all. In fact, one New Humanity has been created out of all opposites which previously had been in conflict, Jew and Gentile, male and female, freedom and slavery, heaven and earth. One New Community, One Mystical Body, One Divine Temple has become a reality for all who serve the Truth, be they Buddhists or Hindus, Muslims or Taoists.

When St Paul came to the end of his message to the Romans, having struggled with the fact that Israel had rejected Christ, he commended the situation to the Divine Sophia. Paul could not fathom how the longed for reconciliation would now come about. Although he could not explain it rationally, Paul still believed that Israel would be part of the universal restoration along with the Gentiles. It was not for him to know the workings of the Divine will, but he had faith that all would be revealed, in time, through the Divine Wisdom. And he uses part of a Wisdom Hymn to seal his message:

> O depth of wealth, wisdom and knowledge in God!
> How unsearchable his judgements,
> How untraceable his ways!
> Who knows the Mind of the Lord?
> Who has been His Counsellor?
> Who has ever made a gift to Him,
> to receive a gift in return?
> Source, Guide and Goal of all that is —
> to Him be Glory for ever!   Amen. (Letter to the Romans 11:33-36)

The Way of Reconciliation

The Ministry of Reconciliation (2 Corinthians 5) is the practical manifestation of St Paul's vision of Sophia-Christ, the most embracing image of All-Unity in heaven and earth that he could imagine. What applies to the firstborn Son of El Elyon applies also to his brothers and sisters. Those who experience this Unity become reconcilers themselves, mediators of the Divine Harmony. This reconciling ministry is so radical that all religious labels cease to have any meaning. Consequently, there are, for example, no 'Christians', or 'Buddhists'. There never can be, at least not by one's own admission. Even to use such words is to go against everything that Christ taught and died for, and the Buddha taught. The Way of reconciliation cannot be labelled, can never become the possession of any one group or religion, no more than Christ can belong exclusively to any one faith, or 'Enlightenment' be the possession of a chosen few. Reconciliation can never be served by 'my Christ', however devoutly one may be drawn to him. 'My Christ' is the Christ of narrow denominationalism and quaint traditionalism, the Christ of misguided exclusivism, triumphalism and of conservative dogma, the petty Christ who has become nothing more than the mascot of competing churches and sects.

The Reconciling One is the Incarnate Lord who came for all people and whose spirit is working in and beyond all religions, the Christ who came to serve everyone and not to create a higher or better or more perfect religion. He is the One who puts an end to all labels, especially ones that speak of 'sacred and profane','us and them', or the 'saved and the damned'. Many religious devotees still refuse to hear this message and continue to make new sacred arrangements for themselves, converting the Wisdom of Crucifixion or Sacrifice into a new religion in the process. Once the Way of Reconciliation speaks of those who are outside as 'non-members, unsaved or ignorant', then it ceases to be the way of reconciliation! Instead, Christ or Buddha becomes a badge of superiority, a sign of power and spiritual one-up-manship. Religion then becomes a barrier between individuals and groups, a sign of division and disharmony. Vladimir Soloviev has this to say on the matter:

> The way to salvation, to the realization of true equality, true liberty and fraternity, is self-denial. But self-denial requires a prior self-assertion. To deny one's own exclusive will, one must first have it. For the particular principles and forces to reunite freely with the absolute principle, they first must have separated from it. They must stand on their own, must aspire to exclusive dominion and absolute significance, for only real experience (where one has come to know thoroughly the contradiction, the radical groundlessness of this self-assertion) can lead to a voluntary self-denial, and to a conscious and free demand for reunification with the absolute principle.   (*Lectures on Divine Humanity*, Vladimir Soloviev, pp. 10-11)

Soloviev's teaching is full of original and challenging insights into the contribution of the Judeo-Christian heritage to the development of the Universal Creed that is still unfolding in our midst, a Creed that in the twentieth century has been greatly enriched by elements from traditional Indian and Oriental faiths.

Sri Ramakrishna (1836-1886), with his doctrine of the Harmony of Religion, made an invaluable contribution as a Hindu to living a spirituality that transcended all faiths. Dr D.T. Suzuki (1870-1996) almost single-handedly introduced Zen Buddhism to the West. Though not a priest in any Buddhist sect, he was honoured in every temple in Japan for the wealth of his spiritual experience and knowledge, Sri Aurobindo (1872-1950) developed a system of yoga that brings the different traditional approaches to the Divine into an integrated whole. The wisdom that his synthesis imparts has been an indispensable tool in my own spiritual discipline for nearly twenty years. Twentieth century-Christianity has not been lacking in pioneers of the emerging Universal Creed. Three in particular remain a constant source of inspiration to me. Dom Bede Griffiths (1906-1993) was an English Benedictine monk who pioneered a Hindu style of Christian monasticism. His Ashram in Tamil Nadu (founded in 1950) became a centre where people of different religions could meet together in an atmosphere of prayer, and grow together towards the Unity in Truth which is the final goal of all religions. Thomas Merton (1915-1968) was an American Trappist monk, committed to the rigours of the Cistercian lifestyle. Before his premature death at fifty-three, he had become deeply committed to world peace, ecumenism and the coming together of Eastern and Western religions. His wide knowledge of Zen Buddhism and Taoism opened up for him new and often unexpected ways of thinking about and experiencing Divine reality. Finally, the life of a Russian Orthodox, Fr Alexander Mem (1935-1990), as a priest grew while under the yoke of Soviet Communism. Influenced by the Russian Sophianists, especially the writings of Vladimir Soloviev, Fr Mem was martyred for his devotion to the Universal Christ. He not only embraced Christians of all traditions without discrimination — 'our walls of divisions do not rise to heaven,' he would say — but was open to the truth in other religions. His faith led him into dialogue not only with atheists but also with open enemies of Christianity. He was severely criticized by the conservative wing of his Church for not conforming to certain expected conventions of Orthodox churchmanship.

The Way of Reconciliation rests on our ability to be with, and for 'the other'. Its authenticity is judged by the way that others see it practised and lived. Working for reconciliation celebrates the surrender of all 'power games' and 'trips', especially theological and ecclesiastical ones. 'Being there' redefines the relationship between individuals of different belief systems, because it means being genuinely engaged by the faith of 'the other'. It means dialogue and not monologue and the ability really to listen to what the other has to say. The latter is no longer there to be saved, a challenge to overcome and conquer. Such a thought is the product of a mentality (perverse, especially when introduced into religion) that needs conquests in order to live and have meaning. People devoid of genuine spirituality are always greedy for success, especially if it can be cloaked in a veneer of religiosity. Traditional evangelism has always provided an ideal way of gaining power and prestige. Such arrogance, especially when sanctioned theologically, breeds the very opposite of Christic qualities of compassion, humility and forbearance. Reconciliation means taking risks for the sake of the Truth, and therefore surrendering the often neurotic need to keep going on and on about 'my belief', and consequently not feeling threatened by the other's faith. Genuine encounters can only take place within an atmosphere of openness and freedom. It means therefore being prepared to be misunderstood, being vulnerable and, at times, being hurt. This is why forgiveness is the life-blood of those who live reconciliation. Forgiveness is unconditional love being honoured even when one feels most wounded or wronged. It can only be truly exercised reciprocally and not hierarchically. It must always be spontaneous and not the prerogative of a religious elite. No one controls forgiveness.

The more one grows in divine humility and in the reality of unconditional love (a process that lasts a lifetime), the more alien becomes the idea of 'taking Christ' or His message to so-called non-believers! Divine love is already at work in the world, in history, in individual lives. No person needs to 'take it' anywhere. It is sheer presumptuousness to think that anyone can be in charge of it. This idea is based on the false assumption that non-Christians do not live in communion with the Divine, but exist, somehow, apart from the presence of the Divine Spirit. And yet many of them (including those who regard themselves as not being religious) can clearly be seen to manifest the fruits of the Spirit in their lives, namely 'love, joy, peace, patience, kindness, goodness, faithfulness, gentleness, and self-control' (Galatians 5:22-23). No one has a monopoly of the fruits of the Spirit, be they religious or not. Every encounter between individuals is pregnant with the Truth. Every meeting can be a new revelation of the way that Divine love works.

What happens to 'my' tradition within the context of a reconciling lifestyle? Should we abandon our personal discipline and devotion for what might be a more inclusive form of worship? Maybe a sacred space more suitable for all religions (and none!) is more appropriate? But the person who devalues his or her own spirituality is unlikely to honour another's. Reconciliation is not about producing a perfect synthesis of religious and spiritual practices. It is about being with others in an atmosphere of mutual trust, friendship and exploration of the Truth. It is only when we are faithful to that which is genuinely divine in our own tradition that we can share with another on his or her spiritual journey.

Christ said, 'When you pray, go into your room, close the door and pray to your Father, who is unseen' (Matthew 6:6). Christ reminds us in these words that at the heart of true spirituality is a person's inner or esoteric relationship with the Divine. It is hidden and veiled, like the intimacy between lovers. It is to be honoured by all and not violated. It is therefore very special when an individual invites another to share sacred space. Both become part of something totally new that will gradually unfold in their midst. One cannot set out to create a sacred space to suit all spiritual tastes. It is the fruit of genuine sharing and growing in the Truth. It is the celebration of true love in action.

Apocatastasis

No limits can be set on love or sacrifice. Renouncing oneself in order to live again in the other — such is the bliss of love. He who loves another loves the Cross as well, since love is sacrificial. Love itself. God, in the Eternal Cross, surrenders Himself for the sake of His love…The bliss of divine love is the sacrificial bliss of the Cross, and its power is a sacrificial power.   (*A Bulgakov Anthology*, p. 171)

The ultimate test of whether one truly believes these words to be true or not, is in relation to the question of whether the loving power of Divine love will have the final word in the history of the universe, or whether the forces of evil will triumph. Some of the greatest teachers in the history of Christianity, among them St Gregory of Nyssa and Fr Bulgakov, believed passionately that Divine love will completely restore (apocatastasis) all things to their divine status at the end of time — including Satan! Sergei Bulgakov writes:

The fullness of the apocatastasis presupposes not only the annulment of the cosmic minus that was introduced by Satan but also the participation of all creation in this new being.

(*Apocatastasis and Transfiguration*, p. 24)

These Christian sages had absolute trust in the reality that St Paul's words celebrate in his Hymn to Love in the First Letter to the Corinthians, viz. 'Love never fails. .it always protects, always trusts, always hopes, always perseveres' (13:7-8). It is the power of this love that Sophianic spirituality never grows tired of celebrating. Consider the words of Hugh of St Victor:

You have great power, O Love; you alone could draw God down from heaven to earth. O how strong is your bond with which even God could be bound. You brought him bound with your chains, you brought him wounded with your arrows…you wounded him who was invulnerable, you bound him who was invincible, you drew down him who is immovable, the Eternal you made mortal…O Love, how great is your victory.

('Symbols of Transformation', *Collected Works of Carl G. Jung, Volume 5*, p. 63

Not to believe in the final triumph of this love makes a mockery of the Good News celebrated in the New Testament. All of creation is to be reconciled together in and through the power of sacrificial love (Colossians 1:20, Ephesians 1:10), in order that the Divine One will be all in all (1 Corinthians 15:28). Mainstream Christian doctrine does not appear to believe in the Totality or Harmony of the Divine Rule of Love, or Universal deification, as Orthodoxy calls it. Traditional dogma maintains that hell is eternal. In its opinion there are aspects of evil that can never be redeemed or made whole. Such evil is destined to eternal damnation and suffering. Such a belief is, in the last resort, unbelief in the power of Crucifixion, and faith, instead, in the power of Evil. Divine love is the ultimate sign of the triumph of Divine Order and not the concept of an eternity of torments. Herein lies one of the greatest contradictions in traditional

Christian dogma. This arises because, in the words of Bulgakov

> To evil is attributed a depth equal to that of good, and to hell is attributed a depth equal to that
> of heaven. But evil...does not exist in and by itself but is extinguished when it is separated from
> being... Evil does not have depth. Evil is exhaustible and exhausts itself, and at a certain stage
> of the ripeness of being, evil inevitably becomes completely impotent. It becomes totally
> exhausted and disenchanted in itself.   *Apocatastasis and Transfiguration,* pp. 26-27

Even at the heart of hell, Bulgakov reminds us, the power of Love is present. Even Satan cannot fully eradicate the remembrance of his state before The Fall, when he was a creature of Light in the Divine Assembly. It is this memory, says Bulgakov, that burns within him, forever purifying all efforts to eradicate it and blow it out. The torments of hell are torments of love, of the love of Satan for his Creator. Satan knows of the Sophianic foundation of creation, of the eternal bond between the Divine and human, the bond embodied in 'the Word made flesh'. Bulgakov sums up:

> This memory enrages him...is the main source of his...frenzied struggle with his own nature,
> the desire to reject and forget his own nature, to replace it with...but with what? With emptiness.
>
> Strange to say this memory makes of him both tempter and tempted. He cannot remain
> indifferent, calmly contemptuous of the appearance of Christ in the world. He loves even the
> holy angels and saintly ones with hate, for hate is the language of love, until this hate manifests
> its true nature in the invincibility and indestructibility of love for what is higher than it. This
> 'memory' is the hand of the Creator's help, which can never be taken away, even from
> rebellious creation.   (pp. 29,30)

The New Ascesis

1.   Not by the Vedas, or an austere life, or gifts to the poor, or ritual offerings can I be seen as
        thou hast seen me. Only by love can individuals see me, and know me, and come unto me. He
        or she who works for me, who loves me, whose End Supreme I am, free from attachment to
        all things, and with love for all creation, he or she in truth comes unto me.

                                                                    (*The Bhagavad Gita,* ll:53-55)

The new ascesis is the ascesis of Divine Love, the creative love that moulds every aspect of creation into one harmonious whole, where homo sapiens is sovereign, the transforming love that enables each person 'to work on oneself' (ascesis), the effort needed that brings about self-mastery. It is the acqusition of true knowledge, or gnosis, that enables men and women to fulfil their potential as mediators or reconcilers within society and human history. Soloviev writes:

> Our personal concern... is a common concern of the whole world, the realization and
> individualization of the unity-of-the-all idea and the spiritualization of matter. It is prepared by
> the cosmic process in the world of nature, and is continued and completed by the historical
> process in humanity.
>
> The idea of unity-of-the-all can finally be realized or embodied only in the fullness of
> completed individualities; this means that the final end of the whole matter is the higher
> development of each individuality in the fullest unity of all.

                                            (*The Meaning of Love,* Vladimir Soloviev, p. 105)

It is the discipline which is the privilege of living the sacredness of Nature in every aspect of life. No longer is it a question of weakening the flesh but of strengthening the spirit for the flesh's transfiguration. No more a neurotic detachment from Mother Nature but her hallowing and perfecting. Instead of destroying or seeking to conquer Nature, the challenge is to raise Nature to divinity. It is part of one's Sophianic vocation to work actively for the reunion of Divinity and Nature, in order that all of creation can become the living body and temple of Wisdom. This is why for Soloviev prayer was an intimate activity which helped to deepen and strengthen the bond between the Creator and creation. The life-blood of such prayer is love. Soloviev never tired of pointing out the mystical significance of love. It is the power that characterizes not only interpersonal relationships but also our relationship with the whole universe, the cosmic environment. Love creates spiritual energies which transform the cosmos itself. Through prayer one loves and links the essences of 'the other' to oneself. One becomes prayer, a growing chain or link in the Sophianic bond of being, uniting Divinity to Nature in all her aspects. As prayer grows, each praying heart becomes more and more spacious with love for creation. A boundless feeling of compassion seizes the heart once one has been struck with Divine Love. Every act of love becomes an act of worship, an offering to the Divine, a Eucharist, a Thanksgiving. One's whole life becomes a celebration of the union between heaven and earth, for earth must be penetrated by heaven and not be ignored or rejected. This truth is one of the great gifts of Russian spirituality to the West, expressed beautifully by Dostoyevsky in *The Brothers Karamazov*. It is a passage worth quoting in full, a liturgical expression of the magick of the Sophianic Age:

Something glowed in Alyosha's heart, something filled it suddenly till it ached, tears of ecstasy were welling up from his soul.. .He stretched out his hands, uttered a cry and woke up... he went out of the cell.

He did not stop on the steps, but went down rapidly. His soul overflowing with rapture, was craving for freedom and unlimited pace. The vault of heaven, studded with softly shining stars, stretched wide and vast over him. From the zenith to the horizon the Milky Way stretched its two arms dimly across the sky. The fresh, motionless, still night enfolded the earth. The white towers and golden domes of the cathedral gleamed against the sapphire sky. The gorgeous autumn flowers in the beds near the house went to sleep till morning. The silence of the earth seemed to merge into the silence of the heavens, the mystery of the earth came in contact with the mystery of the stars. Alyosha stood, gazed, and suddenly he threw himself own flat upon the earth.

He did not know why he was embracing it. He could not have explained to himself why he longed so irresistibly to kiss it, to kiss it all, but he kissed it weeping, sobbing and drenching it with his tears, and vowed frenziedly to love it, to love it for ever and ever. 'Water the earth with the tears of your gladness and love those tears,' it rang in his soul. What was he weeping over? Oh, he was weeping in his rapture even over those stars which were shining for him from the abyss of space and 'he was not ashamed of that ecstasy'. It was as though the threads from all those innumerable worlds of God met all at once in his soul, and it was trembling all over 'as it came in contact with other worlds'. He wanted to forgive everyone and for everything, and to beg forgiveness — oh! not for himself, but for all men, for all and for everything, 'and others are begging for me,' it echoed in his soul again. But with every moment he felt clearly and almost palpably that something firm and immovable, like the firmament itself, was entering his soul. A sort of idea was gaining an ascendancy over his mind — and that for the rest of his life, for ever and ever. He had fallen upon the earth a weak youth, but he rose from it a resolute fighter for the moment of his rapture. And never, never for the rest of his life could Alyosha forget that moment. 'Someone visited my soul at that hour!' he used to say afterwards with firm faith in his words ....

Three days later he left the monastery in accordance with the words of his late elder, who had bidden him 'sojourn in the world'.   (pp. 426-427)

Creation is a living organism, an icon of Divine Wisdom. She is a living, breathing sacrament, a means of Grace. Every aspect of Mother Nature is a manifestation, a sign, of the sacred marriage between heaven and earth. It is because of the Sophianic principle that Divinity extends to the lowest and most easily denigrated dimension of creation. The world thus becomes a cosmic temple, in which men and women can exercise their universal priesthood, as priests and priestesses of Sophia, Divine Beauty preparing the world to become the new earth. It is this beauty, according to Dostoyevsky, that will save the world.

2.   It cannot be seen. It cannot be heard.
        Yet it cannot be exhausted by use.
                    (*Tao Te Ching* 35)
Within the Christian Scriptures, it is in the Fourth Gospel that we encounter teaching that comes to us from the sublime heights of mystical theology. In view of the fact that the Divine One is Spirit, the question it asks of the reader is this:'What kind of worshippers (or servants) does the Divine seek?' The answer? 'Those who worship in Spirit and in truth' (John 4:23-24). This Spirit of Truth is like the wind, 'it blows wherever it pleases. You hear its sounds but you cannot tell where it comes from or where it is going' (John 3:8). It is the Divine Spirit 'that guides us into all Truth' (John 16:17). No one religion has a monopoly on the Truth. It is by the action of the Spirit that we receive Enlightenment, the Spirit that leads us to the mystical heart of all religions. It is through her that Divine beauty radiates, not only in Nature but also in the world's holy books and sacred writings. She is the Goodness that nourishes all those who partake of Her Wisdom.

I never underestimate the gift and privilege of being able to hold in my hands the spiritual heritage of the world's religions, the treasures of those who, in past centuries, sought the Truth and found it. I still find it a deeply moving experience to read the pages of these Scriptures or to be able to look at paintings and sculptures that enable me to become part of the Truth which they embody or point towards. Thomas Merton, while visiting the site of ancient monasteries and shrines during a visit to Sri Lanka (Ceylon), came across a number of famous carved figures of the Buddha. I hope one day to follow in his steps. Here is his account of what he saw:

> The path dips down to Gal Vihara: a wide, quiet hollow, surrounded with trees. A low outcrop of rock, with a cave cut into it, and beside the cave a big seated Buddha on the left, and Ananda, I guess, standing by the head of the reclining Buddha. The vicar general [i.e. of Merton's Order], shying away from 'paganism', hangs back and sits under a tree reading the guidebook. I am able to approach the Buddhas barefoot and undisturbed, my feet in wet grass, wet sand. Then the silence of the extraordinary faces. The great smiles. Huge and yet subtle. Filled with every possibility, questioning nothing, knowing everything, rejecting nothing, the peace not of emotional resignation but of [That] which has seen through every question without trying to discredit anyone or anything, without establishing some other argument, for the doctrinaire, the mind that needs well-established positions, such peace, such silence, can be frightening. I was knocked over with a rush of relief and thankfulness at the obvious clarity of the figures, the clarity and fluidity of shape and line... Looking at these figures I was suddenly, almost forcibly, jerked clean out of the habitual, half-tied vision of things, and an inner clearness, clarity, as if exploding from the rocks themselves, became evident and obvious... The thing about all this is that there is no puzzle, no problem, and really no 'mystery'. All problems are resolved and everything is clear... I don't know when in my life I have ever had such a sense of beauty and spiritual validity running together in one aesthetic illumination.   (pp. 95, 96)

This, and similar writings, form part of our Third Testament, contemporary sacred texts that are themselves witnesses to the continued presence of the life-giving Spirit. The new ascesis celebrates the privilege of working together to fashion a liturgy that honours the many faces of the Wisdom that lies at the heart of our global spiritual heritage. It also encourages the critical exploration of different traditions, in particular comparative religious studies. This is no romantic exercise designed to produce an idealized 'one world' type of religion. Such a mentality implies that distinctive aspects of different religions can be subordinated to an individual or a group's theory or blueprint of what an all-embracing religion should be. There are real and concrete differences between the world's religions. Some appear insurmountable even when confronting such fundamental questions as the meaning of Ultimate reality. But new aspects of Truth are emerging all the time in many disciplines. The twenty-first century may witness the emergence of the likes of Sri Aurobindo and Vladimir Soloviev and in all the major world religions, in order that new theological truths can be revealed, or old ones seen in a new way. This is the way of the Kingdom of Heaven, where 'every teacher of the law who has received instruction is like the owner of a house who brings out of his or her storeroom treasures new as well as old' (Matthew 13:52).

There is a wealth of material on hand, not only for strictly academic purposes, but also as nourishment for those who feel they belong to a new and emerging spirituality. For many of his contemporaries, Bishop John Robinson's most important book after *Honest to God* was *Truth is Two-Eyed* (1979). In it he explores the multi-faceted traditions of Hinduism and the person of Christ within Indian religion. He does this in order to help liberate Westerners from the cultural and religious conditioning that in fact distorts the way that many of them perceive the Truth. Forever the radical, Bishop Robinson knew that 'to plead for a two-eyed vision of reality carries with it a challenge, explicitly to any kind of exclusivism and implicitly to any claim to uniqueness' (ix). This is an earth-shattering declaration, especially to those who have taken the finality of Christ and Christianity, or Buddha and Buddhism, for example, too much for granted. Bishop Robinson remains one of a special group of teachers whose writings can provide guidance for those spiritual seekers who are genuinely committed to an ecumenical (oikumene = of the world) spirituality in the twenty-first century, not the pseudo-ecumenism that is an offspring of a decaying Christianity that is only interested in spreading its own version of the Truth.

It is Klaus Klostermaier's book, however, (*Hindu and Christian in Vrindaban*, 1969) that for me embodies the hope and spirit of the discipline that Sophianic ascesis demands of Her lovers in the new millennium. He sums up the challenge aptly with these words:

> The truth must be suffered. Truth challenges. One has to surrender to truth — truth is like a gigantic wheel which, once set in motion, smashes anyone who does not follow the movement. Strangely enough, truth is never agreeable… Dialogue challenges both partners, takes them out of the security of their own prisons their philosophy and theology have built for them, confronts them with reality, with truth; a truth that cannot be carried home black on white, a truth that demands all… Dialogue in depth shatters the self-confidence of those who regard themselves as guardians of the whole and only truth. Truth has to be searched for in order to be had: the Kingdom of God is arriving, and only those who are on their way will reach it. (pp. 102-103)

3.   The new Christian thought — and the emergence of such is a necessity if Christianity is not doomed to death — will apprehend the relation between the divine and the human in a different way. (*Truth and Revelation*, Nicolas Berdyaev, p. 123)

The search for, and growth in, the Truth is never easy. It is often the stuff of controversy and disagreement, conflict and debate. Integral to this process is the fact that, following more profound theological reflection on

Divine reality, sterile dogmatic patterns of thought and doctrine must regularly be discarded. Theories that may have seemed right in one age suddenly appear totally meaningless in another. This process has been going on in the life of the Church since its inception. During the lifetime of the first followers of Christ, for example, it was a core belief that Christ would usher in the new heaven on earth. He clearly did not. Furthermore, Christ would return soon, in person, to reign in His full glory. He didn't! The Church, however, did not disappear. It adapted very quickly and discarded the idea of Christ's immediate appearing and re-formulated it. Some looked to the distant future for Christ's 'Second Coming'. Others celebrated 'the gift of Eternal Life' in the present, while some highlighted the regular sacramental coming or presence of Christ in the bread and the wine.

Or take another problematic piece of doctrine that has been around for centuries, namely the penal and legal element in the Western Church's teaching on the meaning of the Cross. It has been like a spiritual cancer eating away at the Good News of Christian revelation. The Eastern Church has always had a more positive view of the redemptive process. The Divine honour, quite simply, is not insulted by human sin. It responds to it with an infinite source of mercy and compassion. The Heavenly Parent is no proud monarch who demands the discharge of a debt payment for damages done to its will. But even when the Western Church did begin to re-think about the relation between the Divine and human, it took the even more ludicrous step of propounding a doctrine that still insisted on the payment of a ransom, but this time to Satan! Theologians should not be afraid of admitting that the Church often makes mistakes, even in key aspects of doctrine. It is time to grow up theologically. Salvation cannot be understood in legal terminology. Christ's coming was not as a reparation for sin nor as the offering of a ransom. Christ's coming is a continuation of the creation of the world. Salvation is the attainment of perfection, the awakening of the divine element in homo sapiens and its union with the Divine. What's more, salvation will never fully be realized without the creative response of each human being to the Divine initiative. Divinity looks to humanity to complete the full revelation of salvation itself, since homo sapiens is the mediator between the Creator and the cosmos.

Our way of perceiving the Truth is changing all the time. We can now look back at key figures in the development of Christian doctrine and see how cultural and religious factors affected their personalities and consequently their way of 'doing theology'. We can also appreciate how some individuals were so in tune with Divine Truth that they managed to transcend their cultural conditioning. St Gregory of Nyssa was one of those spiritually minded people who live before their time. He was the greatest philosopher among the early Church Fathers and he endeavoured to raise the dignity of the human being. But he had few followers. His views made little headway in early Christian theology. Nicolas Berdyaev says of him: 'His doctrine of man was the most exalted in the history of Christian thought, and his spirituality anticipates the whole history of Christian mysticism' (*The Divine and the Human*, pp. 186-187). High praise indeed. And yet St Gregory's understanding of human sexuality, for example, was clouded by his fear of the flesh (he denied that Adam and Eve had had sexual intercourse in the Garden of Eden) although his attitude was not as neurotic as many of his contemporaries. We are contradictory beings and many of the most revered teachers in all religions are no exception. In fact, truth often emerges in spite of human contradictoriness. It is often individuals with great personal hang-ups who make important discoveries in all areas of life, including very often in theology and philosophy. Through their writings, many who become 'saints' become an open book, their souls laid bare for all to see. We can observe their inner struggles and see their excesses and errors as well as their unique insights and creativity. We think of Paul, prophet of the Universal Christ, who could not exorcise himself of the idea that pure Divine love also contained anger and wrath. He also had strong elitist tendencies. In some passages he teaches that 'in Christ all will be brought to life' (1 Corinthians 15:22), while later on he qualifies this by referring to those 'who belong to Christ' (v. 25). Even a St Paul had limited understanding in some theological matters. The new ascesis invites us to honour the truth even when it appears in individuals who often failed to integrate the knowledge acquired into a more wholesome personality or balanced theology. Now is the time for the Church Fathers to learn from the Mothers! While acknowledging that the former were limited in their knowledge of certain aspects of personal and interpersonal dynamics, no holistic Western spiritual psychology can develop unless it is firmly rooted within the original esoteric core of Christian Wisdom. This tradition lives on within Eastern Orthodoxy.

Finally, in order to be fully open to the Truth, wherever we may encounter it, it is important to be aware of the tendency in religious and theological debate, to 'take sides', to polarize the situation under examination by regarding the search for the Truth as a contest in which one side will inevitably win and the other will be beaten and defeated. Truth is not served in this way. This happened in one of the greatest theological controversies ever to arise in the Western Church, namely the clash between Pelagius (350-418), a Celtic lay scholar and free-thinker, and Augustine (354-430), one of the Fathers of Latin Christianity. Even today, over a millennium and a half later, Christians are still 'taking sides'. For some, Pelagius has become the patron saint of so-called alternative Christianity — be it humanist, Celtic or Creation orientated — while Augustine, the champion of Orthodoxy, is vilified as the archetypal neurotic male theologian. Augustine's psychological analysis of the human will and its motivations, however, are among the most profound in our culture. Sigmund Freud, as someone once said, could have taught him little save jargon.

Pelagius and Augustine were polar opposites. The insights of both are needed if we are to understand ourselves better. Both came from totally different backgrounds. Pelagius probably grew up in the Christian faith, while Augustine was a convert at the age of thirty-two. Augustine had lived the decadent life that Pelagius was eager to lead individuals out of by a programme of moral reform and spiritual discipline. Pelagius lived a life of free apostleship, with no interest in belonging to, or establishing, a theological school or church. Augustine became a theologian in a highly centralized church that was already imposing a set of beliefs upon its members, whether they had grown up spiritually or not. Many joined the Church out of pressure to conform socially and religiously — a trend that was anathema to Pelagius. There was little that the two theologians could agree on.

The Latin Church had become permeated by a superstitious and magickal view of Divine Grace that led Christians to renounce their own powers of reason and understanding, and in particular the centrality of the human will in enabling the individual to choose and carry out the Good. Augustine's own experience of Divine Grace or Love meant that he reinforced the fact that Salvation was ultimately the gift of Divine intervention. Human effort had no part to play in it. Pelagius visited Rome in AD 394. It wasn't long before Pelagius and Augustine came head-to-head in a major controversy over the relationship between Grace and Freedom.

Pelagius reminds us that all of us have the natural capacity or potential to be holy or perfect. We have the gift of free will to enable us to make our own free choices of right or wrong, and the ability to translate that choice into right action and thus live the virtuous life that the Divine wills for us. In view of the fact that we often make the wrong choice, and sin, Divine forgiveness is on hand, through Christ's example and moral teaching, to guide us to the Truth. This is fine as far as it goes, but it is based on too superficial a view of human nature. Augustine's teaching on freedom, or rather on freedom of the will, goes further, because, with his mystical leaning, his was a more personal awareness of Christ as a living presence in the depth of the human soul, a presence that could work wonders in an individual's life beyond the mere mechanical process of stages to salvation. It isn't enough for the will to desire The Good, i.e. the fact that we have freedom of choice. It must resolve to fulfil the desire. Willing must be joined to The Good itself, which alone makes one's freedom of choice effective. This is why individuals so often fail to put into effect the good choices they have freely made. It is our immersion in the reality of Divine Love which sets us free to fulfil our human potential.

Copy of the painting of Florensky and Bulgakov by M.V. Nesteror

It took the genius of St John Cassian (AD 360-435), one of the most attractive and lovable of the Church Fathers, to bring together the teachings of Pelagius and Augustine into a coherent whole. It may seem obvious to us now, but it isn't a case of either/or in relation to Grace and Freedom but of both working in harmony together, the Divine and human wills wedded in love. It was due to Cassian's dedication that the wisdom of the Desert Fathers and Mothers reached Western Europe. After two years living in a cave near the Church of the Holy Nativity in Bethlehem, Cassian travelled to Egypt to study the path to sanctity and perfection. After many years he returned to southern Gaul (France), where he founded a double monastery near Marseilles at Lerins. His great reputation as a wise and holy man led other monasteries to ask him to write a monastic rule for them. Taken on its own, Augustine's teaching made a mockery of the fact that through spiritual discipline and effort, individuals could grow in virtue and thus into deeper union with the Divine. Co-operation is always required between Divine Love and human freedom. Within the workings of the Divine, room is left for the will to exercise responsibility for the choices made. Grace is not irresistible. 'Grace springs from the desire for it,' as Eastern spirituality would have it. Or as Cassian put it, 'It is ours to will but God's to bring to perfection.' It is this teaching which prevailed within the monasteries of Gaul and the Celtic lands.

NOTES ON CHAPTER SEVEN

Vladimir Soloviev, *Lectures on Divine Humanity*, revised and edited by Boris Jakim, Lindisfarne Press, Hudson, NY 1995

The New English Bible, Oxford University Press, 1970

Vladimir Soloviev, *Lectures on Divine Humanity*

A Bulgakov Anthology, edited by James pain and Nicolas Zernov, SPCK, London 1976.

Sergius Bulgakov: *Apocatastasis and Transfiguration* (Variable Readings in Russian Philosophy, No. 2) translated, edited and with an introduction by Boris Jakim, Variable Press, New Haven, Conn. 1995

'Symbols of Transformation', *Collected Works of Cark Gustave Jung*, Volume 5

The Bhagavad Gita, translated and introduced by Juan Mascaro, Penguin Books 1976

Vladimir Soloviev, *The Meaning of Love*, Floris Books, 1985

Fyodor Dostoyevsky, *The Brothers Karamazov*

Tao Te Ching, translated and introduced by D.C. Lau, Penguin Books, 1963

Thomas Merton, *Varieties of Buddhism*, reprinted in Thoughts From the East, Burns & Oates, London 1996

Klaus Klostermaier, *Hindu and Christian in Vrindaban*, SCM Press, London 1993

Nicolas Berdyaev, *Truth and Revelation*, Geoffrey Bles, London 1953

Afterword

Cervus Fugitivus

The Green Man remains a powerful mediating figure in my life, guardian of intimate dynamics that continue to shape my soul. As I have changed, the Ancient One has mirrored those changes, sharing my transformation, sometimes in the most unexpected way. A treasure house of images, he first revealed himself as a link to the Underworld. But following the theft of rare and beautiful carvings from Pennal Church in 1988, the Ancient One instigated a process that took me from the instinctual depths of my personality to the heights of mystical union. The Stag's disappearance summoned me to The Quest, re-awakening in me the spirit of heroism and chivalry. I began to experience the magick of the new ascesis as a discipline that helped me to weave together different strands of my personality into an integrated and beautiful whole.

I became the Stag.

A profound integrating power, the Stag helped me to understand the way in which every aspect of life is interrelated. I celebrated the union of opposites. In dreams and guided meditations, in deep prayer and in ritual, I entered the world of the Antlered One. I even discovered a set of antlers 'by accident' (!), behind an old fireplace in one of our outbuildings. A visit to a local Garden Centre a few months later brought me face-to-face with a *Platycerium* or Stag Plant. I bought it. It wasn't long before it died from lack of proper nourishment, but I was fortunate to find a second one. Having learnt from past mistakes, its green antlers continue to grow and grow to this day.

I entered different levels of consciousness. I tasted of mysteries that transported me back to the dawn of human awareness, a time when the Stag was revered as a deity or animal spirit. Ancient cave paintings abound with human figures dressed in the skin of wild animals, often a Stag or Deer. Every animal (its meat a source of survival and therefore of life) was regarded as having special gifts to impart. The Stag was particularly revered for its beauty, sensitivity and compassion. Tribes adopted certain animals as their patrons or guardians. Through ritual wise men and women sought the favour of their ruling spirit and thus could tap into its wisdom and draw of its energy. So close became the communion between a tribe and its animal guardian that the hunter and hunted became as one.

The Stag or Hind became a powerful symbol of the Mother Goddess. Often accompanied by her faithful dogs, they would travel on journeys to the Otherworld. In classical culture, Diana was the supreme Goddess of the hunt, her greatest pleasure was in pursuing her prey. The hunt became a special religious and magickal ritual to honour the Divine Feminine. Wisdom literature, in the last centuries BC, also extols the spirit of the hunt, in its case in honour of Sophia. Ben Sirach declares that we should 'Pursue Sophia like a hunter and lie in wait on Her paths' (14:22). Sophia may tabernacle in our midst, but this does not excuse us, in turn, from seeking her out. He goes on to say:

> While I was still a youth, before setting off on my travels,
> At prayer in the temple I sought Sophia.
> In truth I will never give up my search for Her.　　(ben Sirach 51:13-14)

The Wisdom of Solomon shares a similar sentiment:

> I loved her and sought her for my youth,
> and I desired to take her for my bride.
> I became enamoured of her beauty.　　(8:2)

In Arthurian literature, it is not only Arthur who goes in search of the Stag. Sir Gawain's first adventure was the Quest for the White Stag, while in the *Tale of Geraint ap Erbin* (in *The Mabinogion*), Sir Geraint also receives a vision of the Stag:

> 'Tell thy tidings,' said Arthur. 'I will lord,' said he (Sir Geraint). 'A stag have I seen in the forest and I never saw the like of it.' 'What is there about it,' asked Arthur, 'that thou shouldst never have seen its like?' 'It is pure white, lord, and it goes not with any animal for presumption and pride, so exceedingly majestic it is.'   (p. 230)

Much of Celtic literature, however, reflects a time when the Goddess or Sovereignty and Her Wisdom, had all but disappeared. In a patriarchal society She had become marginalized and largely ignored. In some of the Grail stories Christ occasionally appeared to His disciples in the form of a White Stag, while in Medieval Literature the Stag came to represent the human soul or self. It celebrates the secret of growth and self-renewal, in addition to the human search for wholeness and union with a reality greater than itself. Antlers have always been associated with regeneration and growth because of the way they are renewed when damaged or broken off. In a painting housed in the Benedictine monastery at Fischingen, Switzerland, a local saint, Idda, can be seen in the first throes of ecstasy as she prepares for union with the Divine. A Stag with flames on its antlers guides her to a chapel in the forest, while a raven brings a golden ring in its beak as a symbol of mystical marriage.

I pursued the Stag from the underground mysteries of our ancestors to the mystical heights of Medieval Europe. It was in the writings of the Spanish mystic and poet, St John of the Cross (1542-1591) that I encountered the Stag in its most sublime metamorphosis. The transformation that followed sealed my spiritual seeking.

In one of his mystical poems, called 'The Spiritual Canticle', he sings of the soul's yearning for union with Christ, the Bridegroom, and of Christ's desire to bring such a union to pass. He communicates this truth by entering the world of the Stag, which represents for St John the human soul as well as Christ, the Bride as well as the Bridegroom. St John describes the soul's pain when, having tasted the presence of Christ, it becomes profoundly aware of His absence. It is characteristic of Stags to climb to high places, and, when wounded, to go immediately in search of refreshing waters. Similarly, if he hears the cry of his mate and senses that she is wounded, nothing would stop the Stag from seeking her out in order to comfort her. In the tradition of the Song of Songs, St John of the Cross gives the reader the privilege of sharing, in an intimate way, the love affair between the Deer and the Stag, the Bride and the Bridegroom:

Bride:
Where have You hidden,
Beloved, and left me moaning?
You fled like the Stag
After wounding me;
I went out calling You, and You were gone.

Why, since You wounded
This heart, don't You heal it?
And why, since You stole it from me,
Do you leave it so,
And fail to carry off what You have stolen?

O, spring like crystal:
If only, on your silvered-over face,
You would suddenly form
The eyes I have desired.
Which I bear sketched deep within my heart.

Withdraw them, Beloved,
I am taking flight!

Bridegroom:
The wounded Stag
Is in sight on the hill,
Cooled by the breeze of your flight"   (from *The Collected Works of St John of the Cross*)

Tired after much journeying, I sojourned 'in the woods and thickets' that St John mentions in this poem. 'The green meadow, coated, bright with flowers' became my dwelling place. It was here that I finally surrendered to The Beloved and where I obtained the peace supreme, my home in Eternity:

> With what wondrous sweetness the loved one and the Beloved dwell one in the other, and
> how they penetrate each other in such a way that neither of the two can be distinguished
> from the other. But they abide in one another in fruition, mouth in mouth, heart in heart,
> body in body and soul in soul, while one sweet Divine nature flows through them both,
> and they are both one thing through each other, but at the same time remain two different
> selves — yes, and remain so for ever.   (*Hadewijch, The Collected Works*, Letter 9, p. 66)

'It is time to move on. New challenges are beckoning.' I wrote those words in 1993, at the time of the thirtieth anniversary of the publication of *Honest to God*. Much has happened in the ensuing period. My sojourn in the 'in-between' has been demanding, and I know it now as the place where I must continue to exercise my ministry, joining other bridge-builders between the old and new dispensations. It is the space where I can be 'Honest to Goddess'.

The traditions that have helped mould me thus far are now become part of an ever-growing spaciousness. A new and exciting future has already taken hold of Ann and me. With fellow travellers in the Order of Sancta Sophia, we will continue to honour the Universal Christ who calls us to service. In tune with many friends the world over, in the words of the Urania Foundation (Moscow), we join to

help the integration of spiritual energy of pilgrims on their way to Sophia.

I cannot ignore the race marked out for me, nor the pioneering Christ who is always way ahead of those who would aspire to follow Him. Between honesty and hope, uncharted territory must now be negotiated. I enter the next stage of my priesthood without knowing the risks or obstacles I will encounter. It isn't always easy to believe that the Divine Spirit will lead us to all Truth, especially when we have to set out without consulting a road map in advance! But surely this is the essence of the Christic Way? — forever a quest, an adventure, a journey and a voyage of discovery.

No one sums it up better for me than Walt Whitman in Passage to India. His words fire me as much now as they did over thirty years ago. I can think of no better words to celebrate the transition into the third millennium of the Divine Mother:

Have we not darkened and dazed
    ourselves with books long enough?
Sail forth —

steer for the deep waters only.
Reckless, O soul, exploring,
    I with thee and thou with me,
For we are bound where mariner
    has not yet dared to go,
And we will risk the ship, ourselves and all.

O my brave soul!
O farther, farther sail!
O daring joy, but safe!
    are they not all the seas of God?
O farther, farther, farther sail.

NOTES ON THE AFTERWORD

The Mabinogion, translated by Gwyn Jones and Thomas Jones, J.M. Dent & Sons Ltd, London 1968
The Collected Works of St John of the Cross, translated by Kieran Kavanaugh OCD and Otilio Rodriguez OCD, Institute of Carmelite Studies Publishing, Washington D.C. 1979
Hadewijch, The Collected Works quoted in Mysticism (p. 10), a booklet produced by the Churches' Fellowship of Psychical and Spiritual Studies (CFPSS), *c.* 1970

SUGGESTED READING LIST

Vladimir Soloviev

Vladimir Soloviev, The Crisis of Western Philosophy, translated and edited by Boris Jakim, Lindisfarne Press, Hudson NY 1996

God, Man and the World, translated by Donald Attwater, James Clarke & Co Ltd, Cambridge 1974

D. Stremooukhoff, Vladimir Soloviev and His Messianic Work, translated by Elizabeth Meyendorff, Norland Publishing Co Inc, Belmont, Mass, 1980

Pavel Florensky

Pavel A. Florensky, The Trinity – St Sergius, Lavra and Russia, Variable Readings in Russian Philosophy, No. 1, The Variable Press, New Haven, Conn, 1995

Robert Slesinki, Paul Florensky: A Metaphysics of Love, St Vladimir's Seminary Press, Crestwood, NY, 1984

Sergius Bulgakov

Sergius Bulgakov, Orthodoxy and Modern Society Variable Readings in Russian Philosophy No. 4, The Variable Press 1995

Charles Lee Graves, The Holy Spirit in the Theology of Sergius Bulgakov, dissertation presented for the Doctor's Degree to the Theological Faculty of the University of Basle, printed privately at the WCC, Geneva, Switzerland 1972

Winston F. Crum, Sergius N. Bulgakov: From Marxism to Sophiology, pp. 3-25, St Vladimir's Theological Quarterly Vol 27 No ? 1983

Barbara Newman, Sergius Bulgakov and The Theology of Divine Wisdom, pp 39-73, St Vladimir's Theological Quarterly (details to follow)

Aidan Nichols 'Bulgakov and Sophiology', pp. 17-31, Sobornost (Incorporating Eastern Churches Review), 13.2 1992

An Introduction to the Theme of Wisdom and Creation in the Tradition Père Louis Bouyer, pp. 149-161, Le Messager Orthodoxe: Colloque P. Serge Bulgakov, No 98 1.11.1985

Sergius Bulgakov: Bibliographie, Institut D'Etudes Slaves, Paris, 1984

'Wisdom', The Month: A Review of Christian Thought and World Affairs, September/October 1992

Jonathan Maury, SSJE, Jesus-Sophia: Divine Woman Wisdom Made Flesh, pp. 24-25, Cowley (Society of St John the Evangelist, Cambridge, Mass, Vol 22 No 1 Spring 1996

Boris Jakim, 'Sophia', pp29-34, The First Hour

(The Magazine of the Patristic Society) No. 12 Christmas 1995

Nicolas and Militza Zernov, Fellowship of St Alban & St Sergius: A Historical Memoir, Oxford 1979

Khristos Voskrese! A Newsletter for Russian Orthodox Philosophy, Volume 2 No 6, 10 December, 1995

Judith Deutsch Kornblatt and Richard F Gustafson (Ed) Russian Religious Thought, University of Wisconsin Press 1996

Nicolas Berdyaev

Nicolas Berdyaev, The Destiny of Man (1948), The Divine and The Human (1949), The Beginning and The End (1952), Geoffrey Bles, London; Dostoyevsky: An Introduction by Nicolas Berdyaev, Sheed & Ward, London 1936

Writings in the Sophianic Tradition

Evgueny Lampert, The Divine Realm, Faber & Faber, London 1944

Alexis Van Der Mensbrugghe, From Dyad to Triad, Faith Press, London 1935

Contemporary writings about Sophia / Goddess / Divine Mother

Aurora Terrenus, Sophia of the Bible, Celestial Communications: The Publishing House of the Holy Order of Wisdom, Santa Cruz, CA 1988

Caitlin Matthews, Sophia: Goddess of Wisdom, Mandala, London 1991

Divine Sophia: Holy Wisdom, Sophia Foundation of North America, Nicasio, CA 1995

Andrew Harvey, The Return of the Mother, Frog Ltd, Berkley, CA 1995

Arthur Versluis, Theosophia: Hidden Dimensions of Christianity, Lindisfarne Press, Hudson, NY 1994

Gerhard Wehr, The Mystical Marriage, Aquarian Press 1990

John Eaton, The Contemplative Face of Old Testament Wisdom in the context of World Religions, SCM Press, London 1989

Monica Sjoo and Barbara Mor, The Great Cosmic Mother HarperCollins 1991

Edward C. Whitmont, The Return of the Goddess, Arkana, London 1987

Mysticism and Spirituality

William Ralph Inge, *The Philosophy of Plotinus*, in Two
   Volumes, Longmans, Green & Co, London 1918
Sri Aurobindo, *The Life Divine*, in Two Volumes (1977)
   and *The Synthesis of Yoga* (1984), Sri Aurobindo
   Ashram, Pondicherry, India
Anonymous, *Meditations on the Tarot*, translated by
   Robert A. Powell, Element Books 1993
Moshe Idel, *Kabbalah: New Perspectives*, Yale University
   Press, New Haven 1988
Gordon Strachan, *Christ and the Cosmos*, Labarum
   Publishers Ltd, Dunbar, Scotland 1985
Robin Amis, *A Different Christianity*, State University
   of New York Press 1995
John Macmurray, *Reason and Emotion*, Faber & Faber
   Ltd, London 1972
John A.T. Robinson, *Truth is Two-Eyed*, SCM Press,
   London 1979

Biblical Studies and Theology

Hans Urs Von Balthasar, *The Glory of the Lord*,
   Volumes 4 and 7 (1989), Volumes 5 and 6 (1991),
   T&T Clark, Edinburgh
Karl-Josef Kuschel, *Born Before All Time? The Dispute
   Over Christ's Origins*, translated by John Bowden,
   SCM Press London 1992
John Ashton, *Understanding the Fourth Gospel*,
   Clarendon Press, Oxford 1993
Celia M. Deutsch, *Lady Wisdom, Jesus and the Sages*,
   Trinity Press International, Valley Forge, PA 1996
Graham Shaw, *The Cost of Authority: Manipulation
   and Freedom in the New Testament*, SCM Press,
   London 1983
Daphne Hampson, *After Christianity*, SCM Press,
   London 1996

INDEX